Trekking in the Indian Himalaya

Garry Weare

Trekking in the Indian Himalaya

2nd edition

Published by
Lonely Planet Publications Pty Ltd (ACN 005 607 983)
PO Box 617, Hawthorn, Vic 3122, Australia
Lonely Planet Publications Inc
PO Box 2001A, Berkeley, CA 94702, USA

Printed by
Colorcraft Ltd, Hong Kong

Photographs by
Rob Cheves (RC)
Garry Weare (GW)
Front cover: Campsite at Humpet, in the Kanital Valley, Kashmir (GW)
Back cover: Pack animals climbing the Upper Warvan Valley, Kashmir (GW)

First Published
April 1986

This Edition
July 1991

Although the authors and publisher have tried to make the information as accurate as possible, they accept no responsibility for any loss, injury or inconvenience sustained by any person using this book.

National Library of Australia Cataloguing in Publication Data

Weare, Garry
    Trekking in the Indian Himalaya

    2nd ed.
    Includes index.
    ISBN 0 86442 093 5.

    1. Hiking – Himalaya Mountains – Guide-books. 2. India, Northeastern – Description and travel – Guide-books. 3. Himalaya Mountains – Description and travel – Guide-books.
    I. Title.

915.40452

text © Lonely Planet 1991
maps © Garry Weare / Jane Besley, and Lonely Planet 1991
photos © photographers as indicated 1991
illustrations © Jane Besley 1991

Garry Weare

Garry has had a close association with the Indian Himalaya since he first trekked in Kashmir in 1970. Since then he has returned regularly, leading many treks throughout Kashmir, Ladakh and Himachal Pradesh. He has also been a consultant to a number of TV documentaries, and has been the presenter of a film for Indian television. He is a Director of World Expeditions (formerly Australian Himalayan Expeditions), and continues to return to India to research and lead treks each season.

From the Author

Trek contributions for this edition came from a number of sources. In Kashmir and Ladakh, the route descriptions were compiled by the author with help from Meraj Din, Firdous Khan, Jitender Kaul, Ferous Ahmed, and Rouf Tramboo (Kashmir); Wangchuk Shamshu and Rigzin Jowa (Ladakh); Iqbal Sharma (Manali) and Yetish Bhaghuna (Uttar Pradesh); together with Harsh Vardhan and Narpat Singh (Delhi).

The author would like to thank Dr Jim Duff (Hobart) for the time he spent writing the medical section of this book, and Rosemary Worthington (Sydney) for compiling much of the material for the present edition. For the illustrations the author is indebted to Jane Besley (Sydney). Many thanks also to Anne Mathews (Sydney), whose editorial advice and assistance is gratefully acknowledged.

Other advice has been from Terry Ryan (Adelaide), Judy Parker (Melbourne), Andrew and Sallee Robinson (Sydney), Simon Balderstone (Canberra), and Cass Pinney (Darwin) – trek companions of many kilometres. Thanks also to the Badyari family, whose houseboats are still without equal on Nagin Lake.

Dedication This book is dedicated to India Weare and India Duff – may they spend many happy seasons discovering the Himalaya.

From the Publisher

This edition of *Trekking in the Indian Himalaya* was edited at the Lonely Planet office in Australia by James Lyon. Valerie Tellini was responsible for the design, cover design and map corrections. Thanks also to Sue Mitra for proofreading and editorial guidance, and to Sharon Wertheim for the index.

Thanks

Letters and contributions are also acknowledged with thanks from Rob Stevenson (UK) for details on Kashmir; Valeria Valli (Italy), on Ladakh; Greg Buckman (Australia), on Himachal Pradesh; Neil Daniel (UK); Darrell High (UK); Pierre Willems (Belgium); Aprampar Singh (India); Roger Macklin (UK); Paul Adams (UK); Hendrik van Prooije (Netherlands); Stewart Johnson (Australia); and Bill Aitkin and Wade Richardson (Canada), on Uttar Pradesh and the Garhwal.

Warning & Request

Things change – prices go up, schedules change, good places go bad and bad places go bankrupt – nothing stays the same. So if you find things better or worse, recently opened or long since closed, please write and tell us.

This edition of *Trekking in the Indian Himalaya* will again be upgraded over the seasons, and any suggestions, corrections or additions will be gratefully received at either the Lonely Planet office, or directly to the author, c/o World Expeditions, 441 Kent St, Sydney, NSW, Australia. The best letters will be rewarded with a free copy of the next edition, or any other Lonely Planet book of your choice.

Contents

Introduction

For people considering a first-time trek to the Himalaya, India provides some superb opportunities. While the numbers visiting the Indian Himalaya are still small in comparison with those trekking in Nepal, there has nonetheless been a surge of interest. Trekkers are discovering that there are opportunities for treks which are as long and demanding as those to Everest Base Camp or the Annapurna Ranges.

In India, as in Nepal, the Himalaya is undoubtedly one of the most spectacular and impressive mountain ranges in the world. To fully appreciate this, there is no substitute for undertaking a trek. Trekking brings you into direct contact with the country and its people, and helps to foster an understanding of the importance of preserving mountain environments. It is a responsibility we all share. Our concern should be translated to

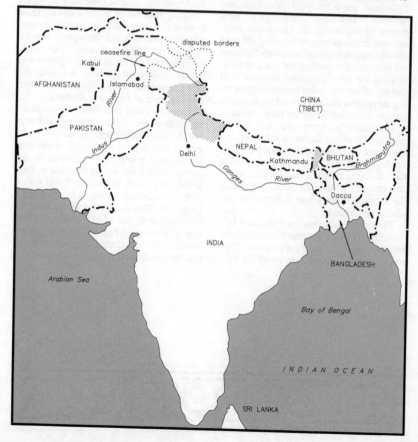

the governments and various tourist organisations to ensure that the Himalaya's most valuable asset is not destroyed.

On a positive note, fees have at last been introduced to help contribute towards the physical wellbeing of some of the more popular Indian trekking valleys; while in Uttar Pradesh plans are still in force to limit the numbers trekking to the Valley of the Flowers and to the Nanda Devi Sanctuary. Similar schemes are afoot in Himachal Pradesh, which has some of the most delightful treks anywhere in the Himalaya, yet the amount of garbage found along the popular trails raises questions about the enforcement of local regulations. There will be little chance of preserving the Himalayan environment unless people undertaking the treks are also prepared to make an effort. This does not just include cleaning the camp areas as you go, but also impressing the local staff that we all have a vested interest in preserving the pristine delights of walking the trails, not just for ourselves but for future trekkers.

This guide has been classified into the regions of Kashmir, Jammu and Ladakh, and the states of Himachal Pradesh and Uttar Pradesh, each with an overall assessment of their trekking possibilities. There is also a new chapter outlining the trekking options in the Indian Himalaya east of Nepal, in Darjeeling and Sikkim.

The trekking regions are introduced by a description of their geographical and historical features, followed by a rundown of the treks covered, the season in which the trails can be followed, and any hazards or difficulties that should be borne in mind. There is information on how to get to the various trek starting points, accommodation before setting out, and an assessment of the trekking arrangements, including the cost and availability of supplies, porters and horses.

Finally, there is a stage by stage description of each trek.

The treks outlined cover many of the more popular routes in India. The structure of the trekking sections starts with treks in Kashmir and Jammu, and continues on to Ladakh and Himachal Pradesh. For example a trek out of Kishtwar (in Jammu) finishes at either Chamba, Kashmir or in the Zanskar. There is no reason why the treks cannot be completed in reverse. A trek through the Zanskar finishes in Lahaul. Treks from Kulu, Chamba and Lahaul can extend right the way across Kashmir or Ladakh: it is only for convenience that many of the itineraries start from the state of Jammu & Kashmir.

There are many possibilities for combining treks in the various regions, and it is hoped that by linking some of the routes you will be able to have a fulfilling experience. For instance a trek out of Kashmir up the Warvan Valley and across the Bhoktol Pass to the Suru Valley can be combined with a trek continuing on to Rangdum and Lamayuru. This in turn can be extended by trekking on to the Markha Valley before finally arriving in Leh. It is up to you to combine the treks according to the time, interest and funds that you have available.

Facts about the Region

HISTORY & CULTURE

From near the Nun Kun mountains and from no other spot in Asia, we go westwards through countries entirely Mohammedan, eastward among none but Buddhists, and southwards over lands where the Hindu religion prevails to the extremity of the Indian peninsula.

Frederick Drew *The Northern Barrier of India* 1877

The Indian Himalaya marks the crossroads of Asia's three main cultures. The Kashmir Himalaya is the cultural boundary of Islam, the foothills of Jammu, Himachal Pradesh and Uttar Pradesh define the northern limits of Hinduism, while Ladakh is predominantly Buddhist.

From the earliest records, the Himalaya was revered as the abode of the gods. From the time the Aryans migrated to northern India between 2500 and 1500 BC, the mountains were held in awe. In about 1000 BC these people composed the Vedas, a set of hymns devoted to the gods: Agni the god of fire, Surya the god of the sun, Vago the god of the wind, and Indra the mighty god of the sky. All resided in the Himalaya, an arena where immortal beings could determine the destiny of the world.

The power of these gods was revealed in an elaborate system of ritual and sacrifice. For the Aryan warriors the sacrifice was of paramount importance, particularly when needed to secure the favour of the gods in times of war. The ceremonies were taken as sacrosanct, with the priests – the Brahmins – assuming a crucial role. The sacrificial rites naturally increased the power of the Brahmins, and gradually they were able to dominate the village and local communities in their interests. A caste system was instituted that has remained an integral part of life in India until the present day.

The powerful position of the Brahmins and their exclusive rituals gave rise to other popular alternatives. The teachings of the Buddha spread, and had a wide appeal across northern India from the 5th century BC. Two centuries later, the Emperor Ashoka patronised the third Buddhist Congress in Kashmir, while the Emperor Kanishka also encouraged the discussion of Buddhist fundamentals during the fourth Congress in Kashmir in the 1st century AD. During this time Buddhist teachings spread far beyond the Himalayan foothills, and as far as China.

Despite of the spread of Buddhism, it did not undermine the position of the Brahmins. Some of the original Vedic gods fell out of favour while others, such as Shiva, Vishnu and Brahma, came to the fore. Brahma was seen as the creator, Vishnu the preserver and Shiva the destroyer.

In the 1st century AD, two epic poems were composed to commemorate the history and heroes of India, the *Mahabharata* and the *Ramayana*. They were not written as religious treatises, but as they gained popularity these works were revised by the Brahmins. The poems were given a religious status and their heroes, including Rama and Krishna, became associated with incarnations of Vishnu. Shiva was linked with the popular fertility cults of the bull and the worship of the lingam. It was an association which gained wider appeal with the spread of Tantric cults and the worship of the Mother Goddess.

The cult of sexual union was raised to divine status, with each god being assigned a female partner. For example, Shiva was associated with Parvati and Vishnu with Lakshmi. Pilgrimages were undertaken to the Himalaya, the home of the gods. For the pilgrim, the trek to the Amarnath Cave symbolised the essence of the Mother Goddess, with the ice statue inside the cave representing the divine lingam. This sign of cosmic creation has become part of the Himalayan tradition.

The traditional Hindu values were not undermined until the coming of Islam. In the 11th century the Mahmud of Ghanzi overthrew the local Hindu rulers of a small principality just south of Kabul. From this base Islam spread across the Hindu Kush and north-west India, with the Sultanate of Delhi being established a century or so later. Kashmir's conversion to Islam came during the following century. Essentially this conversion was peaceful, and independent of the Turkish forces that had by then assumed power across the north Indian plains.

Despite these religious changes, Ladakh remained Buddhist, and continued to trace its cultural origins to the time when the Tantric sage Padmasambhava wandered from India to Tibet in the 8th century. From that time on, the animistic Bon Po beliefs fell into decline, and by the 10th century the kings of Western Tibet, or Ladakh, had been fully converted.

While the wave of Islam was to spread to other nearby Himalayan regions such as Baltistan, the hill kingdoms from Jammu across the foothills to the Garhwal were able to maintain their cultural heritage. The three distinct cultural worlds of Buddhist Ladakh, Islamic Kashmir, and the Hindu hill states had almost evolved into their present-day situation.

The founding of the Moghul Empire realigned cultural boundaries. After consolidating his power over the Indian plains and the Rajput territories, the Moghul Emperor Akbar invaded Kashmir in 1588. The Moghuls also extended their influence to the Indian hill states, and demanded tribute to their courts.

To the north, Ladakh had carved out a sizeable empire for itself, but after a war with Lhasa its boundaries were confined again to the Indus Valley. This war would have reduced the Ladakhi borders even further had it not been for the intervention of the Moghuls. Aurangzeb, the last of the great Moghul emperors, called for the Ladakhi king to pay a nominal tribute to his court – the mosque at the end of the Leh bazaar.

Following the decline of the Moghuls, a complex political situation evolved. Kashmir was invaded by the much-feared Afghani forces while Jammu gradually secured a position of autonomy in the foothills. The nearby state of Kangra also extended its influence, across the Kulu Valley as far as the Sutlej River, while the Gurkhas of Nepal had expanded their borders over the Kumoun and the Garhwal as far as the Simla hill states. To complete the picture, by the second half of the 18th century the Sikhs had established an empire across the Punjab, while the East India Company was setting its sights far beyond the established trading posts of Calcutta.

The state of Kangra, the Sikhs, and the Gurkhas all had ambitions to control the Punjab Himalaya. The Gurkhas sought the assistance of the Sikhs, but the Sikhs had their own plans to extend their territory beyond Lahore. The Gurkhas therefore led a united front with the deposed hill rajahs against the Kangra army. These forces retreated to the Kangra fort, and called on the Sikhs for assistance. The Sikhs complied, the Gurkhas withdrew to the Sutlej, and the Sikhs took control of most of the hill states which were soon to include Kashmir.

The British were wary of the extent of Sikh influence, and were equally aware that a combined Gurkha-Sikh empire stretching from Sikkim to Kashmir would be a formidable force to deal with. The British were determined to forge a neutral zone between the Sikhs and the Gurkhas, which they achieved as a result of the Gurkha wars in 1815. The Gurkhas were restricted to the eastern banks of the Karnali River, the present boundary between India and Nepal – leaving the districts of Garhwal, Nainital, Kumaon, and Dehra Dun under British control.

By the 1830s the Sikhs, with assistance of the Dogras of Jammu, had taken Kishtwar, Ladakh, and Baltistan. An historic manoeuvre followed. After the death of the noted Sikh ruler Ranjit Singh, the British gained control of the Punjab during the Sikh wars in the mid-1840s. Under their leader, Gulab Singh, the Dogras remained neutral. The political evolution of north-west India was almost complete.

On 9 March 1846, following the Treaty of Amritsar, the Sikh Durbar agreed to cede 'the hilly and mountainous country' between the Beas and Indus rivers. One week later, a separate treaty was entered into between the British and the Dogra leader, Gulab Singh. Essentially, this treaty transferred to the Dogras the region between the Ravi and Indus rivers. By granting rule to the Dogras the British had, in effect, found a means of exercising control over the northern barrier of India. Gulab Singh became the maharajah of a vast state encompassing Jammu, Baltistan, Ladakh, and Kashmir — boundaries that were to remain until Indian partition in 1947.

A boundary commission was established in 1847 to survey the lesser known regions of the Indian Himalaya. Their principal concern was the region of Ladakh, Zanskar and Baltistan. This vast area was of considerable interest, in respect of both access to Tibet and the possibility of a backdoor invasion by Russia. The commission consisted of

Indian Himalaya (Political)

© Compiled and drawn by G. Weare and J. Besley

Cunningham, Thomson and Strachey. Cunningham was to produce the most extensive geographical survey of Ladakh. Strachey received reports from the borderlands of Tibet. Thomson's travels took him across the Umasi La to Leh, from where he continued his journey, and distinguished himself by being the first European to ascend the Karakoram Pass.

The Ground Survey of India, conducted during the 1850s and 1860s, began to fill the gaps of the Commission's exploration. All important valleys were explored, and every major peak surveyed, including those of K2 and the Karakoram.

It was then the turn of the forest officers and administrators to upgrade many of the mountain trails. During this time, rest houses and Public Works Department (PWD) huts were constructed in remote valleys many stages from the nearest roadhead. Many of these still retain their charm and character. Other intrepid travellers, such as the geologist Alexandra Drew, took service with the Kashmir maharajah and published surveys of the state's mineral wealth. By the turn of the century guidebooks had appeared, complete with the walking stages from Srinagar to Astor and Gilgit.

After Indian partition many of these walks were no longer possible. For example, treks to Baltistan now ventured into Pakistan, while Ladakh was closed to foreigners.

In 1947 the Maharajah of Kashmir, Hari Singh, was forced to choose between joining India or Pakistan. On paper the choice was clear. Kashmir was predominantly Muslim, and Pakistan became the natural cultural alternative. However, Hari Singh remained indecisive. As a Hindu, he had little feeling for Pakistan, while as a maharajah he had even less inclination to lose his kingdom to India. His true desire was for an independent maharajah's kingdom – an utterly impossible dream. Pakistan seized upon the urgency of the situation, and 'organised' a coup by dispatching Pathan tribespeople to capture Srinagar. Hari Singh called on India for support, and paid the political price – a full-scale war which was not settled until 1 January 1949, and the division of Kashmir between India and Pakistan.

The Kashmir line of control was a matter of constant dispute between India and Pakistan, and further conflicts arose in 1965 and 1971. The result in India is the state of Jammu & Kashmir, where Jammu is predominantly Hindu, Kashmir Muslim, and Ladakh Buddhist – a state born more out of political accident than cultural design.

The hill states of Chamba, Kangra, Kulu, and Lahaul came under the Punjab administration after 1947. In 1966 the administration was reorganised and Kangra, Kulu and Lahaul were merged with the Simla hill states to form Himachal Pradesh. In 1971 Himachal Pradesh was given full statehood in the Indian Union, and is an essentially Hindu state devoid of the cultural complexities of Jammu & Kashmir.

To the east of Himachal Pradesh, wedged between the high Himalaya and the kingdom of Nepal, are the northern reaches of Uttar Pradesh. In 1947 the hill states of Garhwal and the Kumaon merged with the regions on the upper reaches of the Jamuna and Ganges to form the state of Uttar Pradesh, one of the most geographically diverse states in India.

GEOGRAPHY

The Himalaya is one of the youngest mountain ranges in the world. Its evolution can be traced to the the Jurassic era (80 million years ago) when the world's land masses were split into two: Laurasia in the northern hemisphere, and Gondwanaland in the southern hemisphere. The land mass which is now India broke away from Gondwanaland and floated across the earth's surface until it collided with Asia. The hard volcanic rocks of India were thrust against the soft sedimentary crust of Asia, creating the highest mountain range in the world. It was a collision that formed mountain ranges right across Asia, including the Karakoram, the Pamirs, the Hindu Kush, the Tien Shan and the Kun Lun, while the Himalayan mountains at the front of this continental collision are still being formed, rising and assuming complex profiles, as anyone who has flown over them will testify.

For the ancient geographer the complexities of this vast mountain range were a constant source of speculation. From the earliest accounts, Mt Kailash was believed to be the centre of the universe with the river systems of the Indus, the Brahmaputra, and the Sutlej all flowing from its snowy ridges, and maintaining courses that they had followed prior to the forming of the Himalaya.

It was not surprising therefore that 19th century geographers experienced formidable difficulties in tracing the river systems, and defining the various mountain ranges that constitute the Himalaya. Even today, with the advent of satellite pictures and state-of-the-art ordnance maps, it is still difficult to appreciate the form and extent of some of the ranges that constitute the Himalaya.

The main Himalayan range is the principal mountain range dividing the Indian subcontinent from the Tibetan plateau. From Nanga Parbat in the west the range stretches for over 2000 km to the mountains bordering Sikkim and Bhutan in the east. In the West Himalaya

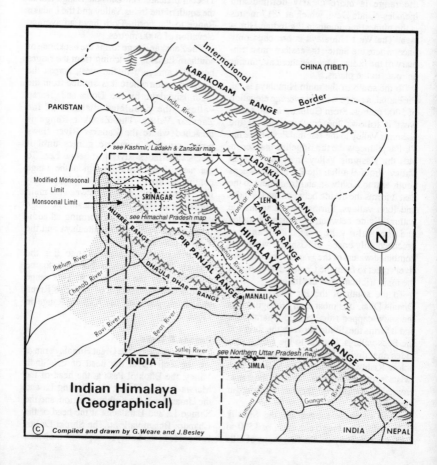

Indian Himalaya
(Geographical)

© Compiled and drawn by G. Weare and J. Besley

it is the range that divides Kashmir and Himachal Pradesh from Ladakh. In Uttar Pradesh the Himalaya divides the headwaters of the Ganges, while in Nepal the main ridgeline frequently coincides with the political boundary between Nepal and Tibet.

In Kashmir the ranges give way to subsidiary ridges such as the north Kashmir range beyond Sonamarg and the Kolahoi and Armanath ranges. In Himachal Pradesh the snowy boundaries broaden to encompass some of the ranges in Lahaul, Spiti, and Kinnaur. In Uttar Pradesh and the Garhwal the range is more clearly defined and includes Nanda Devi, which at 7817 metres is the highest mountain in the Indian Himalaya. The West Himalaya is breached only once, where the Sutlej, the eastern-most tributary of the Indus, breaches these mountains en route to the plains.

To the south of the main Himalaya is the Pir Panjal, a range with an average elevation of 5000 metres. From Gulmarg in the northwest it follows the southern rim of the Kashmir Valley to the Banihal Pass. Here the Pir Panjal meets the ridgeline that separates the Kashmir Valley from the Warvan Valley. From Banihal the Pir Panjal sweeps south-east to Kishtwar, and from there to the east it forms the divide between the Chandra and Ravi valleys. Further east it forms the natural divide between the Chandra Valley and the Kulu Valley. The Pir Panjal is breached only once – at Kishtwar where the combined waters of the Warvan and Chandra rivers meet to form the Chenab River, one of the main tributaries of the Indus.

To the south of the Pir Panjal lies the Dhaula Dhar. It is most easily recognised as the snow-capped ridge behind Dharamsala, and it forms the divide between the Ravi and the Beas valleys. Further to the west it provides the divide between Chenab Valley below Kishtwar and the Tawi Valley which twists south to Jammu. This is the range crossed at Panitop on the Jammu-Srinagar highway.

South of these ranges are the Siwalik Hills, with an average elevation of 1500 to 2000 metres. They are the first range of hills

encountered en route from the plains and they are geologically separate from the Himalaya. They include the Jammu Hills and Vaishnu Devi, and extend to Kangra and further east to the range south of Mandi. In Uttar Pradesh they extend from Dehra Dun to Almora before heading across the southern borders of Nepal.

To the north of the Himalaya lie the Zanskar and Ladakh ranges, commonly referred to as the Trans-Himalaya region. Geologically, this marks the transition zone between the Indian subcontinent and the Tibetan plateau. The Zanskar Range lies to the south of the Indus Valley and the Ladakh Range to the north. Both have an average elevation of 5000 metres.

The Zanskar Range forms the backbone of southern Ladakh, stretching from the ridges beyond Lamayuru in the west, across the Zanskar·region where it is divided from the main Himalaya by the Doda and Tsarap valleys, the populated districts of the Zanskar Valley. The Zanskar Range is breached where the Zanskar River flows north, creating awesome gorges until it reaches the Indus River just below Leh. To the east of the Zanskar region the range continues through Lahaul and Spiti, providing a complex buffer zone between the main Himalaya and the Tibetan plateau. The range extends to Uttar Pradesh, forming an additional range between the Himalaya and the Tibetan plateau.

North of the Zanskar Range lies the Ladakh Range, which is bordered to the north-west by the Karakoram. This range extends eastwards, north of the Indus River, until it merges with the Kailash Range in Tibet.

Passes & Trails
The main passes in the Great Himalaya range are the Zoji La at the head of the Sindh Valley, the Bhoktol Pass at the head of the Marwa-Warvan Valley, the Chilung La and the Umasi La in the Kishtwar region, and the Shingo La and Baralacha at the head of the Chandra-Bhaga valleys. The Shipki La lies to the side of the Sutlej River, while the Mana

La at the head of the Alaknanda Valley is the main pass linking the Garhwal and Tibet.

Of the West Himalayan passes, the Zoji La and the Baralacha are only open to vehicles for up to six months of the year as the heavy snows make them impassable during the winter months. The other glaciated passes, however, remain trekking objectives from mid-June until mid-October.

In the Pir Panjal the main passes are the Pir Panjal Pass due west of Srinagar, the Banihal Pass which lies at the head of the Jhelum River at the southern end of the Kashmir Valley, and the Sythen Pass linking Kashmir with Kishtwar. In Himachal Pradesh the main passes are the Sach which links the Ravi and the Chandra valleys, and the Rhotang which links the Beas and Kulu valleys with the upper Chandra Valley and Lahaul.

Roads are being constructed over all these passes – the Banihal is now tunnelled and work is in progress on roads over the Pir Panjal Pass in Kashmir and the Sach Pass in Himachal Pradesh. The roads over the Sythen and Rhotang passes are open during the summer months. There are plans to tunnel through the Pir Panjal west of the Rhotang Pass, to make Lahaul accessible by road from the outside world within the next decade. For trekkers there are many options for exploring the range, notably the Kugti, Kalicho and Chobia passes between the Ravi Valley and Lahaul, while the Hampt Pass links the Kulu Valley with Lahaul. Similarly, the Dhaula Dhar has many foot passes by which to explore this delightful range when trekking from Dharamsala over to the Ravi Valley.

The Siwalik Hills are lower, broader, and more accessible, with roads linking the northern Indian plains with Kangra, the Kulu Valley, Simla and Dehra Dun.

On the Zanskar Range, the Fatu La, on the Leh-Srinagar road, is considered the most easterly pass, while the Singge La, the Charchar La and the Rubrang La are the main trekking passes into the Zanskar Valley. For the hardy Ladakhis, the main route in winter between the Zanskar Valley and Leh is down the ice-bound Zanskar River gorges. Further to the west, many of the Zanskar Range passes are close to the Indian-Tibetan border, and are closed to trekkers.

In the Garhwal, roads are being constructed to the main places of pilgrimage in the heart of the Himalaya. These include Yamunotri Gangotri at the head of the Bhagirathi Valley, Kedarnath at the head of the Mandakini Valley, and Badrinath in the Alaknanda Valley. While most treks are followed from the roadhead to the river sources, alternative trek routes are available across the many mountain ridges that separate the headwaters of the Ganges.

Rivers

One of the distinguishing characteristics of the Himalaya is that the main river courses existed prior to the evolution of the mountains. The Sutlej was able to maintain its course flowing directly from Tibet to the Indian subcontinent, while the huge gorges on both flanks of the Himalaya reflect the ability of the Indus and the Brahmaputra to follow their original courses. The Indus flows west until it rounds the Himalaya by the Nanga Parbat massif, while the Brahmaputra flows eastwards for nearly 1000 km before cutting through to the Ganges basin.

The Indus River and its tributaries provide the principal drainage system in the western Himalaya. The catchment area is huge. The Kabul river system drains the Hindu Kush to the west, while the Shyok, Gilgit and Hunza river systems drain the Karakoram to the north. As the Indus flows to the plains it is fed by the Jhelum, the Chenab, the Ravi and the Sutlej rivers whose headwaters drain the entire West Himalaya.

The hill ridges at Simla mark the continental divide between the rivers that flow into the Indus and those that flow into the Ganges. Eastwards from the Sutlej the rivers drain into the Ganges basin. First there is the Tons which flows into the Yamuna, which in turn joins the Ganges at Allahabad. As the sacred Ganges continues its journey eastwards across north-east India, so it is fed by the main river systems of Nepal before reaching the Bay of Bengal.

The Brahmaputra is the third major system of the subcontinent. Like the Indus and the Sutlej it has its source close to Mt Kailash. From here, where it is known as the Tsangpo, it flows eastwards draining the Tibetan plateau and the headwaters of rivers north of the Himalaya, until it sweeps around the Assam Himalaya and descends to the Bay of Bengal.

CLIMATE

Climatically, the Indian Himalaya can be divided into three regions. The first contains the ridges and valleys to the south of the Pir Panjal Range, and the monsoonal hill states from Jammu to the Kumoun; the second includes the region south of the main Himalaya but beyond the Pir Panjal – it encompasses the Kashmir Valley and the valleys of Lahaul and Spiti, and has a modified monsoon climate. The third region, that of Ladakh and its environs, lies beyond the Himalaya and has a high altitude desert climate.

TREKKING SEASONS

The seasons to trek these regions are as follows. In the monsoonal hill states of Kangra, Kulu, Simla and the Garhwal, the trekking season is the month of June and from September until mid-October. In Kashmir it is from late May to October. The Lahaul/Spiti area offers good trekking from late May to October, although it is difficult to gain access to these regions until mid-June. In Ladakh the season is from May until October.

Spring in the valleys of Kashmir and Kulu begins in mid-March and continues through to the end of May. At this time Kashmir experiences its heaviest rainfall, with storms breaking over the Pir Panjal. In the valleys heavy rain can fall for two to three days while in the mountains snowfall can play havoc with early trek schedules. Late snow on the passes restricts extended treks until at least early June, while those that rely on passes

across the main Himalaya are rarely open until late June or early July.

Late snows can also interrupt pre-monsoon treks in Kulu and road access over the Rhotang Pass to Lahaul, so extended trek itineraries out of Kulu that continue to the Zanskar cannot normally be undertaken until late June or early July.

While the Kulu Valley experiences rain in July and August, the Kashmir Valley becomes hazy and humid. During these summer months temperatures often reach 30°C. In Kashmir the mountain trails are generally clear, while in the Kulu region it is recommended to go over the Rhotang Pass into Lahaul. Treks here are possible anytime between mid-June and October.

Autumn is the most settled period. The months of September and October are typically clear with a minimum of rain. Treks can be made throughout the Pir Panjal and the Himalaya from Kashmir, Kangra, Kulu and the Garhwal. Night time temperatures begin to drop by mid-October and early snows settle on the passes. However, this does not preclude valley treks, and many of the mountain valleys remain clear until December.

The winter months from December to March are marked during some years by heavy snowfall in early December. In other years the snows don't fall heavily until as late as the end of January. Downhill skiing in Gulmarg can be reliably undertaken from then until April, while those on cross country trips should plan ahead till late March and April.

Ladakh is isolated from most of the Indian climate patterns. Humidity is always low, and rainfall no more than a few centimetres a year. Until a few years ago, Ladakh was cut off completely for over six months of the year – from the time the snows fell on the passes in October until they melted again the following June. Rarely would the mail runner risk the avalanche-prone Zoji La in the middle of winter. Nowadays the commercial flights to Leh allow visitors to travel to Ladakh throughout the year, although the region is not particularly comfortable during the winter. Indeed, for many Ladakhis the flight is an opportunity to escape the cold and get down to the plains, so inbound flights carry only a few civilian passengers.

Ladakh experiences some of the coldest temperatures anywhere in the world, and it doesn't warm up till the spring in late April or early May. In June, July and August, daytime temperatures frequently rise to the high 20s, and the snow on the passes melts. Occasional heavy rain can be experienced in July and August, and care needs to be taken on river crossings. By September, the conditions are perfect and normally continue until late October, even though night time temperatures may fall below freezing. By November, the early winter snows fall on the passes closest to the Himalaya. In winter the Ladakhis still travel, enduring the intense cold to follow the valley floors where river crossings are no longer a problem. For the well-prepared trekker, there are possibilities of exploring the Indus and Zanskar valleys in the winter months.

NATURAL HISTORY & ECOLOGY

Over the last decade there has been an increasing awareness of the delicate ecological balance in the Himalaya. Some regions that have been overgrazed or denuded of timber have been designated as national parks or sanctuaries, while there are plans to impose restrictions on many of the other alpine valleys in the Indian Himalaya.

Until 1947 the balance of wildlife in the hills was closely regulated. Sport was a prime attraction of the area and close control was kept on hunting regulations. Since 1947 however, enforcement of the rules has lapsed and many of the protected species, including the snow leopard and the Kashmir stag, have been drastically reduced in number. It is only over the last decade that concerted action has been taken against poachers and fur traders.

In his book *The Wildlife of India*, the noted naturalist E P Gee refers to the diminishing numbers of the Kashmir stag in the Dachigam Sanctuary near Srinagar. In 1947 the population was estimated at between 1000 and 2000; by 1954 it had dropped to 300; by 1964 to less than 200; and by 1970

to less than 150. Strong measures backed by the Jammu & Kashmir Wildlife Directorate and the World Wildlife Organisation have been responsible for checking this decline, and the numbers today have increased to more than 500.

In 1984 the Uttar Pradesh government introduced restrictions on movement through the Valley of the Flowers and the Nanda Devi Sanctuary. Both the local shepherds and climbers have caused a gradual erosion of the flora and fauna, and a suitable period is necessary for these regions to regenerate.

In the high Himalayan valleys in Kashmir and Himachal Pradesh proposals have been made to regulate the shepherd migrations in the valleys that border the main Himalaya. The regions north-east of the Warvan Valley, and north-west of the Chenab up to the main Himalayan watershed have been designated. This ambitious scheme would effectively control the movement of the Bakharval and the Gaddi with their huge flocks of sheep and goats that have damaged the alpine hillsides. Alternative grazing areas have to be found, and the numbers strictly controlled, before the plans will achieve any degree of success.

In the meantime, the Dachigam Sanctuary is an example of successful regeneration by restricting movement through the area. The rich variety of wildflowers has been restored and, as a natural progression, the wildlife has returned and multiplied. This area had previously been overgrazed by the buffalo owned by the local Gujar shepherds. The sanctuary extends from the shore of Dal Lake to the 4000 metre high ridges beyond Tarsar Lake.

A day-trek can be made to the lower sanctuary beyond Harwan, just 20 km from Srinagar. Alternatively, a week or more could be profitably spent trekking to the upper sanctuary, either from Harwan, Tral (near Avantipura), or from the ridges of Tarsar Lake. If accompanied by an able guide, the experience is likely to be highly rewarding, and the chances of sighting the Kashmir stag and other rare wildlife species are quite high. Permits are necessary to visit the sanctuary; they cost Rs 20 per person per day, and can be obtained from the Wildlife Directorate in Srinagar.

While demands on the mountainside are being made by both conservationists and shepherds, trekkers have also made their mark over the past 20 years. While trekkers are likely to have a stronger awareness of the mountain ecology than those who visit the Himalaya by jeep or bus, there is still a need for regulation. In the most popular trek areas of the Kulu Valley and the Sindh and Lidder valleys, the trails and campsites are showing signs of deterioration. Garbage is seldom buried or burned, rain ditches are rarely filled in, and trees are often felled indiscriminately. In the West Himalaya the severe winters have, until now, been the one saving grace. Heavy snowfalls make the mountain regions wilderness areas for over half the year, and this gives the flora a chance to regenerate. There is also an abundance of dead wood for fires, so forest erosion is not as acute as in other Himalayan districts, such as the Khumbu region of Nepal. Yet the demands of both graziers and trekkers will soon exceed the environment's capacity.

It is hoped that with the recently established Himalayan Environment Foundation in Delhi, both foreign and local trekking companies will become more aware of the delicate ecological balance of these mountain areas.

Flora

The West Himalaya can be broadly classified into three main vegetation zones at various altitudes.

The highest is the alpine zone, the open grazing areas and flowered meadows above the treeline. The elevation of this alpine zone varies from 3500 to 4500 metres, though plant life is actually sustained to the margins of the permanent snowline at about 5000 metres.

Immediately below this is a transitional zone, or subalpine region, where birch groves, juniper and dwarf rhododendron grow at elevations of between 3400 and 3800 metres.

The temperate forest zone occurs in the lowest region. Generally, conifers are found on the higher levels, to 3500 metres, while the deciduous trees come at elevations lower than 3000 metres. Below 3000 metres many tree varieties – pines, firs, spruces, holly, oaks, ash, and alder – are interspersed. Each tree grows in its own specific elevation band, for example the blue pine, the deodar, and white oak grow between 1500 and 2500 metres, while the silver fir and brown oak are found between 2500 and 3500 metres. Bordering the forest regions are farming settlements with orchards and walnut groves. Cornfields are found at higher altitudes, to 3000 metres, while rice paddies are cultivated up to 2000 metres.

While these forest and vegetation categories are useful indications of elevation south of the main Himalayan range, to the north of the Himalaya in Ladakh, Zanskar and to some extent Lahaul, there are other relevant factors.

First, there is altitude. While the highest village in Kashmir is at no more than 3000 metres there are few villages in Ladakh below this elevation, so the forest regions of the latter are limited to willow, poplar, and sage bush. The lack of rainfall is the second factor. The vegetation is adapted to a drier climate and the alpine zone is characterised by plant species that have little resemblance to those of Kashmir or Himachal Pradesh.

Bearing this in mind, the alpine regions of Kashmir, Himachal Pradesh and Uttar Pradesh provide the best scope for appreciating the wild species of flora, many of which are similar to the mountain flora of Europe and the USA. For identifying the hundreds of varieties of wildflowers in the mountain districts of the subcontinent, you should consult *Flowers of the Himalaya* by Polunin & Stainton.

The flowering season is dependent on the spring snow melt and can vary considerably from year to year. In the regions over 3500 metres the alpine meadows become clear of snow sometime between mid-June and late July, depending on the harshness of the winter.

By summer, mid-July to late August, the alpine meadows of Kashmir, Himachal Pradesh and Uttar Pradesh are at their best. In Kashmir occasional storms break over the Pir Panjal, while Himachal Pradesh and the Garhwal region of Uttar Pradesh are subject to the monsoon. However, compensations abound for the well-prepared trekker.

In Kashmir, the region beyond Sonamarg, to Vishensar, Krishensar and Gangabal, is always a popular locality for those seeking wildflowers, and the trekking trails into the main Himalaya pass through alpine meadows that support a wide variety of flora. For those based in Srinagar a short trek to the upper Dachigam Sanctuary is recommended, and the valley above the Gujar village of Satlanjan, en route to the Kolahoi Glacier, is also worth visiting.

In Himachal Pradesh the alpine plateaus above the Kulu Valley are notable for wildflowers. The higher stages of the trek up the Jakatsukh Valley are particularly recommended, as the flora is subject to monsoon rains and abounds with exotic varieties. The trek up to Beas Kund is also recommended, particularly if it is undertaken in the middle of summer. The trek stages up to the Sach Pass beyond Chamba and the meadows below the Kugti Pass are also renowned for wildflowers. In Uttar Pradesh the alpine meadows between Yamunotri and Har-ki-Dun are recommended, and anyone who has read Frank Smythe's *The Valley of the Flowers* is sure to be attracted to the Bhyundar Valley in the heart of the Garhwal.

In Ladakh the wetter regions to the immediate west of the Himalaya, such as the Pensi La and the grazing grounds en route to the higher passes, support many wildflower species. As you move further away from the Himalaya, the alpine zones contain fewer flowering species.

Fauna

The migration of wildlife in the Indian Himalaya, while dependent on the seasons and the respective vegetation zones, has also been considerably influenced by the migration of shepherds and villagers to the mountain regions. As a general rule, the more remote the area, the greater the chance of seeing animals in their natural state. The only outstanding exception to this is the wildlife found in the Dachigam Sanctuary.

In the West Himalaya, wildlife such as the black and brown bear, the red fox, the stone-marten and members of the cat family (including the panther and snow leopard) inhabit the upper forest regions during the summer months. In spring, as soon as the snow at 3000 to 3500 metres begins to melt, the animals migrate higher to the birch groves and open meadows. The animals are less wary of human encroachment during this period and it is an ideal time to trek up the valleys from Phalgam, Sonamarg or Manali on skis or snowshoes.

The period between the snow's melt and the migration of shepherds to the high pas-

tures is an ideal time to explore the more remote valleys in the high conifer, subalpine zones. In May and early June it is common to see both black and brown bears, with their cubs, foraging for food above the Lidder Valley or in the Kulu region. The wild sheep and goat herds, including the urial and the markhor, inhabit the thicker birch and conifer forests – a habitat they share with the Kashmir stag and the musk deer. The bharal and ibex seek higher altitudes, particularly in Ladakh where they head for the most remote plateaus for their summer grazing. During the summer months the rare snow leopard, the wolf and the brown bear also roam here in search of prey – wild goats or those tended by shepherds. The alpine and subalpine zones are also the habitat of the marmots, the most common animals in these regions. You can hear them whistle from their burrows as soon as they sense danger. The common langur is often seen in the Himalaya, and its upward migration through the valleys to the conifer zones normally takes place very early in the season. Family groups of these

arboreal monkeys will occasionally wander close to campsites.

From midsummer until early autumn the bears are attracted to the valleys and villages by the ripening cornfields. Many tales are told of the destruction they cause, and the measures adopted to control them. The black bear is the main culprit, and is not on the list of protected wildlife. The rarer brown bear is protected, but tends to stick to the higher terrain until early winter.

Most of the animals make their own way down in late autumn, after the shepherds have departed down the valleys. In Ladakh, the rarer wild goat and sheep species descend to the security of the remote valleys, and their migration can be appreciated in late October. They are followed by packs of wolves and lone snow leopards. After the first winter snows wolf tracks are easy to follow, and their migration has been well documented in the Zanskar and Markha valleys. The snow leopard, the most elusive of the cat species, also descends to the highest villages in Kashmir and Himachal Pradesh.

Facts for the Trekker

VISAS

All nationalities, including Commonwealth citizens, are required to have a visa for India. Visas are issued at Indian embassies. They are valid for 90 days and can be extended for a further 90 days. Visas must be obtained no more than six months before your arrival in India. Indian visas are usually triple entry so you can travel to Nepal or Sri Lanka and return on the same visa.

Note that if you apply to visit Sikkim, the Punjab, or any politically restricted area, your visa application may take a minimum of three months, and sometimes far longer, to process. If you have any doubts as to whether this will fit into your plans, forget it. Once you have applied to visit a restricted area you cannot reapply for an ordinary tourist visa until your original application has been cleared.

Within India, visas can be extended at the Foreigners' Registration Office in Delhi or Srinagar, or at any other office of the Superintendent of Police, in Leh or Manali for example. The application is usually straightforward, and no particular problems are encountered. It is not advisable to leave India and apply for a new 90 day visa: the embassy in Kathmandu, for instance, is wary of re-applications and may restrict a new one to a few weeks.

If you stay in India for more than 90 days, be sure to hold on to your bank exchange certificates as you will need a tax clearance before leaving the country. An exemption form must be completed in the area in which you registered, ie if you were registered in Srinagar you must get a clearance from the local tax office there, and then you may need to get the relevant certificate re-endorsed at your port of exit in Delhi. Allow a day or so to complete formalities.

Restricted Areas

Special permits are not required for visiting Kashmir, Ladakh, Himachal Pradesh or Uttar Pradesh. However, it is important to remember that all Himalayan border regions are politically sensitive. The area of Ladakh from one mile (1.6 km) north of the Leh-Srinagar road is a restricted zone from which foreigners are barred. The same restrictions apply to the area one mile east of the Leh-Manali road beyond the Baralacha. At the time of writing it is possible to travel along this road, although it is important, as always, to check local regulations. The Rupsu region in Ladakh is now open to trekkers, but the region of Spiti is closed, as is the nearby region of Kinnaur. In the Garhwal, similar restrictions apply as you get closer to the Indian-Chinese border, and as a double check it is advisable to go to the police headquarters in Mussorie before proceeding. It should also be noted that certain other trekking areas such as the Nanda Devi Sanctuary are at present closed to trekkers.

It is necessary to carry your passport with you at all times. This is your only bona fide means of identification, and it will need to be shown at strategically placed checkpoints in Ladakh, Zanskar and Lahaul. No trekking permits are necessary for walking in the Indian Himalaya, although a permit system may be instituted in the next few years.

Postscript 1990

The political situation that erupted in Kashmir in January 1990 has dramatically reduced the number of people trekking in the region. Apart from the worries about safety there is also the problem of trying to ascertain whether or not Kashmir is actually open to tourists. In July 1990 certain areas of the Kashmir Valley were declared 'disturbed areas'. That is to say the Indian military and reserve police forces in Kashmir were given extraordinary powers of arrest etc, similar to the situation in the Punjab after 1984. However tourists were still permitted to go to Kashmir and there are no restrictions on their movement except the ones which were already in force, such as the ban on travel to areas close to the India/Pakistan ceasefire line, or to areas under curfew.

While the current political situation leaves much to be desired, people who have travelled to Kashmir this year have done so without incident. It must be emphasised that neither the state government nor the Kashmir separatist forces have any objection to foreigners visiting the region. The Kashmir tourist office is still open and the Mountaineering & Trekking Division was prepared to go out of their way to assist in arrangements.

For those that did give it a go there were the obvious rewards of having the mountain trails almost to themselves. For individuals planning to trek there were often delays in getting around. It could take the best part a day or two to catch a bus to Phalgam. Here the main bazaar was practically deserted except for the odd provision store. The hotels, including the lodges on the far side of the Lidder, were closed. Yet the horsemen were still anxious to work for anyone undertaking a trek up the Lidder Valley. For trekking further afield they were more reluctant, not wanting to wander too far from home.

Should the current political situation in Kashmir continue, then Ladakh is the obvious destination for trekkers undertaking an extended walk throughout the summer. With the exception of Lahaul and Kishtwar, all other regions are subject to the direct influence of the monsoon. In Himachal Pradesh and the Garhwal region of Uttar Pradesh itineraries are mainly restricted to the valleys in the pre-monsoon season in June, while the rains preclude trekking until the post-monsoon season in September and October

INSURANCE

Whether you're going alone or with a trekking agency, it is imperative to take out some cover against sickness, injury or loss of baggage. Most policies also cover the reimbursement of cancellation fees and other nonrecoverable expenses if you are forced to cancel your booking because of an accident or illness of a close family member. If you are trekking to a more remote location, more than a few days from the nearest roadhead, then an evacuation cover must also be seriously considered. Evacuation by helicopter can be very expensive – up to US$5000 or more, and a helicopter will not be sent unless the Indian Air Force has some guarantee of payment. Most reputable agencies who run treks to the Himalaya can organise policies to cover emergency evacuation, indeed many insist that this is taken out as a condition of booking. Do not rely on your consulate or embassy in Delhi to help.

Most insurance companies will cover a trekking trip for a premium equal to, or only slightly more than, the insurance for a normal holiday in India. A substantially higher premium is involved if you are intending to go mountaineering or skiing.

If you purchase insurance and incur a loss of baggage or personal items, you must submit proof of this in order to make a claim. If you have a medical problem it is important that you save all your bills and have a doctor's letter stating that you were sick. If you lose something covered by insurance you must file a police report and obtain a copy to send to the insurance company, no matter how remote the location. Insurance companies will generally not consider claims without this documentation. Read your policy carefully and make sure you understand all the conditions.

MONEY

The current exchange rates are as follows:

A$1	=	Rs 14.9
C$1	=	Rs 16.5
NZ$1	=	Rs 11.3
DM1	=	Rs 12.6
UK£1	=	Rs 37.0
US$1	=	Rs 19.3

The Indian rupee (Rs) is divided into 100 paise. There are coins of 5, 10, 20, 25 and 50 paise, and Rs 1, 2, and 5. Notes cover Rs 1, 2, 5, 10, 20, 50, 100 and 500. The rupee was once divided into 16 annas, and you may occasionally hear prices quoted in annas in bazaars and markets: 4 annas equal 25 paise.

Due to problems of fraudulent use, some banks, principally the State Bank of India, do not accept American Express travellers' cheques. Apart from this, major travellers' cheques are all easily exchanged in India, although US dollars and pounds sterling are the most well known foreign currencies. In out of the way centres you may find that these are the only currencies that are acceptable. Exchange rates tend to vary from bank to bank. Anything to do with paperwork in India is inevitably time-consuming, so you may find it easier to change a larger amount at one time (more than you would in other countries) simply to minimise the time wasted in banks. Get some small denomination notes as lack of change can be a problem in India.

Deciding on how much money to bring is a difficult consideration. If you are on a scheduled itinerary with most hotels, meals and sightseeing and/or trekking included, then you need little extra. A few hundred dollars will easily cover additional expenses such as alcohol, laundry and airport taxes.

If, however, you are handling your own arrangements, you will naturally need to budget for the unexpected. A good idea is to double your original budget, and itemise transport, food and equipment. Remember that government rates for accommodation can usually be bargained down, while actual costs for horsemen and porters are generally higher than the government recommended rates, especially when taking into account relocation costs of the horses and staff. Don't forget that the cooking gear and additional food for staff, together with their clothing and equipment, boosts the costs even further. A contingency fund should also be considered for unforeseen delays and emergencies.

Try to avoid having money transferred to you while you are in India. If this cannot be avoided, then have funds transferred by cable or telex, and not by mail.

There are two particular points to be careful about with Indian money. Firstly,

avoid grubby or torn notes – they may be unusable, particularly in remote locations. Secondly, try not to carry notes of large denominations. It can be difficult to use Rs 100 notes in a village, although don't worry unduly about having a month's supply of Rs 1 and Rs 2 notes, as most payments to horsemen, porters etc are made at the end of a trek and will require payments in higher denominations anyway.

Away from the major centres, changing foreign currency or travellers' cheques may be difficult, if not impossible. There are no facilities, for instance, for changing foreign money in the Zanskar or in Kishtwar while changing money in Leh or Kargil can take most of the day.

TOURIST INFORMATION

The Government of India tourist office maintains a number of overseas branches where you can obtain brochures, leaflets and some general information about India. The tourist office leaflets contain plenty of detail and are well worth getting hold of.

As well as the major offices the following list also includes smaller 'promotion offices' in Osaka (Japan), and Dallas, Miami, San Francisco and Washington DC (USA).

Australia
    Carlton Centre, 55 Elizabeth Street, Sydney, NSW 2000 (tel (02) 232 1600)
    Elder House, 111 St Georges Terrace, Perth, WA 6000 (tel (09) 321 6932)
Canada
    Suite 1016, Royal Trust Tower (PO Box 342), Toronto Dominion Centre, Toronto 1, Ontario (tel (416) 362 3188)
Japan
    Pearl Building, 9-18 Ginza, 7 Chome, Chuoku, Tokyo (tel 571 5062/3)
Singapore
    Podium Block, 4th Floor, Ming Court Hotel, Tanglin Rd, Singapore 10 (tel 235 5737)
Sweden
    Sveavagen 9-11 (Box 40016), 103-41 Stockholm 40 (tel (08) 215081)
Thailand
    Singapore Airline Building, 3rd floor, 62/5 Thaniya Rd Bangkok

UK
  7 Cork St, London WIX QAB (tel (071) 437 3677/8)
USA
  30 Rockefeller Plaza, 15 North Mezzanine, New York, NY 10020 (tel (212) 586 4901)
  201 North Michigan Ave, Chicago, Illinios 60601 (tel (312) 236 6899)
  3550 Wilshire Blvd, Suite 204, Los Angeles, California 90010 (tel (213) 380 8855)

Within India there are a number of Government of India Tourist offices that should be useful for general information, and these are listed below. However, for advice on trekking, particularly in Kashmir, it is advisable to wait until you reach the area. Reliable sources suggest that information, particularly from the Delhi office, has tended to be less than objective.

Bombay
  123 M Karve Rd (tel 293144)
Calcutta
  4 Shakespeare Sarani (tel 441402)
Jammu
  Gulab Bhavan (tel 5121)
Madras
  35 Mount St (tel 86240)
New Delhi
  88 Janpath (tel 320005)
Srinagar
  Residency Rd

There are also State Tourist offices, with staff specifically designated to cater for the needs of trekkers.

Jammu & Kashmir
  Trekking Officer in Charge, Tourist Reception Centre, Srinagar, Kashmir
Himachal Pradesh
  Trekking Officer in Charge, Tourist Office, Simla, Himachal Pradesh
Uttar Pradesh
  Trekking Officer in Charge, Tourist Office, Mussorie, Uttar Pradesh

GENERAL INFORMATION
Mail
The Indian postal services and poste restante are generally excellent. Expected letters almost always arrive, and letters that you send almost invariably reach the address you put on the envelope. American Express, in its major city locations, is an alternative to the poste restante system, but the latter is quite OK. Have letters addressed to you with your surname in capital letters and underlined. Many lost letters are simply misfiled under first names, so when in doubt check under both.

You can often buy stamps at good hotels, avoiding the interminable queueing in crowded post offices.

Telecommunications
Making a phone call from Kashmir to Delhi can involve a considerable wait, while to make an international phone call from Kashmir you need connections if you are to avoid hours at the local exchange. This is also the case for Kulu, Simla and Dharamsala. If there is an emergency it is best to go to Delhi where the international phone service is as good as anywhere else in the world. The alternative is to send a telegram which is a reliable service if the message is sent from a main post office.

Time

India is 5½ hours ahead of GMT, 10½ hours ahead of New York, 13½ hours ahead of the west coast of the USA, 4½ hours behind Sydney, and 15 minutes behind Nepal.

Business Hours

Government and airline offices are normally open from 10 am to 5 pm from Monday to Friday, and for a half day on Saturday. Take into account, though, the many holidays and festival dates, both local and national.

BOOKS & BOOKSHOPS

The many bookshops around Janpath and Connaught Circle, New Delhi provide India's largest stock of books on the Indian Himalaya, including many of the reprints listed below. Closer to the hills, the Kashmir bookshop on Sharvani Rd, Srinagar, has a comprehensive selection on Kashmir and Ladakh. In Leh, the Artou bookshop stocks an outstanding selection of volumes, and is on a par with some of the best Himalayan bookshops in Kathmandu's Thamel. In Simla there are a number of good bookshops on the Mall.

Guidebooks

Trekkers Guide to the Himalaya and the Karakoram by Hugh Swift (Hodder & Stoughton, London, 1982) gives an overview of trekking possibilities in the Himalaya.

Trekking in the Nepal Himalaya by Stan Armington (Lonely Planet, Melbourne, 1991) describes trekking routes out of Kathmandu.

Kashmir, Ladakh & Zanskar – a travel survival kit by Rolf & Margret Schettler (Lonely Planet, Melbourne, 1988) is a useful guide to general travel in the region.

India – a travel survival kit by Crowther, Raj, Wheeler et al (Lonely Planet, Melbourne, 1990) is recognised as *the* guide to travel throughout India.

Himalaya – a practical guide by Geiner & Ahluwalia (Himalayan Books, Delhi, 1985) should also be consulted.

Himalaya – Playground of the Gods by Mohan Kolhi (Vikas, Delhi, 1983) is also worth a look.

Guide to Kashmir, Ladakh & Skardu by Arthur Neve (Civil & Military, Lahore, 15th edition, 1933). If you are fortunate enough to come across this book, hang on to it. The guide ran into 17 editions between the wars and is still informative as to the state of the trails 50 years ago.

General

Where Men and Mountains Meet and *The Gilgit Game*, both by John Keay (John Murray, London, 1977 & 1979) are two indispensable books on the history of exploration in the Western Himalaya during the 19th century.

Foreign Devils on the Silk Road, *Trespassers on the Roof of the World* and *Setting the East Ablaze*, a trilogy by Peter Hopkirk (OUP, 1980, 1982 & 1984) are good background reading on the areas bordering the Himalaya.

The Abode of the Snows by Kenneth Mason (Diadem Books, reprint 1987) is the classic on Himalayan exploration and climbs.

Mountains of the Gods by James Cameron (Century Publications, London, 1984) is another well written guide to the history of Himalayan exploration.

Plain Tales from the Raj and *A Mountain in Tibet* (London, 1980), both by Charles Allen, also provide popular introductions to the history of the region.

The Wonder that was India by Basham (London, 1984) and *The History of India*, Volumes 1 and 2 by Romila Thapar and Percival Spear (Penguin, London, 1966) both offer a general historical introduction to India.

History and Culture of the Himalayan States, Volumes 1-3 on Himachal Pradesh, and Volumes 4-5 on Jammu by Charak (Light & Life Publications, New Delhi) provide historical accounts of the West Himalayan states.

The two collections of Mountain Travel books by Eric Shipton & H W Tilman (Diadem Books, 1985, and The Mountaineers, Seattle, 1985) are highly recommended for background reading on exploration in the Indian Himalaya and beyond.

For social and cultural perspectives the following are good reading:

A Portrait of India by Ved Mehta (Penguin, London, 1968)

An Area of Darkness by V S Naipul (Penguin, London, 1968)

India, the Seige Within by M J Akbar (Penguin, London, 1985)

Kashmir

Kashmir by Rughubir Singh is the best illustrated book on the Kashmir Valley, followed by *Kashmir*, by Francis Brunel (Rupca, Delhi, 1979).

This is Kashmir by Pearce Gervis (Universal Publications, Delhi, 1974) is a storehouse of historical information.

Travels in Kashmir by Bridgid Keenan, (OUP, 1989) provides a highly readable account of the history and handicrafts of the Kashmir Valley.

Ladakh

Ladakh by Heinrich Harrier, (Penguin, Verlag, 1980) is the best of the many illustrated books on Ladakh.

The Cultural History of Ladakh Volumes 1 and 2, by Snellgrove & Skorupski (Vikas, Delhi, 1977 & 1980) provide the most comprehensive cultural background.

The Lion River by Jean Fairly, and *Journey Through Ladakh* by Andrew Harvey (John Day, New York, 1875) are also recommended.

Himalayan Art by Madajeet Singh (Macmillan New York 1968) is an excellent guide to the various art styles that have evolved in the Himalaya, and includes sections on Ladakh and Lahaul.

Ladakh by Alexandra Cunningham, (Sagar Publications, Delhi, 1977) written in the mid-19th century, provides a comprehensive survey of all things Ladakhi and is a wealth of information.

A History of Ladakh by Francke (Sterling Publications, Delhi, 1977) is also available as the standard history on Ladakh.

Hiking in Zanskar and Ladakh (Artou, Switzerland 1987) is a useful trekking guide.

Himachal Pradesh

Himalayan Hill Districts of Kooloo, Lahaul & Spiti by Harcourt (Vivek Publications, Delhi, reprint 1982) was the first account of the rich history of the Kulu Valley.

Kulu – the End of the Habitable World by Penelope Chetwold (Allied Publications, Delhi, 1980) is widely available.

Over the High Passes by Christina Noble (Collins, London, 1987) also picks up on the background of the Kulu & Kangra valleys, while tracing the migration of the Gaddi shepherds.

Uttar Pradesh

Garhwal by G & M Thukral (Frank Bros, Delhi, 1987) is a wonderfully illustrated book on the region.

Valley of the Flowers by Frank Smythe remains a classic on the area. Also refer to:

Beautiful Garhwal by Ruskin Bond (EDB Publishers, Dehra Dun, 1988).

The Ascent of Nanda Devi by H W Tilman and *Nanda Devi* by Eric Shipton are both now available in the collection of *Six Mountain Travel Books* by Shipton, and *The Seven Mountain Travel Books* by Tilman (Diadem Books, 1985 and The Mountaineers, Seattle, 1985).

India by Jim Corbett, edited by Hawkins, is recommended for anyone who doubts the feats of true adventure in the Indian foothills.

19th Century Accounts

Travels in Hindustan and the Punjab by Moorcroft & Trebeck (OUP, reprint 1979) is indispensible background reading on travels in the western Himalaya in the 1820s.

Travels in Kashmir, Ladakh, and Iskardo by Vigne, (Sagar Publications, Delhi, 1978) who covered much of Kashmir, Ladakh and Baltistan in the 1830s.

Western Himalayas and Tibet by Thomson, (Cosmo Publications, Delhi, 1978) and *Ladakh* by Alexandra Cunningham (Sagar Publications, Delhi, 1977) are both references from the Ground Commission of the late 1840s.

Other volumes which are interesting, but not always available, include:

The Northern Barrier of India by Drew

The Valley of Kashmir by Lawrence (Kaser Publications, Srinagar, 1967). Lawrence was the Land Reform Commissioner in Kashmir in the 1880s.

20th Century Accounts

Kashmir by Younghusband (Sagar Publications, Delhi, 1970),

Kashmir in Sunlight and Shade by Tyndale Biscoe (Sagar Publications, Delhi, 1971)

Thirty Years in Kashmir by Arthur Neve (Asia Publications, Lucknow, 1984).

Natural History

Indian Hill Birds by Salim Ali (OUP) is still the best bird book available.

Flowers of the Himalaya by Polunin & Stainton (OUP) is essential for anyone interested in the flora of the region.

The Stones of Silence by G B Schaller (Vikas Publishing, New Delhi, 1980) provides the best illustrated guide to the wildlife of the region.

The Wildlife of India by E P Gee contains a section on the Dachigam Sanctuary, while the superbly illustrated *Indian Wildlife* (Insight Guides, 1987) also has a chapter on this region.

MAPS

The trekking maps in this book are basic ridge and river profiles, based on the Ground Survey of India 1:250,000 maps. The Ground Survey maps have local information supplied by the tourist department, and have the advantage of being very clear. They are available through the Jammu & Kashmir tourist departments in Delhi and Srinagar, and consist of two sheets – one for Kashmir and one for Ladakh, at Rs 20 each. For Himachal Pradesh there are three similar sheets, one for Chamba-Kangra-Kishtwar, a second for Kulu-Lahaul-Spiti, and a third for Kinnaur-Simla.

The US Army maps (U-502 series) 1:250,000 are the best commercially available contour maps. The originals, published in 1948, were in colour, but the series reprints are in black and white and somewhat difficult to follow. It is best to colour in the river and glacial systems to get a general profile of the region. The most relevant to Jammu & Kashmir are 43.6 Srinagar, 43.7 Kargil, 43.8 Leh, 43.11 Anantnag, and 43.12 Padum. The most useful for Himachal Pradesh and Uttar Pradesh are 43.16, 44.13, 43.4, 44.1 Himachal Pradesh and 44.6 Nanda Devi. These are generally available through Stanfords, 12-14 Long Acre, London, UK. Stanfords is a leading map supplier which regularly prints updates on what is available in the U-502 series, and also on new maps of the Indian Himalaya published in Europe.

DISTANCES & ALTITUDES

An average group will cover two to three km in an hour along a jeep track but considerably less, perhaps 1½ km, on a demanding pass ascent. Bearing this in mind, a five or six hour day will average 12 to 14 km – sufficient to appreciate the trek while still achieving a decent day's walk.

Altimeters have a disadvantage in that the trekker cannot unduly exaggerate his or her performance after returning home. However, there is always some leeway. I have watched Leh rise and fall nearly 100 metres in one day, not from any strange hallucinations but simply by recording altimeter readings on a stormy day. Barometric pressures change considerably in mountain regions, and I have not yet spent sufficient time with an altimeter to record every pass and valley in a variety of weather conditions. When altitude figures are given for passes or villages, these are estimates, and should be taken as such. Spot heights referring to mountains on the maps are more accurate, and have been taken from the Ground Survey of India.

Remember that compass bearings in the Himalaya are only as good as the maps you are following.

WHERE TO TREK

Once you have decided to go to India, the next step is to decide where you want to trek, whether it is the right season for a particular area, and whether that area is the most attractive in terms of walking conditions and culture. Check out the guidebooks and follow this through with background reading on the region. Write off for travel brochures and information from the Indian tourist office, and talk to people who have recently returned – compare their experiences with your own expectations, and see how they measure up. Be as flexible as possible at this stage; there are many opportunities in the Indian Himalaya and some careful thinking at the outset will go a long way towards ensuring a successful trek.

Ultimately, of course, it is a question of what is available and what you can afford. Itemise the cost of organising the trek independently. Calculate how much you need to spend on clothing, equipment, medical supplies, insurance, food, cooking gear and the additional cost of horses and perhaps a cook and a guide. Then compare and consider the alternatives and the variables: the number of people who are interested and can share costs, and their degree of commitment. Compare these with the costs of an organised trip through a trekking company and decide which plan of action suits you.

For many, the alternatives are also limited by time. Consider how long you are going to be away and the length of the trek. Never follow a too ambitious itinerary if time is limited by travel or work commitments. You must structure your plans to meet the pace of India. For example, you may experience delays waiting for flight connections or for guides or horsemen to assemble at the right spot on the right date. Plan an itinerary but be prepared to modify it. Remember that the stages in this guide are based on schedules to allow for inclement weather, acclimatisation, sickness and other delays.

Your outdoors experience is also a factor, and you must assess this for yourself. Trekking in India is more of a wilderness experience than trekking in Nepal. Attention must be paid to pass and river crossings: sound common sense is essential and it can be a lifesaver. Remember to structure your trek around the weakest member of your party. A weekend bushwalk is one thing, but a trek in the Himalaya for a week or more is quite another. A trek can be exhilarating, but it can also be frustrating for those who are not fully aware of what it is actually like to camp for weeks at a time. Friendships can often become strained unless each person is actually aware of what they are letting themself in for.

After considering the cost, the time available and your outdoors experience, it is worthwhile to at least examine the various options open.

WHAT STYLE OF TREK
Adventure Travel Company
Over the last decade or so many companies have extended their programmes from Nepal to the Indian Himalaya. The Indian tourist offices have a file of recommended organisations. Points to bear in mind when considering these companies include their experience in handling trips to India, the leaders they employ, the type of food, equipment, medical kits, and information they provide, the evacuation/insurance cover, and the specialist interests they cater for. Ultimately, any travel company is only as good as its local ground agent, and this should be carefully considered before making any commitment.

Local Agent
You could of course try to bypass the overseas travel company, and deal directly with the local agent. This can be done by writing to the Indian state tourist offices who will be able to supply you with the names and address of local agents. You can contact these agents beforehand or on arrival in India. Quotes should be taken from two or three companies, and from this you will have to ascertain their degree of expertise and competence in dealing with your party. You must of course carefully check what is included, as well as the exact details of your trek itinerary, so that you end up paying for, and going, where you planned to. This takes time, and has to be weighed up against the do-it-yourself option.

Do-it-Yourself
At a hill station or trekking-off point you can arrange your own equipment, food and staff. If you have sufficient time and patience to organise things, either directly or through a local person, then this can be a highly rewarding experience, besides saving you money.

You must, however, be aware of the problems of dealing with a culture that is vastly different from that of the West. This will colour many of your negotiations. Don't expect things to happen quickly, or expect a straight answer when it comes to times and stages. It's an open bargaining situation. The horsemen will naturally want to go on the less demanding route, and will lose little time in explaining to you that the relevant passes you wish to cross are snowbound, blocked by bears or any number of other obstacles. The result is that you may have to alter your ambitious plans and accept an easier, less challenging, alternative. Generally, no staff or horsemen are prepared to go on an extended trek on their own. They will insist on taking a work companion with them, and this will obviously increase the cost. It is worth considering the possibility of having other people join your party and share some of the costs.

A cook is a valuable asset who will save

you the expense of buying pots and pans, and can recommend what food is the most suitable to bring with you. A cook can also bargain hard for you in the market, saving large amounts of otherwise wasted time. In return, they will expect some clothing allowance, normally local walking boots, plus a decent tip at the end of the trek.

Your choice of guide is vital. You are dependent on their experience and reliability, which can either make or break your trek. It is essential that, before hiring a guide, you check their experience in the area you are going to, their attitude and connections with other staff, and their general knowledge of the region. Once the rate has been fixed, the guide is your representative, and should be reminded of this when negotiating with the cook, the horsemen or the various other suppliers.

As the contractor of your trek you will also be held in the position of employer should something go wrong. It is particularly necessary that you have additional funds with you to deal with an emergency, and carry a medical kit that can cover most eventualities.

Backpacking

This can be easily undertaken on short treks where the payload is light and the stages easy. On a long trek, your backpack may weigh you down to the point where you see more of your feet than of the mountains. In Nepal this style of trekking has become quite popular because you can trek from teahouse to teahouse. In India there is no direct counterpart of this system. The British rest houses, or the dak bungalow equivalents, are a long way down the line, and food supplies en route tend to be unreliable. In the Zanskar a teashop-cum-travellers inn system has evolved in the last few seasons, but the facilities are limited in comparison to those provided in Nepal. It is one thing to carry your own gear for a few days, but quite another to carry it for two weeks or more. Some trekkers compromise, but a porter or horseman is generally necessary unless you're very fit and experienced in the wilderness.

Whatever option you choose, whether it be backpacking, joining an adventure travel company group, or something in between, the magic of the Himalaya should always be experienced, and shared with the local people. A local crew can enhance your experience in a way that is sometimes not appreciated by people wary of anything that hints of the 'Raj'. However, work with a trekking party is a valuable source of employment for the local cooks, guides and horsemen, and their involvement and sense of humour can remain with you for a long time after you return home. Experiences in the Himalaya are shared experiences, and there is nothing finer than having these enhanced by a great crew.

CLOTHING

Clothing considerations differ widely from trek to trek. A short hike up the Lidder Valley in the middle of August could be undertaken in shorts, T-shirt, a warm pullover, sandshoes and a sun hat; a traverse from Kashmir to Ladakh in June, however, would require a far more comprehensive clothing list. One of the most important considerations is the manner in which you trek – if you are using packhorses then weight is not such a problem as when carrying all your gear in your backpack. The checklist below must therefore be interpreted liberally. Experienced bushwalkers will already have a good idea as to what they believe is most suitable, but for those with less outdoors experience the following hints may prove useful.

In all mountain areas you should be prepared for inclement weather. On the other hand, excessive clothing takes some of the simple delight out of trekking and it can also be very expensive. Remember that most of the clothing that you would take on a weekend bushwalk is also suitable for trekking the Himalayan foothills. During the period in which you will be walking in India, heat will be just as much a consideration as the cold. For the majority of treks you will not be walking in snow, and it is not necessary to equip yourself with double boots and heavy down gear as if you were about to climb Everest. A sturdy pair of boots is always recommended, as is a good wind- and waterproof jacket and a comfortable backpack which is adequate for your needs. An invaluable extra is a sturdy walking stick – useful on muddy trails and for warding off over-friendly shepherd dogs.

If you are travelling exclusively in India and are not prepared to carry huge quantities of trekking gear around all the time, you can practically equip yourself in India. A local tailor can make up a pair of shorts and comfortable long trousers in an afternoon. Raw wool pullovers, long johns, string vests, gloves, socks, and balaclavas can be purchased in the bazaars, while local hunter boots are just about adequate for a short valley trek. A windproof/waterproof jacket and a decent backpack are therefore the minimum requirements. The tourist office in Srinagar has a stock of boots and jackets for hire, but as yet there are none of the local trekking and clothing shops which are found in Kathmandu.

Clothing Checklist
Walking Boots These are the most important item when considering your trekking gear. Boots must give good ankle support and have a sole flexible enough to meet the anticipated walking conditions. A sole fitted with a three-quarter length shank is not necessary unless you intend to tackle extensive snow and glacial terrain. Ensure that your boots are well walked-in beforehand, and don't forget to bring spare laces and some waterproofing application such as Dubbin.

Jacket Unless you have a very tight budget it is worthwhile investing in a top range Gortex jacket. This will serve your needs in the Himalaya, and be an invaluable asset on any outdoor trip you undertake when you return home.

Down Vest Recommended for those chilly mornings. If you already have a full down jacket then there is no harm in bringing it along, although the temperatures on your trek are seldom likely to call for its use, unless you really feel the cold.

Wool Shirt or Pullover A thick woollen shirt is worth its weight in gold. This is an item that does not cost the earth but can contribute greatly to your total wellbeing. As an alternative, raw wool pullovers can be purchased locally in Srinagar, Leh and Manali for about Rs 150.

Breeches A pair of woollen walking breeches is ideal. Ex-army woollen pants are another option. Pile trousers provide a satisfactory alternative, or even track suit bottoms if you are not likely to be going above 3500 metres. A lighter pair of reinforced cotton ex-army pants is also a useful item. Jeans are totally unsuitable in wet conditions.

Over Trousers A strong nylon pair is indispensable in wet weather.

Shorts Ideal for most trekking, although they should not be worn in villages, monasteries or others places were they may cause offence to the locals.

Shirts T-shirts are OK, but include some cotton shirts with collar and sleeves to give much-needed protection in the sun. Ex-army shirts with plenty of pockets are ideal.

Thermal Underwear Both the vest and bottoms can make a significant difference to comfort. A double layered vest is especially recommended, particularly if you are unsure of the adequacy of your sleeping bag. Also include a normal quantity of regular underwear for the trek.

Gloves & Balaclava Both items can be purchased locally in the Srinagar, Manali and Leh markets. A balaclava is particularly important as considerable body heat is lost through the head.

Socks A sufficient supply of thick and thin pairs should be taken. Use cotton inner socks and woollen outer socks when on the trail.

Sandshoes For campsites and days when you have blisters.

Sunhat Absolutely essential.

Tracksuit A bit of luxury for sitting in the mess tent in the evening.

Snow Gaiters Recommended, especially during the early part of the season when there is likely to be snow on the passes.

Snow Goggles/Sunglasses Good quality snow or ski goggles are necessary to combat the side glare on the snow. Even if you are not actually walking on snow, the side glare from snow on the ridges can make goggles necessary. For non-snow conditions sunglasses are adequate.

EQUIPMENT

Over the last few seasons a number of outlets in Delhi and Srinagar have begun to stock lightweight equipment for hire. In Delhi it is best to check with the Government tourist office in Janpath for up-to-date lists of stockists. In Srinagar the tourist office has a stock of sleeping bags and boots for hire, while Choomti Trekkers on the Bund are doing their best to equip trekkers with lightweight stoves, cooking utensils and such, and are a mine of information as to where you may be able to get that extra tent or insulated mat. However, in the middle of the season most stocks of anything useful are depleted, and serious trekkers making their own arrangements are advised to bring their own tent, sleeping bag, insulated mat, stove, and backpack with them. For those undertaking an inclusive trek, professional agencies usually provide these basic essentials, although it is advisable to double check before you leave for India as to exactly what is provided.

Equipment Checklist

Holdall A strong duffel bag or holdall is necessary for carrying your gear on the packhorses. The bag should be large enough to contain all your personal gear.

Stuff Bags To protect your clothes from the elements you should bring a few stuff bags, as most holdalls are not totally waterproof. Strong plastic bags are an ideal alternative.

Backpack Internal frame backpacks are ideal for longer walks. Ensure that the sack is large enough to carry your toilet gear, camera, waterproof jacket and sweater, as the packhorses may not be at hand during a sudden change of weather. It is not recommended to bring a large backpack as a means of packing gear onto horses, as the condition of the backpack will deteriorate rapidly after a few weeks of rough treatment by over-zealous horse handlers.

Water Bottle An aluminium or ex-army make is recommended, although plastic bottles can be purchased locally.

Swiss Army Knife The pride of any shepherd's possessions, and always useful for peeling fruit and opening tins; one with a small screwdriver is invaluable for carrying out camera repairs.

Torch (Flashlight) & Candles Available in India, but don't forget spare batteries and bulbs.

Umbrella For the rain, and shielding yourself from the sun; also handy when making discreet calls of nature. Available locally.

First Aid Kit Refer to the Health chapter for recommendations on what to include.

Miscellaneous Toiletries, toilet paper, waterproof matches, sun block, towel, laundry soap, sewing kit, safety pins, a length of cord, and some small plastic bags to carry toilet paper and litter until you can dispose of it properly.

Optional Extras Altimeter, compass, binoculars, notebook and pens.

Equipment for Independent Trekkers
The following is a checklist for trekkers going it alone:

Tent A doubled walled tent is necessary on most treks, except for a short ramble up the Lidder Valley, as there are few of the teashops or overnight hotels that are so common in Nepal.

Sleeping Bag A good quality sleeping bag is imperative. Fibrefill bags dry a lot faster in wet conditions, although a down bag is more compact and lighter.

Insulated Mat A closed cell mat should provide adequate insulation from the ground. A space blanket can double as a ground sheet. A Thermarest is a real luxury and well worth bringing, even if you do encounter hardy Wilfred Thesinger types in the hills.

Rope Whatever trek you are undertaking, a 40 metre length of rope is highly recommended for ensuring safe river crossings, particularly in Kashmir, Kulu and the Garhwal in the early part of the season, and in Ladakh and the Zanskar in midsummer.

Cooking Utensils Cooking pots and pans, enamel mugs, plates and cutlery, in fact all kitchen utensils, can be purchased in India. Camping Gaz containers or refills are not available. Local kerosene stoves provide a cheap and efficient alternative, although most locals use wood fires for cooking the evening meals. Remember to take spare parts and an ample supply of stove pins.

Miscellaneous Plastic drums for carrying kerosene, mustard oil etc can be purchased locally. Large canvas mess tents can be hired for your crew to sleep in during the trek.

High Altitude Treks For exploring glaciers or undertaking minor climbs you'll need to bring your own ice axe, crampons, harness, carabiners, rope and other hardware, as most of these items are not readily available in India.

PHOTOGRAPHY
Ideally you should bring two single reflex cameras with you – one for colour, and one as a reserve. As far as lenses are concerned, you could bring a wide angle for village profiles and monastery interiors, a macro lens for wildflowers, a telephoto for dramatic mountain shots and people close-ups and a zoom lens for on the move photography. A flash unit, light meter and tripod should also be carried, together with a Polaroid camera so that every mother and child in every village can have a memento of your visit. All this, of course, requires at least 10 rolls of colour film per day to cover the wide variety of interests that abound when you are trekking.

In practice, most of us have to settle for less, and get by with an Instamatic or SLR camera with a standard 50 mm lens. If you have never used a camera before, then a trip to the Himalaya is an ideal opportunity to start. If you have previously used a camera, I would advise a reliable SLR body with a wide angle and zoom lens. A zoom lens is ideal for nonintrusive people photography. You can get a full-frame photograph of a shy villager without them noticing that you have taken their picture. If you can afford it, buy a zoom lens that is of the same make (dedicated) as your SLR camera. A wide angle lens is great for taking shots of interiors, and campsites with a full panorama of the mountains.

Bring a change of UV filters, while extra camera and flash batteries are essential, plus a blower brush and cleaning equipment. The temperatures in summer do not necessitate the camera being 'winterised'. If, however, you are going to ski in Kashmir or trek in Ladakh in the winter, then this process should be considered. Don't forget, waterproof containers are essential to protect your film and camera gear in prolonged rainy conditions, while an X-ray bag is highly recommended for taking your film through the many airport security checks in the Indian subcontinent.

Film is very expensive in India and you should bring all your colour film with you. If possible, allow a roll a day. Otherwise try to ration your film so that you don't use half of your supplies before you set off on the trail. Some fast film, ASA 400, is necessary,

especially if you're using a zoom or telephoto lens in low light conditions. Slide film is cheaper than the print variety, and your best slides can be reprocessed as prints. Don't send film back from India by post – it will probably get there but it may be delayed or subjected to damage, heat or opening for customs inspection. Keep it cool and secure until your return home. Colour film can be processed in Bombay and Delhi, but the quality is uneven.

If you are buying new equipment, check it out thoroughly beforehand and make sure you know how to use it. Keep a record of light conditions and compare the results when the photos are developed. If you haven't used your camera for a while, have it serviced before you leave.

Finally, consider that you will be carrying the majority of your photographic gear with you each day. Your camera gear will almost certainly be the heaviest component of your daypack, so don't weigh yourself down with too much gear. Taking photographs should complement the enjoyment of your trek, and not be viewed as end in itself.

Health & First Aid

The material on trekkers' health and first aid in this section was prepared by Dr Jim Duff, a doctor with wide experience of medical treatment in remote areas.

PRE-DEPARTURE PREPARATIONS
Preliminary Considerations
Having a suitable temperament is the most important consideration for undertaking a trek in the Himalaya. If you have any doubts about whether you can cope with the stresses of being away from it all for a period of weeks, then it is advisable to restrict your initial outdoors experience to a shorter trek nearer to home.

I have led many groups over the last 20 years, and I am convinced that if someone has the will to complete a trek, then they will do so. Encouragement is often necessary, but most problems arise in the head rather than in the feet. Trekking is not an activity exclusively for the young – age is no barrier. In fact people of more mature years often do better than the young. It is essential to approach the Himalaya with a sound and tolerant attitude.

Having made the decision to go to the Himalaya, get fit! Jogging, swimming, cycling – in fact any regular physical exercise – is desirable. Begin your programme preferably three months before your trek, and try to exercise daily for at least half an hour. The fitter you are, the more you get out of your trek. If you do nothing beforehand, you will probably finish the trek but feel completely exhausted for the first week on the trail. Most people have never felt better than after two or three weeks of continuous walking in the mountains. Rarefied air, exercise and wholesome food are the ideal combination for rejuvenating both the mind and the body.

Health Insurance
A travel insurance policy is vital if you are going trekking. While most general travel insurances cover you against sickness while on a trek, not all cover you for emergency evacuation, which can run into many thousands of dollars if a helicopter is required. Remember that, should evacuation be necessary, some proof of insurance and of your ability to pay, will save time, and even a life. Bear in mind also that most embassies and consulates in Delhi will authorise evacuation only after contacting your next of kin, and that again can take days.

Medical Check-up
It is recommended that you have a physical examination before undertaking your trek. Anyone with long-term symptoms (indigestion, chest pain, wheezing or coughing, back or joint problems, recurrent infections, or dental problems) should have them thoroughly investigated before leaving home. All problems are exacerbated by altitude and strenuous exercise, and seem more serious in proportion to your distance from medical help.

Immunisation
Vaccinations provide protection against diseases that you may be exposed to in India. Plan ahead for getting them, since some require an initial shot followed by a booster.

Smallpox
> This has now been eradicated worldwide, so immunisation is no longer necessary.

Cholera
> The vaccination provides only limited protection.

Tetanus
> A booster is recommended if it's more than 10 years since the last one.

Polio
> Have a booster if it's more than 10 years since your last one.

Typhoid
> A primary course or a booster is recommended if it's more than three years since the last one.

Infective hepatitis
Gamma Globulin gives prophylaxis against Hepatitis A. One 5 ml dose lasts four months.
Meningitis
The vaccine gives two years protection.
Malaria
Chloroquine 250 mg, two per week and Maloprin, one per week, should be sufficient for the malarial areas of northern India. Start two weeks before, and continue for four weeks after leaving the area. (They're best taken after food at night.)

FIRST AID KIT

The kit you take on your trek will depend on a number of factors. It will depend on whether you are going on your own, or whether a kit is provided by the company which is making your ground arrangements. It will also depend on the degree of confidence you have in handling medical situations, and also on the remoteness of your trek itinerary, the availability of drugs and cost of compiling the kit.

The following list has been prepared as a guide, and needs to be varied depending on the above considerations. Consult a doctor about which drugs you should carry and in what quantities. For details of dosage and administration of these drugs, follow the instructions of the manufacturer or the doctor who prescribes them.

Drugs are listed with their generic names followed, in some cases, by trade names.

Pain, Inflammation & Fever
Aspirin
For relieving mild pain, reducing fever, and as a mild anti-inflammatory. Side effects include rashes and indigestion.
Paracetamol
As an alternative to aspirin, with no common side effects
Codeine Phosphate
For moderate to severe pain. It sedates coughing and slows diarrhoea. Side effects include rashes, constipation, nausea and respiratory depression.
Pentazocine
A strong pain killer which is more effective as an injection. Side effects include nausea, vomiting, hallucination and respiratory depression.

Diarrhoea
Electrolyte salt sachets eg Gastrolyte, Repalyte
Used to treat or prevent dehydration due to diarrhoea, vomiting, shock, heat exhaustion, bleeding, burns etc. No side effects. Follow the instructions and give enough to produce plenty of clear urine.
Immodium (Lomotil)
Slows diarrhoea. A side effect is constipation. Do not use if diarrhoea is bloody. Aim to slow the bowels down, not to stop them.

Infection & Antibiotics
Metronidazole (Flagyl, Fasigyn, Tinidazole)
Used as a treatment for amoeba, giardia, vaginitis, or acute appendicitis. Side effects are nausea, fatigue, rashes and weakness.
Trimethoprim sulfa-methoxasole (Bactrim DS, Septrin forte)
An antibiotic for treating diarrhoea and ear, skin, sinus, chest or urinary tract infections. Side effects are a rash in sulpha-sensitive persons.
Ampicillin
An alternative antibiotic to Bactrim. Side effects are a rash and diarrhoea.
Erythromycin
An alternative antibiotic to the previous two, with similar indications. Specific for streptococcal sore throat. Side effects are the same as Ampicillin.

Nausea & Vomiting
Metoclopramide (Maxclon)
Prochlorperazine (Stemetil)
To control nausea and vomiting. Suppositories are for use if tablets cannot be kept down. It is also available as an injection. One side effect is drowsiness.

Constipation & Piles (Haemorrhoids)
Dulcolax tablets
For relief of constipation.
Rectinol, Haemorex, Anusol creams
For the treatment of internal and external piles. Apply to the anus, or insert into the rectum using the plastic nozzle, immediately after having a crap, or three times daily.

Allergy, Skin Infection & Antiseptics
Diphenydramine HCl (eg Benadryl)
An antihistamine for hay fever, drug rashes and insect bites. Also treats the swelling which may occur with acute allergic reactions. Side effect is drowsiness. The drug can be used as a mild tranquilliser.

Antihistamine cream (eg Anthisan)
> For local application to bites and rashes to help control itching.

Hydrocortisone cream (eg Hydrocort)
> As for antihistamine cream, and it may be used as an anti-inflammatory in allergic rashes.

Betadine, Dettol, Lugol's iodine solution
> For the treatment of superficial skin infections, or cleaning wounds and abrasions.

Canestan cream
> Antifungal cream for conditions such as ring-worm, tinea, or vaginal thrush infections.

Eye & Ear Infections

Soframycin eye & ear drops
> The side effects include allergy. Dose: two drops every hour.

Burns

Silvazine cream
> Apply to burnt area after removing charred clothing or skin.

Respiratory Problems

Strepsil lozenges
> For sore throat, to be sucked slowly.

Drixine
> A nasal decongestant.

Indigestion

Antacid tablets
> One or two, chewed or swallowed.

Acute Mountain Sickness

Acetazoleamide (Diamox)
> One tablet morning and night as a preventative for AMS.

Equipment

Hardware
> Five syringes (2 ml) and needles; 20 alcohol swabs; scalpel blade plus holder; scissors; tweezers; packaged kit with needle holder & sutures (two large, one medium); low reading thermometer

Dressings
> Butterfly steristrip; 45 cm (18 inch) wire mesh splint; large roll cotton wool; 10 pieces of 10 cm gauze; large trauma dressings; triangular bandage; band-aids; moleskin; 2.5 cm (one inch) adhesive tape; 10 cm (four inch) adhesive bandage; 10 cm elastic bandage; two crepe bandages.

DAY TO DAY HEALTH
Basic Considerations

Common sense is perhaps the most valuable asset when undertaking a trek. Personal hygiene, including the regular washing of hands before handling food, will go a long way to reducing the chances of sickness. If you have a choice, stay at the cleanest looking hotel or guesthouse.

For many trekkers, the fresh air and exercise, combined with a good diet, will minimise the chance of sickness. If you do get the 'runs', drink plenty of fluids, avoid coffee and alcohol and eat simple food sparingly. Diarrhoea is nature's cure for bowel infections. Don't consider treatment for at least 48 hours unless dehydration is occurring.

Water

The adage of 'don't drink the water' applies equally in the Himalaya as elsewhere in India. Boiling will reduce the number of germs, but at higher altitudes where water boils at a lower temperature, such as in Ladakh, a water purifier or iodine solution is also necessary.

An iodinisation kit in your bag allows you to fill your water bottle from a nearby stream, treat it with four to eight drops of Lugol's iodine solution per litre of water, and 30 minutes later have cold, safe drinking water. Add more iodine if the water is very cold or particularly polluted. If the water is heavily contaminated, either add more iodine solution or wait for longer than 30 minutes before drinking.

Do not use iodine sterilisation for prolonged periods, ie longer than three months.

Food

Remember that a healthy diet makes for a healthy trek. The freshly made chappatis and whole grains contribute towards a highly nutritious eating pattern. When trekking, try not to depend on tinned or imported freeze dried foods. Selective shopping, or a list of preferences made out initially to the cook, will stand you in good stead.

Besides the fruit and vegetables available

in the local markets, fresh meat, eggs, pulses (seeds of pea, bean or lentil), cheese, ghee, flour and rice are generally available anywhere in the Himalaya. Butter and dried milk are available in tins. Nuts and raisins, honey, peanut butter, jams, tea and coffee, sugar, biscuits and chocolate can also be purchased locally. The cost of locally produced food such as rice, flour, fruit, vegetables and pulses is low, while the meat, tinned goods, butter, cheese, fish and dried fruit are on a par with Western prices.

It is important to have a balanced diet of carbohydrates, proteins and fats on the trek; it is equally important not to miss the delicacies of Indian cooking. Try delicious puris and paratha with honey for breakfast, instead of white bread and biscuits. A succulent mutton curry cooked with local vegetables and dhal is more appetising and interesting than roast mutton and boiled vegetables. Sausage, beans and chips may be OK, but a simple chicken or vegetable pulao for lunch, with chutneys and local curd, tastes so much better. During your time in India try the local honey rather than the weak blends of peanut butter; and try Kashmiri kawa instead of coffee.

Eric Shipton, the British explorer who specialised in small lightweight expeditions in the Himalaya, reduced his requirements to just oatmeal. Food was simply calculated by multiplying the number of days out on a trek by the quantity of oatmeal per day. Apparently, he spent considerable time debating whether salt was a luxury that could be dispensed with.

For us lesser mortals it is easy to exist quite happily for three or four weeks at a time on a substantial diet of porridge, puris and honey in the morning, with daytime snacks of nuts, raisins and tea, and an evening meal of rice, dhal and vegetables. On such treks I have found little need for freeze-dried food, and tinned or packaged items.

FIRST AID IN REMOTE AREAS

The following section includes an outline of some of the more common accidents that can occur on a trek, and appropriate first aid should the accident occur in a remote location. It also includes a consideration of some of the most common diseases that can occur in the Indian Himalaya, and a variety of travellers' illnesses and their treatment.

It has been compiled as an insurance to help you if something goes wrong. The chances of you either having an accident or contracting disease are minimal. Both Garry Weare and I have led treks for a month at a time without having to open the group medical kit.

However, if this section encourages you to undertake a first aid course and learn the basics of CPR, for example, then this might go some way to helping someone in difficulty should the occasion arise away from immediate medical help. A sensible and informed approach may save the life of a trekker or a villager in times of an emergency when there is no one to turn to but yourself.

Read the sections carefully: there is a great deal of information condensed into the next few pages, so try to read it a couple of times in order to absorb it properly. It is also recommended that you refer to *Medicine for Mountaineering*, edited by James Wilkinson, and published by The Mountaineers, Seattle, Washington, USA.

Initial Examination

If one of your party falls sick, take your time and make a detailed history of the complaint, any previous occurrence of symptoms, their duration, degree and location, and the factors which help or make things worse. Continue your analysis by asking about cough and chest pains, palpitations, headaches, numbness, tingling, abdominal pain, urinary or bowel symptoms and whether the member of your party is taking any drugs, or is allergic to any.

When examining the person, a well lit, quiet place is ideal. Remember also that a confident, reassuring approach works wonders when a patient is injured or sick. As a matter of course, take their temperature, pulse and respiration rate, feel the abdomen, and record the urine output and colour.

Cardio-Pulmonary Resuscitation (CPR)

This special technique of cardio-pulmonary resuscitation (CPR) is a reminder for those with training, and an incentive to train for those who haven't.

An unconscious person does not respond to shaking or being shouted at. If breathing, they should be placed on their left side with the right knee drawn up, their head tilted back and jaw pulled forward to clear the tongue from the airway and keep the mouth open.

If breathing stops, lay them on their back and, with the airway maintained, give them five quick breaths mouth to mouth with the nose pinched closed. If there is no response, then continue mouth to mouth once every five seconds.

Feel the carotid pulse in the neck (it lies in the groove alongside the windpipe) and if it is absent this means the heart has stopped and that heart massage should be started. Compress the lower one third of the breast bone four or five cm (1½ to two inches) 80 times a minute. Check for a carotid pulse every two to three minutes. Kneel beside the patient, rock from the hips, arms locked straight, heel of palm on lower one third of the breast bone, one hand on top of the other hand.

Heart massage and mouth to mouth resuscitation may be combined. Give one breath for every five compressions if two people are administering CPR, and one breath every 15 compressions if there is only one person.

This is a specialised technique which requires training on dummies. Do not practise on living persons.

Remember

Don't panic. Don't shake the patient or shout at them.

Clear Airway if unconscious
Mouth to Mouth if not breathing
Heart Massage if no carotid pulse

Head & Spinal Injury

Treat the patient as if the neck or spine is broken until you are sure that the injury is not this serious. Support the head, keep the pelvis, shoulder girdle and head in alignment, and use a stretcher to avoid sideways bending or rotation of the spine.

If the patient is unconscious, nurse them on the left side with the airway open. This prevents vomit from entering the lungs. Remember to keep the head tilted back and jaw pulled forward.

Close head wounds and examine the pupils of the patient's eyes, which may have become unequal in size or unresponsive to a light shone in them. Both are signs of cerebral trauma and need urgent medical attention.

Fractures

Bones break in several ways – the main varieties for our purposes are simple and compound. In compound fractures the bone is exposed to the air through the wound.

Broken bones need first aid and then medical treatment. Straighten the limb back to its normal position. Do this gently, firmly and as soon as possible. Check the circulation, and readjust the position if a good pulse cannot be felt.

Apply a well-padded splint, and check every 20 minutes to make sure the splint is not restricting circulation. A cold, numb, painful, pulseless, white or purple limb with pins and needles and loss of use will tell you the circulation has been cut off, and you should loosen the splint. Air splints should be partially deflated before air evacuation.

If the fracture is compound, proceed as above but give an antibiotic (Septrin or Ampicillin), thoroughly clean any wounds and close them with appropriate dressings.

Musculo-Skeletal Problems

General aches and pains may be the onset of flu, or stiffness caused by unaccustomed exercise. Administer Aspirin or Panadol, massage the area and/or apply liniment.

Sahib's Knee

The knee joint may become painfully inflamed while walking, especially while descending. Stop as soon as possible, and apply cold compresses, elevate the leg and apply a compression bandage. Give aspirin, two every four hours, until the pain settles down.

Sprained Ankles

A sprained ankle needs treatment similar to that for 'sahib's knee', but with the application of a good adhesive support bandage. If severe, this injury may take two to three weeks to clear up. It is often difficult to tell whether the ankle is sprained or broken.

Burns

Burns are classified according to their depth. Burns are extremely painful and can cause shock due to pain or fluid loss. Seek medical help after rendering first aid.

Burns should be dunked in cold water immediately, and covered with Silvazine or other burn cream.

Second degree burns, where there is blistering of the skin, are treated as for first degree burns, but a dressing should be applied. Change the dressing daily and treat any infection with an antibiotic.

Third degree burns, where there is charring and destruction of the skin, are more serious and need medical attention. First aid is as for first and second degree burns.

In all cases pain may be severe, and needs to be controlled using Pentazocine or Fortral which may be given by injection. Milder pain may be treated with Codeine or Paracetamol. Dehydration occurs in extensive burns and should be treated vigorously (see the section on the treatment of diarrhoea).

Lacerations

Cuts to the skin need to be cleaned with Dettol, clean water, or Betadine solutions, and closed with a firm bandage, butterfly strips or stitches.

Stitching (suturing) a wound is best carried out using a pre-packaged surgical needle, needle holder and thread. If surgical needle and thread are unavailable, substitute an ordinary needle and thread, sterilised by boiling for 10 minutes. Use a local anaesthetic if you have one, and place one stitch

every cm, bringing the cut edges cleanly together. Remove the stitches after one week.

Clean and dress the wound daily. If infection sets in, apply an antibiotic preparation to the wound, and give the patient an oral antibiotic.

Respiratory Problems

Respiratory problems include sore throat – a common problem at altitude – which is often associated with a cough. Stop smoking, gargle warm salt water, and use steam inhalations and antiseptic lozenges. If the problem is severe or persistent, use an antibiotic.

Sinusitis

An infection of the sinus cavities around the nose, sinusitis has symptoms of facial pain (with either a sudden or slow onset), fever and nasal discharge of pus. The treatment is the same as for a sore throat, with special attention to nasal washouts with warm salt water, and the use of an antibiotic and a nasal decongestant such as Drixine.

Bronchitis

This infection of the respiratory tubes is marked by a productive cough, especially early in the morning when large amounts of phlegm may be coughed up. Treatment is with steam inhalations and antibiotics (Bactrim, Ampicillin or Tetracycline)

Pneumonia

An infection which has invaded the lung tissue, pneumonia is indicated by shortness of breath, fever, headaches, and often chest pain. Treatment is as for bronchitis, plus descent and evacuation.

Urinary Tract Problems

In any urinary problem, increase the fluid intake until there is frequent passing of clear urine.

Infection of the lower urinary tract is called cystitis. The symptoms are the onset of a burning pain when passing urine, and the urine will be cloudy and often foul smelling.

Upper urinary tract (kidney) infections have symptoms of back pain, fever, and cloudy, foul smelling urine.

Treatment is the same for both problems. An antibiotic is recommended for four days for cystitis, or seven days for upper tract infections, using of Bactrim DS or Ampicillin.

Eye Infections

Infection will cause pain and redness in the eyes, and a discharge that will stick the lids together overnight. Insert antibiotic eye drops (Soframycin), but beware of allergy to these drugs if the symptoms persist or worsen.

Superficial foreign bodies should be removed with a cotton wool bud or the blunt end of a sterilised needle. Cover the eye, and use an antibiotic eye drop if infection occurs. If the foreign body has penetrated the eye, put a cover dressing on the infected eye, and evacuate the patient as soon as possible.

Ear Infections

Infection of the ear can cause pain, discharge of pus, or both. If there is a discharge, use an antibiotic ear drop. If the ear is very painful with no discharge, use an oral antibiotic.

Boils & Abscesses

Both boils and abcesses appear as red, pus-filled pimples, but can be larger. Do not squeeze them. Keep the area clean and use hot compresses frequently until they discharge themselves. If they are growing, spreading, very painful, or located on the head, give the patient an antibiotic and seek medical assistance for incision and drainage.

Vomiting

Prolonged vomiting can cause dehydration and exhaustion. Common causes are food poisoning, meningitis, hepatitis, or acute mountain sickness. Sips of rehydration fluid (see the section on the treatment of diarrhoea) between bouts of vomiting will help, as a little is absorbed each time. Stemetil tablets, suppositories or injection may be used.

Shock

Shock is caused by a drop in blood pressure, and can be due to loss of blood or other body fluids (following diarrhoea, vomiting or burns), heat exhaustion or pain. The patient feels faint or is unconscious, and the pulse is feeble and rapid.

The patient looks pale and feels clammy. Place them on their back (on the left side if unconscious) and raise their legs to an angle of 30 degrees. Rehydrate with electrolyte solution, and treat pain adequately. Fear makes shock worse so reassurance is vital. Treat the cause of the shock.

Painful Belly

The main concern is to decide if the patient must be evacuated. Severe abdominal pain lasting for more than six hours is usually serious. Conditions requiring evacuation and urgent medical treatment include:

Appendicitis Symptoms are central abdominal pain, low fever, vomiting and loss of appetite. Pain moves to the right lower abdominal quadrant with marked tenderness. Treat with immediate rehydration and a combination of antibiotics such as Ampicillin and Metronidazole, and evacuate by stretcher or helicopter.

Perforated Peptic Ulcer Symptoms are a long history of indigestion and the sudden onset of severe pain, collapse and shock.

Other Causes Prolonged, severe abdominal pain can also be caused by incarcerated hernia, acute gallbladder disease, pancreatitis or kidney stones. In all cases, evacuation and urgent medical treatment is essential.

Nonserious belly pain can be relieved by Codeine and is commonly caused by:

- diarrhoea, dysentery and food poisoning
- menstrual pains
- indigestion, peptic ulcer (sharp upper abdominal pain)

Death

If someone dies in the mountains, take their details and their passport to the nearest police post. The police will help with arranging evacuation or burial, and advise you on the necessary procedures.

ACUTE MOUNTAIN SICKNESS (AMS)

Acute mountain sickness (AMS), also called altitude sickness, is a not uncommon and potentially fatal disease caused by the failure to acclimatise to the low levels of oxygen at high altitude.

Acclimatisation to altitudes over 3000 metres (10,000 feet) takes time. The body undergoes a number of physiological changes. Some are immediate, such as increased pulse and respiratory rate, while others, such as the increase in red blood cells or changes in the acid base balance, take days or weeks.

These changes, plus the effects of intense sunlight, hard walking and dehydration may cause any of the following mild acclimatisation symptoms:

- loss of appetite
- fatigue
- headache
- nausea
- dizziness
- sleeplessness
- mild shortness of breath on exercise
- interrupted breathing while asleep, followed by gasping (Cheyne-Stokes breathing)

If you suffer from these symptoms while ascending, slow your ascent rate or take a rest day till they clear.

Acute mountain sickness is the appearance of fluid (edema) in the lungs and/or the brain, resulting from failure to acclimatise to the low tissue oxygen levels encountered at altitude. Fluid in the lungs is called high altitude pulmonary edema (HAPE). Fluid in the brain tissue is called high altitude cerebral edema (HACE). These may occur together or separately, rapidly or gradually over a period of days.

Symptoms of AMS

The following are symptoms of pulmonary edema (HAPE) and cerebral edema (HACE), but may also be caused by other factors:

- Headache which becomes more severe and does not respond to moderate painkillers. It is often aggravated when lying down (HACE)
- Nausea and vomiting which may become pronounced and prolonged (HACE)
- Shortness of breath which persists at rest (HAPE)

There are a number of symptoms which are more specific to AMS:

- Frequent coughing, often with a frothy blood stained sputum. (HAPE)
- Loss of co-ordination (HACE)
- Loss of higher mental abilities; test by asking simple mathematical problems (HACE)
- Double vision or failing vision (HACE)

To examine a person for AMS, take a good history and ask about specific symptoms mentioned:

- Have they been taking drugs?
- See if they are breathless at rest. (HAPE)
- Listen to the chest for wet sounds; compare with a healthy person. (HAPE)
- Can they perform mental arithmetic? (HACE)

Treatment of AMS

The best treatment is prevention. Avoid rapid ascent. Take acclimatisation symptoms seriously, using adequate rest days.

If you suspect someone of having early symptoms of AMS, keep them at that altitude, or descend until the symptoms clear.

If symptoms are severe or worsening, or if the patient is very ill, then descend immediately. Try to go down 400 metres (1500 feet) or more. This is the best treatment, and if necessary must be done whatever the weather or time of day.

Drugs Drug therapy is no substitute for descent, and may be used only to buy time in moving patients eg if the terrain is extremely rough or you are on a plateau and it will take some time to lose altitude.

Drugs such as Lasix and Dexamethasone should be administered only under close medical supervision.

Diamox (acetazoleamide) 250 mg tablets
    May be given morning and night for acclimatisation symptoms. It appears to prevent AMS in some people. It will not mask the onset of AMS. If the person is getting worse, descend. Continue Diamox for five days or until descent to lower altitudes if symptoms recur. Side effects are numbness or tingling of digits and lips. They are not serious.
Lasix (Frusemide) 20 mg tablets
    This drug is a powerful diuretic, ie: it will make a person pee one to three litres of urine within one to two hours of absorption. It buys a little time for descent in very ill people by temporarily drying out the waterlogged tissues. Its main side effect is dehydration, so give plenty of electrolyte solution, and monitor the urine output. It is useful in both HACE and HAPE. You must be sure of what you are doing before administering this drug, as its effect is powerful.
Dexamethasone
    A potent steroid given by injection for the treatment of HACE. It is mentioned here for completeness. Anyone carrying this drug (or Lasix for that matter) should be conversant with their indications, administration and side effects from a wider source than these brief notes.
Oxygen
    If available, should be given at two to six litres per minute, depending on the patient's condition.

Once again, the only guaranteed treatment is early and adequate descent.

CLIMATIC & GEOGRAPHIC CONSIDERATIONS
Hypothermia (Exhaustion Exposure)
Cold, wet, windy conditions may cool a person down enough to kill them. This can occur after immersion in cold water (acute hypothermia), or in the mountains on cold, wet and windy days over a period of hours or days (chronic hypothermia). Core body temperature drops below 37°C, and the brain starts to malfunction. Behaviour becomes erratic and the patient uncooperative . They shiver, lose co-ordination, their speech may become slurred, and fatigue is intense. Finally unconsciousness occurs, followed by death.

Prevention is by using windproof clothing and eating energy-giving food with warm drinks. Seek shelter if conditions are bad, and go by the abilities of the weakest person.

If the patient is unconscious, treat them with the utmost gentleness or the heart may stop. Shelter them from the elements, remove wet clothing and put them in a well-insulated sleeping bag.

Add heat from stoves or peoples' bodies. Warm the armpits, neck and groin with suitably insulated bottles of hot water.

Using CPR, attempt to resuscitate anyone found apparently dead from hypothermia: remarkable recoveries have occurred after several hours of CPR and rewarming.

Frostbite
This is a freezing of body tissues. Initially the affected part is white, numb and frozen solid. Later it will turn black and blister. Rewarm it in water at 45°C (hot but bearable to your hand) and protect from injury with plenty of dressings. Do not walk on frostbitten feet after rewarming. Do not massage or rub snow on frostbitten parts.

Snow Blindness
Caused by UV light reflected from snow or ice, this is a very painful condition. Use good sunglasses with protection underneath and at the sides. Symptoms include red, watery eyes and blindness. It lasts for two or three days, and is treated with cold compresses and analgesics.

Sunburn
UV light is much stronger at altitude. Use a hat with a brim, a good sun block and lipseal. Apply burn cream or calamine lotion to burnt areas.

Prickly Heat
This is an itchy rash caused by excessive perspiration trapped under the skin. Keeping

cool, bathing often and using a mild talcum powder should relieve the symptoms.

Heat Exhaustion

Prolonged exercise in a hot environment can result in electrolyte and circulatory disturbance, which may cause a fall in blood pressure and fainting. Keep the patient in the shade and rehydrate them with electrolyte solution.

Heat Stroke

This is a more serious condition and must be treated as an emergency. Prolonged exercise in a hot environment, and/or failure of the sweat mechanism, can cause the person to collapse, become unconscious and possibly to start to have fits. The skin feels dry and hot, and the temperature is elevated. Put them in cool water (not cold), or strip them and use sponges and fans to reduce their temperature. Rehydrate them with electrolyte solution when they are able to swallow.

Fungal Infections

Fungal infections, such as tinea, are most likely to occur between the toes and the fingers (athlete's foot), or in the groin (jock itch or crotch rot). To prevent fungal infections, wear loose comfortable clothes, wash frequently and dry yourself carefully. If you get an infection, wash the area daily with medicated soap and dry well. Apply an antifungal preparation such as Canestan cream. Try to expose the infected area to air and sunlight, and wash all towels and underwear regularly.

DISEASES OF INSANITATION
Diarrhoea

Diarrhoea is increased looseness and frequency of stool; a common and often debilitating complaint with a folklore all of its own. The infecting agents are viruses, bacteria, and protozoa (amoeba or giardia).

Your gut teems with billions of bacteria which, under normal conditions, are essential to health. Disease-causing organisms enter your gut and displace the normal bacteria, causing the bowel wall to secrete fluid

and dissolved electrolyte salts. This flushes the invading bacteria from the bowel. On occasions, mucus, blood or both will be secreted. The gut wall also produces antibodies against certain viruses and bacteria, which accounts for the immunity to diarrhoea acquired by locals or experienced trekkers.

The diarrhoea-causing organisms are transferred by the simple act of consuming food or drink contaminated with infected stool. This is called faeco-oral contamination, and is common in areas which have not developed high standards of sanitation and food preparation.

Prevention Here are some basic points to remember:

• wash your hands with soap and water frequently, especially after using the toilet and before meals
• sterilise drinking water by boiling or filtering, and/or by iodine treatment: four to eight drops of Lugol's iodine solution per litre of water, depending on the degree of contamination
• drink tea or bottled drinks
• food should be peeled, washed or soaked in iodine solution for 30 minutes (½ teaspoon Lugol's solution per two litres of water)

Treatment Rehydration is the key to treatment, and applies to all the varieties of diarrhoea detailed below. Encourage fluid consumption so there is regular passing of clear urine. (Note that the urine can be coloured by jaundice, some vitamin B tablets and coloured cordial drinks). Add a proprietary electrolytic salt mixture if available (Jeevan Jal, Gastrolyte, Staminade etc) or make one up (½ teaspoon salt plus a squeeze of lemon juice per litre of water, or ½ teaspoon salt plus 10 or 15 teaspoons of boiled ground rice per litre)

If dehydration is occurring, or stool frequency is distressing, use Immodium or Lomotil tablets to slow but not constipate the patient. Do not use these drugs if blood appears in the stool, as they would prevent the flushing out of the disease-causing organism.

The more serious or prolonged (10 days or more) diarrhoeas will need drug treatment to cure them, ideally after a stool test has been undertaken to identify the organism. A test will require a ½ teaspoon of stool in a clean labelled container, delivered to the laboratory within two hours.

Fasting, bland foods (rice, porridge, black tea) or yoghurt are additional aids to recovery. Avoid cheese, milk and alcohol

If diarrhoea, debility and weight-loss persist, consult a doctor with specialised knowledge for detailed investigation.

Travellers Diarrhoea

This is a nonspecific diagnosis (doctors like to label things) describing a self limiting diarrhoea of two to five days duration. It is often caused by a virus on which antibiotics would have no effect. Symptoms are abdominal discomfort and frequent loose stools. Fever, if present, is mild. The treatment is rehydration, bland diet and rest. An anti-diarrhoeal may be used as indicated, and if the diarrhoea persists or is worsening after 48 hours, then Bactrim DS is the drug of choice. If the patient has an allergy to sulpha drugs, Ampicillin is an alternative.

Giardia

Giardia is caused by a protozoa with a whip-like tail. Symptoms are abdominal pain and discomfort after eating, with rotten egg burps and farts. These symptoms may be of long duration if untreated. The treatment is a two-gram dose of Tinidazole per day for three days.

Bacillary Dysentery

This is caused by salmonella, shigella or other pathogenic bacteria. It is more persistent and more severe than other forms of diarrhoea, with an abrupt onset of profuse watery stools and fever. Occasionally mucus, and less frequently, blood, will appear in the stools. Treat as for travellers diarrhoea. If symptoms are worsening after

48 hours, use an antibiotic such as Bactrim DS, Ampicillin etc.

Cholera

This is a specific form of severe bacillary dysentery, usually associated with natural disasters where drinking water becomes contaminated by sewage. Treat as for bacillary dysentery, with special attention to rehydration.

Amoebic Dysentery

Amoebic dysentery is slower in onset than bacillary dysentery, with two to three stools of a porridge consistency, sometimes with mucus or blood. There is marked pain on moving the bowels. If untreated, weight loss and lassitude become marked. Treatment consists of a three day course of Tinidazole, one two-gram dose per day. Follow up with stool tests and a 21 day course of Diodoquine on return to civilisation.

Viral Gastroenteritis

As the name indicates, viral gastroenteritis is caused by a virus, not a bacteria, and is characterised by stomach cramps, diarrhoea, and sometimes vomiting or a slight fever. All you can do is rest and drink lots of fluids.

Hepatitis A or Infective Hepatitis

This is another disease caused by a virus, and it is passed by the faeco-oral route. It starts with flu-like symptoms, loss of appetite and vomiting. It may be mild or severe, with the virus attacking the liver after 10 to 40 days of incubation. After a week or so jaundice may occur, causing yellow urine, skin and eyes, and chalky stools. A person is usually noninfective 10 days after the onset of jaundice. The disease takes three to six weeks to clear up, and up to six months for the liver to fully recover.

Rest, and a carbohydrate protein diet with no fats constitute the basic treatment. Prevention is by Gamma Globulin injections every four months. Do not share eating utensils with an infective person.

Typhoid Fever

Typhoid is caused by salmonella and spread by the faeco-oral route. Incubation takes 10 days, then a flu-like illness develops with headache, sore throat, and a fever which increases daily up to 40°C (104°F). The pulse rate does not increase, and in the second week a fine pink rash appears on the trunk. If complications do not occur, the illness usually clears by the third or fourth week. Vomiting and diarrhoea may occur. Treatment is a 10 day course of Bactrim DS, one tablet twice a day, plus rest and rehydration.

Worms

These intestinal parasites spread by the faeco-oral route, resulting in a number of vague symptoms such as fatigue or abdominal pain. Their presence is often suspected only when they appear in the stool, or are coughed or vomited up. A stool test should be performed to identify the parasite, and to make sure it has been eliminated by the appropriate drug.

DISEASES SPREAD BY PEOPLE, ANIMALS & INSECTS

Tetanus

Tetanus occurs when a wound becomes infected by a germ which lives in the faeces of animals or people, so all cuts should be cleaned. Tetanus is also known as lockjaw, and the first symptoms may be discomfort in swallowing, stiffening of the jaw and neck, then painful convulsions of the whole body. Keep your tetanus vaccination up to date.

Rabies

Rabies is spread by bites from infected animals. Avoid startling dogs, or dogs that are fighting. Rabid dogs attack without warning, and often bite several people. Clean the wound thoroughly: this is important. Return to the nearest centre of population for antirabies treatment. Even if the dog is not rabid, all bites should be treated seriously, as they can become infected and result in tetanus.

Meningitis

This is an infection of the brain's lining, which can occur in epidemics. Vaccination gives protection against some forms of the disease (Meningitis A and C). Symptoms are fever, a severe headache which is made worse if the knees are bent up to the chest, nausea, vomiting and loss of consciousness. Treatment is by penicillin, or a combination of any two available antibiotics such as Bactrim DS and Ampicillin.

Tuberculosis

TB is prevalent throughout the Himalaya, and is spread by droplet infection. It usually affects the lungs, producing a cough, often with bloodstained sputum, low fever and weight loss. It is a chronic disease, ie it develops slowly and can last a long time, and a healthy person is less likely to contract it than someone who is run-down and debilitated. It needs hospital diagnosis and treatment by a medical specialist.

Malaria

This mosquito-borne disease is prevalent below 1000 metres through most of the Himalaya. The patient starts to feel unwell, and develops a fever which produces shivering fits and then drops to near normal before rising again. Treatment is normally given after hospital diagnosis. Prevention is by avoiding mosquito bites use repellent, long sleeved shirts, nets, screens and mosquito coils.

Antimalarial drugs do not actually prevent the disease, but suppress its symptoms. The usual malarial prophylactic is Chloroquine (one tablet once a week for two weeks prior to arrival in the infected area and for six weeks after departure) plus Maloprin (one tablet per week for the same period).

Leeches & Ticks

Leeches may be present in damp rainforest conditions, and attach themselves to your skin to suck your blood. Trekkers often get them on their legs or in their boots. Salt or a lighted cigarette end will make them fall off.

Do not pull them off as the bite is more likely to become infected.

Vaseline, alcohol or oil will persuade a tick to let go. You should always check your body thoroughly if you have been walking through a tick-infested area, as these creatures can spread typhus.

Typhus

Typhus is spread by ticks, mites or lice and begins as a bad cold, followed by a fever, chills, headache, muscle pains and a body rash. There is often a large painful sore at the site of the bite, and nearby lymph nodes are swollen and painful. Seek local advice on areas where ticks pose a danger, and always check yourself carefully for ticks after walking in a forest area.

Insect bites

Do not scratch insect bites: use an antihistamine cream. Keep the bites clean and dry. Fleas and bed bugs can be discouraged by airing sleeping bags in the sun.

Snakebite

Keep the victim still, and apply a compression bandage over the wound and up the limb. This should be tight but not so constrictive as to cut off the circulation. Use analgesics, and evacuate by stretcher. If breathing stops, administer mouth to mouth resuscitation, and CPR if necessary.

WOMEN'S HEALTH
Gynaecological Problems

Poor diet, lowered resistance due to the use of antibiotics for stomach upsets, and even contraceptive pills can lead to vaginal infections when travelling in hot climates. Keeping the genital area clean, and wearing skirts or loose-fitting trousers and cotton underwear will help to prevent infections.

Yeast infections, characterised by a rash, itch and discharge, can be treated with a vinegar or even lemon-juice douche, or with yoghurt. Canestan cream is the usual treatment.

Trichomonas is a more serious infection; symptoms are a discharge and a burning sensation when urinating. Male sexual partners must also be treated, and if a vinegar and water douche is not effective medical attention should be sought. Flagyl is the prescribed drug.

Pregnancy

Most miscarriages occur during the first three months of pregnancy, so this is the most risky time to travel. The last three months should also be spent within reasonable distance of good medical care, as quite serious problems can develop at this time. Pregnant women should avoid all unnecessary medication, but vaccinations and malarial prophylactics should still be taken where necessary. Additional care should be taken to prevent illness, and particular attention should be paid to diet and nutrition.

CHILDREN'S HEALTH

Children are being taken to remote and wild places more and more frequently, and there are some important considerations. Some drugs, such as Tetracycline, should not be given to children under 12 years, and all drugs should have their dose reduced. Consult the maker's instructions. As a rough guide when in doubt, and a drug seems unavoidable:

- children 6 to 12 – ½ dose
- children 3 to 6 – ⅓ dose
- children 1 to 3 – ¼ dose

TREATMENT OF LOCAL PEOPLE

On the trail, villagers and shepherds will ask you for medications, usually for headaches, colds and bowel complaints. Many believe that every Westerner is a doctor, and therefore equipped with wonder drugs that are a cure-all for anything. If your guide is with you, ask him or her to explain that this is not the case. It cannot be over-emphasised that the practice of freely dispensing drugs for headaches and illness will cause more harm than good.

The Indian state governments have instituted a system of paramedics to help villagers who do not need to be referred to physicians. These paramedics are normally based in isolated regions and need support. To freely dispense medications on the trail will seriously undermine the role and status of the paramedics who are trying to establish themselves in the community, and it also endangers the likelihood of recovery should the villager be suffering from a serious illness.

In isolated emergency cases, when no paramedic or doctor is available, trek doctors or nurses should be wary of prescribing drugs or administering first aid until an interpreter is at hand. In any case, no medical aid should be given unless the ailment is clearly diagnosed. If you start treating someone, be prepared to evacuate them if necessary.

AFTER YOUR JOURNEY

Some illnesses which may be picked up while travelling may have a slow onset of symptoms, or become chronic (long lasting). These include gut parasites, TB, malaria, giardia, and amoebic dysentery.

If you are not feeling well after your return home, or are having symptoms of indigestion, weight loss, diarrhoea, fever, or general fatigue and malaise, consult a doctor and, if necessary, ask for a specialist consultation.

Getting There

Delhi is the gateway for the majority of treks in India. This chapter outlines some of the fares to Delhi, and the various alternatives of getting from there to Kashmir, Himachal Pradesh and Uttar Pradesh. Trekking areas in Darjeeling and Sikkim can be accessed from Calcutta as well as from Delhi, and for details of how to get there see the Darjeeling & Sikkim chapter.

AIR
Round The World Fares
Round the world (RTW) fares have become increasingly popular in the last few years. Basically they are of two types – airline tickets and agent tickets. An airline RTW ticket usually means two or more airlines have joined together to market a ticket which takes you round the world on their combined routes. Within certain limitations of time, and the number of stopovers, you have a year in which to travel as you please, provided you keep moving in the same direction. Compared to full fare tickets, which permit you freedom to change sectors to any IATA carrier as long as you don't exceed 'the maximum permitted mileage', these tickets are much less flexible, but are considerably cheaper.

As an indication of prices, RTW fares are around A$2000 from Sydney, £1000 from the UK and approximately US$1800 from the USA.

The other type of RTW ticket, the agent ticket, is simply the combination of cheap airfares strung together by an enterprising agent. This will probably use a wider variety of airlines, and may provide routes that 'off the shelf' tickets cannot offer.

From the UK
There is a six month excursion fare of £634 low season and £736 high season. Alternatively, check out one of the many bucket shops in London, and the travel pages in the *Times*. Typical fares being quoted here range from £230 one way to £350 return. Fares are very much dependent on the carrier, with Middle Eastern carriers giving the best deals.

From the USA
There is a four month excursion fare of US$2100 from New York to Delhi. Out of San Francisco a similar ticket costs US$1500. Some travel agencies will discount up to 10% on these fares, so it is worth shopping around.

From Canada
There is a four month excursion fare of C$1900 from Toronto to Delhi. This is slightly higher if travelling out of Vancouver.

From Australia
From Sydney or Melbourne, a three month excursion fare costs A$1210 in the low season and A$1540 in the high season. From Darwin or Perth, a three month excursion fare is A$1040 low season and A$1200 high season.

From New Zealand
Three month excursion fares are available from Auckland to Delhi and Bombay for NZ$1988 low season and NZ$2309 high season.

OVERLAND
The classic way of getting to India from Europe has always been the overland route, though political problems in Iran and Afghanistan may prevent travel by land through those countries. Check Lonely Planet's *West Asia on a shoestring* for more details.

Similarly, from Australia you can travel country to country through South-East Asia to India – see *South-East Asia on a shoestring* for the complete picture.

GETTING TO THE TREKKING REGIONS

Air

Indian Airlines is the main internal carrier. There are flights from Delhi to Srinagar several times a day (US$77), and from Delhi to Leh, either directly (US$115) twice a week, or via Srinagar, five times a week. Flights from Srinagar to Leh cost US$58.

If you're undertaking a trek in the Kulu Valley it is possible to fly from Delhi to Bhuntar, just below Kulu, by Vayudoot Airlines (US$67). The service is daily during the main trek season, and two or three times a week at other times of the year.

Vayudoot also fly from Delhi to to Simla daily (US$53), and to Dehra Dun (US$40).

Note that since July 1990 payments for all internal fares in India, whether purchased overseas or in India, must be in foreign currency. Payment in Indian rupees on production of the relevant exchange certificate is no longer permitted.

A major problem with flying in India is the Indian Airlines reservation system. If your international ticket combines the internal sectors then it is advisable to reconfirm your reservation on arrival in India. Similarly, the rule regarding reconfirmation is strictly adhered to in India, and you would be wise to double check that your name appears on the manifest. A portion of seats are now held for foreign tourists up to 72 hours before departure on most of the Indian airline sectors. It is too early yet to see how this system will work, but anything that reduces the inconvenience of the normal Indian Airlines service is to be commended.

Overland

It is also possible to travel to the trekking regions of India by rail or bus, or a combination of the two. Beware of theft, particularly at long distance bus terminals, or at New Delhi railway station, which has an unenviable record in this matter. It is not uncommon for passports and money to be stolen by organised gangs just as the train departs.

If you are taking the bus, the Central bus station at Kashmir Gate in Delhi is the place to go. Both private and state buses operate throughout the day, and many have reclining seats, videos and air-conditioning – your only problems now are the Indian roads and drivers!

To Jammu & Kashmir To reach Kashmir by land you have the option of travelling by train to Jammu and from there by road to Srinagar; or by bus directly from Delhi to Srinagar. Both trips take 24 hours.

The trains to Jammu leave Old Delhi and New Delhi stations in the evening and arrive in Jammu the following morning. The trains connect with the bus to Kashmir which arrives in Srinagar that evening.

Train tickets from Delhi to Jammu cost Rs 567 (air-con class), Rs 256 (1st class) and Rs 78 (2nd class sleeper). The buses from Jammu to Srinagar cost Rs 120 (super deluxe), Rs 60 (A class) and Rs 45 (B class). Taxis from Jammu to Srinagar cost Rs 900 but may be sold on a per-seat basis.

The bus from Delhi to Srinagar costs around Rs 250.

To Himachal Pradesh To reach Chamba and Dharamsala it is best to take the Jammu train as far as Pathankot (3 hours before Jammu). From Pathankot get the local bus to Dharamsala, which takes about 3 to 4 hours, or to Chamba (5 to 6 hours). Both buses operate from the Himachal Pradesh bus stand.

The train fares from Delhi to Pathankot are about 10% less than those to Jammu (see above). The local bus to Dharamsala is Rs 20, and to Chamba Rs 30. There are regular buses to Kulu and Manali from the central bus stand. Cost varies from Rs 75 to Rs 250 and the journey takes about 18 hours.

To Uttar Pradesh There are regular bus services from Delhi to Mussorie, Hardwar or Rishikesh. Fares range from Rs 50 upwards, depending on the bus operator and the journey takes some 5 to 6 hours.

There is also a train service from Delhi to Rishikesh and Dehra Dun which takes about the same time as the bus. Fares from Delhi to Dehra Dun are Rs 335 (air-con class), Rs 145 (1st class) and Rs 57 (2nd class).

Buying Train Tickets Indian Railways has a 'tourist quota' on some trains – a proportion of seats are reserved for foreign tourists. To reserve a seat in the tourist quota used to be a bureaucratic adventure, but the quota is now available direct from New Delhi station. You can ask at the enquiry desk at the station, but it is worthwhile checking first with the Indian tourist office in Janpath, New Delhi, as regulations in India are apt to change.

LEAVING INDIA

Cheap flights are available from many of the smaller travel agencies around Connaught Place in New Delhi. However, the price of the ticket is not likely to be a considerable saving, except for those who have come out overland and are preparing to go on to Australia. One-way fares to Australia, after concessions, vary around Rs 9000 from Delhi to Sydney. Fares from Delhi to London are about Rs 6000.

If you purchase a cheap ticket, you must first pay the full official fare in foreign currency, and your concession is then refunded to you in Indian rupees – the last currency that you want if you are about to leave the country. It is therefore wise to purchase your fare far enough in advance to use up your rupees, or save your currency exchange certificates so you can change the rupees into foreign currency at the airport on departure.

It is important that you reconfirm your international booking out of India as soon as you are sure of your return date. Reconfirmation must generally be done in Delhi. Apart from an Air India office in Srinagar, there are no other airlines represented for reconfirmation. You could confirm your flight by telex or telegram but there is no guarantee that your message will not be garbled.

Departure tax from India is Rs 300 if flying out of the Indian subcontinent, and Rs 150 if flying within the subcontinent, eg to Nepal, Pakistan, Bangladesh or Sri Lanka.

Kashmir

For nearly six months of the year Kashmir is a natural destination for anyone undertaking a trek in the Indian Himalaya. As soon as the spring snows melt the alpine trials present some superb trekking opportunities. Trails extend across the mountain ranges encircling the Vale of Kashmir with many strenuous options across the main Himalaya passes to Ladakh.

The trekking possibilities were fully realised by the British colonialists who would trek for weeks at a time on their annual vacation. Evidence of their activities can still be seen 50 years later in such hill stations as Phalgam, where the rates for bath tubs and huge tents are displayed on the outfitters boards. The British also established their presence in the Kashmir Valley. The houseboats were built along the banks of the Jhelum River, while big game and fishing agencies lined the Bund. The Residency, now the Government Arts Emporium, was built nearby while the shops in Polo View and Nedous hotel reflected the commercial interests of the day.

The British presence in the later part of the 19th century also revitalised an interest in Kashmir's history. Scholars such as Aural Stein translated the *Ratatarangini*, a huge volume originally compiled in the 12th century, which was the definitive guide to Kashmir's early history. At the same time one of Kashmir's most noted administrators, Land Reform Commissioner W R Lawrence, was able to detail the land policies that had been adopted in Kashmir since the time of the Moghuls.

Geologists such as Frederick Drew were able to compile comprehensive geographic accounts of the valley. According to his findings the Kashmir Valley was a lake until quite recent geological times. The Jhelum River was temporarily blocked below Baramulla and the valley filled, with a lake forming some 200 to 300 metres above the present valley floor. According to legend the

Nagas, half human, half serpent beings, dwelt in the lake, and when the waters eventually subsided they escaped to the higher mountain lakes.

The belief in the Nagas remained as an integral part of Kashmir's history. As the Aryans migrated up the Indus Valley to Kashmir, the Aryan and Naga priests were able to maintain an accord. Even the introduction of Buddhism during the time of Ashoka in the 3rd century BC did not undermine the relationship. The Buddhist viharas were soon reconstructed as temples to commemorate Shiva or Vishnu, while every lake, spring and stream was sanctified by the Naga priests.

The culture of Kashmir was preserved for many centuries and reached a high point during the time of the great Utpala and Karokta dynasties, when the power and influence of Kashmir stretched far beyond the confines of the valley. During the 8th and 9th centuries huge temples, such as those at Avantipura, Parihasipura and Patan, were built to commemorate the kings. Then a series of weak rulers hastened a period of cultural and political decline.

It was against this backdrop that Kashmir was converted to Islam in the early part of the 14th century. This was a peaceful conversion, with many of the followers of Shah Hamadan, the noted Persian leader, seeking refuge in the valley. Among the enlightened rulers was Zain ul Abundin who, after returning in his youth from the Moghul courts of Samarkand, introduced many of the famous handicrafts to Kashmir, including carpet weaving and papier-mâché.

In 1585 Kashmir came under the vast Moghul Empire. The Emperor Akbar upgraded the administration and instituted more equitable systems of land distribution. During Akbar's time the lower ramparts of the fort around the Hari Parbat hill were constructed, while his son Jahangir and grandson Shah Jehan were responsible for

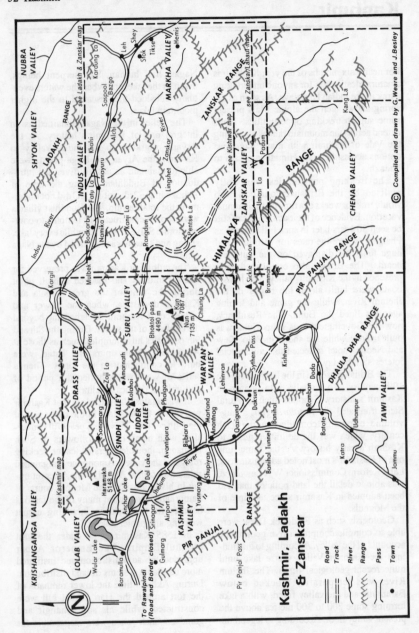

Kashmir, Ladakh & Zanskar

© Compiled and drawn by G. Weare and J. Besley

Road
Track
River
Range
Pass
Town

the famous gardens including those at Nishat and Shalimar on the banks of Dal Lake.

With the gradual decline of Moghul rule, the local administration again fell into decline. In the 1750s the valley was invaded by the despotic Durranni rulers from Afghanistan, and later by the Sikhs who constructed the impressive Hari Parbat fort above the old city.

Following the Treaty of Amritsar in 1846 Kashmir, together with the adjoining regions of Jammu, Baltistan and Ladakh, became part of the maharajah's state of Jammu & Kashmir. The four Dogra maharajahs, Gulab Singh, Ranbir Singh, Pratap Singh and Hari Singh ruled Kashmir. In May each year they moved from Jammu to Srinagar to conduct their summer administration. The Dogras shared a peculiar relationship with the British. The British assumed control over the state's external affairs while the maharajahs were able to determine their own domestic policy. Indeed the British were unable to own land in the valley, hence the development of the houseboats.

During the 1930s there was a Kashmiri movement against the maharajah. A Quit Kashmir campaign evolved, similar to that of the Quit India movement which faced the British in other parts of India. It was a movement that drew considerable support from the Kashmiris, the majority of whom were Muslim with very little in common with the Hindu maharajah.

The Indian partition in 1947 brought the Kashmir situation to the fore. Maharajah Hari Singh wanted an independent Kashmir, yet Kashmir was predominantly Muslim and culturally closer to Pakistan. Economically its strength was tied up with India. To break the deadlock a Pathan force from the Pakistan-occupied region of Baltistan was sent to liberate Kashmir. The manoeuvre failed, Hari Singh called in the Indian forces to protect him, and he retreated to Jammu. A full scale war between India and Pakistan resulted, lasting until a UN ceasefire came into effect on 1 January 1949.

In 1957 Kashmir was formally made part of the Indian Union, despite protests from Pakistan. In 1965 India and Pakistan were again at war over the issue, with the Pakistan forces nearly taking Srinagar. In 1971, during the conflict over Bangladesh, it was India who took the offensive and Pakistan was pushed back to a position not far from the original ceasefire line.

To complete the picture, India was in an earlier conflict with China in 1962, when it was found that the Chinese had managed to invade the remote Aksi Chin region of Ladakh. The ensuing conflict eventually ground to a halt, and another ceasefire line was drawn – this time with China.

The result is that much of the border regions of Kashmir and neighbouring Ladakh and Baltistan are no-go areas for trekkers. Ladakh was opened to tourists only in 1974, and regions such as the Zanskar from 1976 onwards. Other areas, 1 km north of the Leh-Srinagar road and east of the Leh-Manali road, are closed to foreigners. Dreams of trekking the length of the Indus Valley, or wandering from Kashmir across to Baltistan and the Karakoram, will remain just that, with land borders across Kashmir from India and Pakistan remaining closed since 1947.

Trekking Areas
The following section includes the two main trekking regions in Kashmir. The first outlines the popular treks in the vicinity of the Lidder and Sindh valleys. These include treks out of Phalgam along the historically important route to the Amarnath Cave, as well as trails to the Kolahoi Glacier, Tarsar Lake and the passes to the Sindh Valley. The treks out of Sonamarg continue across the 'lake district' of Kashmir to a camp below the sacred Haramukh massif. The second section includes the more strenuous treks that go from the Kashmir Valley to the Warvan Valley, and over the less-trodden glacial passes into Ladakh.

Trekking Agents
Reliable local agents are still at a premium. Many who have been to Kashmir recommend a particular houseboat family to set

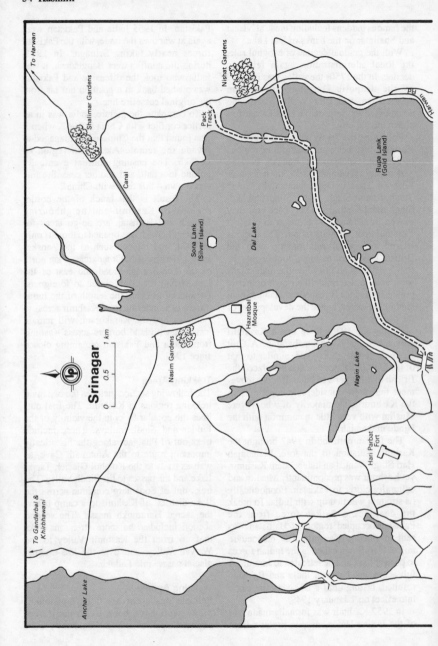

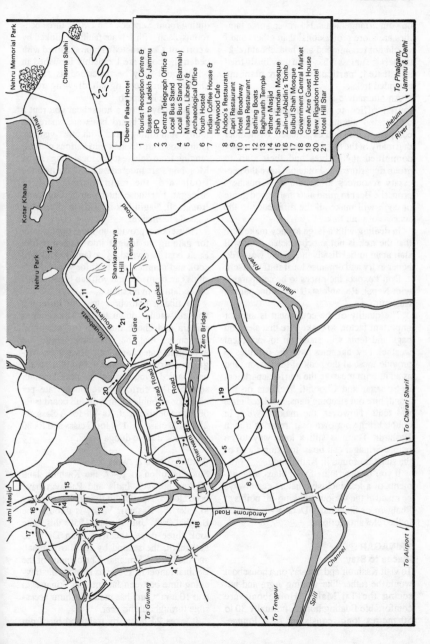

1 Tourist Reception Centre &
  Buses to Ladakh & Jammu
2 GPO
3 Central Telegraph Office &
  Local Bus Stand
4 Local Bus Stand (Batmalu)
5 Museum, Library &
  Archaeological Office
6 Youth Hostel
7 Indian Coffee House &
  Hollywood Cafe
8 Ahdoo's Restaurant
9 Capri Restaurant
10 Hotel Broadway
11 Lhasa Restaurant
12 Bathing Boats
13 Raghunath Temple
14 Pather Masjid
15 Shah Hamdan Mosque
16 Zain-ul-Abidin's Tomb
17 Bulbul Shah Mosque
18 Government Central Market
19 Green Acre Guest House
20 New Rigadoon Hotel
21 Hotel Hill Star

up your arrangements. However, some families are more professional than others and I would not recommend any houseboat trekking service unless it has been previously tried and tested, particularly when planning extended treks.

An alternative is to wander down to the tourist office to view their list of recommended agents. It then up to you to compare quotes and experience. Remember that many of the better agencies have already committed themselves and their staff to group departures, and may not have the necessary resources to handle your business properly. Bear in mind also that a good guide or cook will make all the difference to the success of your trek.

In dealing with a large agency make sure that the trek is not subcontracted. You will start at an initial disadvantage and would do better to try and organise local staff yourself.

Don't expect the prices to be comparable with Nepal. Reliable staff are better paid in Kashmir.

The quality of the equipment is another important factor, so make sure that sleeping bags and tents will stand up to inclement weather. Few agencies have the facilities to provide these at the peak of the season, and as an interim measure the tourist department in Srinagar and Choomti Trekkers on the Bund, hire out sleeping bags, insulated mats and tents. However, the maxim 'when in doubt, bring your own gear' remains true in Kashmir. There is still a long way to go before Srinagar can boast trekking shops of the standard found in Kathmandu.

If you're uncertain of your plans, arrangements of a less inclusive nature can always be made at the various trekking-off points at Phalgam or Sonamarg. Details are covered in the relevant sections.

SRINAGAR
Places to Stay
To visit Kashmir and not stay on a houseboat would be rather like visiting Agra and not seeing the Taj Mahal. Houseboats are comfortable floating homes, normally 30 to 50 metres long, consisting of a lounge, dining room, sundeck and two or three bedrooms, each with private facilities, linked by a corridor. Constructed of pine and lined with cedar, the boats are inevitably furnished in what could only be described as '1930s chintz', but the English drawing room atmosphere is superb.

When staying on a houseboat you rent a room on a full board basis and share the lounge and dining room with other visitors. Houseboats are divided into various classes, ranging from deluxe to the local dunga style. Most boats are moored on Dal Lake near the Boulevard, the main thoroughfare of Srinagar. For those intent on getting away from it all, Nagin Lake, 7 km out of town, is a good alternative.

Houseboats provide an ideal opportunity for gaining an insight into Kashmiri life. Each boat is owned by a family who will cook and maintain the boat for you. Friendships can be made, and you can become part of the family in no time.

To find a houseboat to your taste and pocket, wander down to Dal Lake, hire a shikara and check out the 'To Let' signs. Remember that the government rates are maximum rates, and can always be bargained down as many boats remain unoccupied even during the peak summer season. The current government rate per night for a double room with full board is Rs 600 for a deluxe boat, Rs 400 for A class, Rs 250 for B class, Rs 150 for C class and Rs 80 for the local-style dunga boats.

Getting There & Away
Since partition in 1947, the Kashmir land borders between India and Pakistan have been closed. Apart from flying, the only way to enter the Kashmir Valley is through the Banihal Pass. Until the late 1950s this route took three days, the first from Delhi to Pathankot, the second by road to Banihal, and the third to Srinagar. The opening of the Banihal tunnel in 1958 has reduced the travelling time between Jammu and Srinagar to 8 to 10 hours, and has made Kashmir accessible throughout the year.

It takes 24 hours by train and bus from

Delhi to Srinagar. The trains from Delhi to Jammu leave from both the New and Old Delhi stations in the evenings, and arrive in Jammu the following morning. The bus leaves Jammu after the train arrives and reaches Srinagar late that evening. The train from Delhi to Jammu costs Rs 567 air-con class, Rs 256 1st class, and Rs 78 2nd class. The super deluxe bus from Jammu to Srinagar costs Rs 120, the A class is Rs 40, and the B class is Rs 30.

To complete the picture, there are several flights from Delhi to Srinagar each day. The flight takes 1 hour and costs US$77 one way.

Getting Around

You can explore Srinagar by foot, cycle or shikara. Walking is the only way to get around the back alleys of the old city and to Hari Parbat and the Shankaracharya hills. It is also recommended that you walk across the causeway across Dal Lake to or from the Moghul Gardens. Sooner or later, however, you will succumb to the delights of being paddled across the lakes by shikara, Kashmir's answer to the gondola. For those shunning the easy way, small shikaras can be hired from your houseboat or the small boys that hang around Dal Lake. It is then up to you to master your strokes – it's not as easy as it looks – and paddle around to Nagin Lake, or the Moghul Gardens. There are cycles if you want to hire one and go further afield to places like Harwan, or the quieter rural villages beyond Srinagar.

From Srinagar there are three ways to travel to the hill stations before embarking on a trek. You can go by taxi, which is convenient but expensive; by local tourist bus which is cheaper and permits some sight-seeing on route; or by local bus which is very slow, and very crowded with local people. The drive to Phalgam or Sonamarg doesn't take too long: a couple of hours by car, three or four by bus. To give you an idea of the cost, a taxi to Phalgam is at present Rs 450 one way and Rs 500 return. The tourist bus costs Rs 25 one way and Rs 35 return; and the local bus is Rs 9 one way.

Lidder & Sindh Valleys

The alpine country between the Lidder and Sindh valleys is the most popular area for trekking in Kashmir. The trails follow the outer ridges of the main Himalaya to where they merge with the Amarnath, Sonamarg and Kolahoi ranges. The picture postcard scenery, not too demanding trails and comparative ease of arranging treks from Srinagar, Phalgam and Sonamarg have helped to popularise this region.

The region is essentially a wilderness area for over six months of the year. During the short summer grazing season, from June to mid-September, the Kashmiri shepherds, the Gujar buffalo herders and the Bakharval goat herders take their animals up the Lidder and Sindh valleys. This is an annual migration that has followed a traditional grazing pattern for many generations.

The 'locals' are the Kashmiri shepherds who confine their grazing to the lower altitudes, settling in the pastures within a few km of Phalgam or Sonamarg. The Kashmiri shepherd is easily distinguishable by his *ferun* – the woollen smock he wears and under which he carries his traditional clay firepot or *kangri*.

The Gujar, with their herds of huge water buffalo, migrate higher up the valleys. They subsist by selling buffalo milk in the local villages, and usually have a small flock of sheep to supplement their income. They originally migrated many centuries ago from Gujarat to the Himalayan foothills. As the pressure of land usage built up on the plains, so the Gujar migrated higher to the hills, crossing the Pir Panjal Range each summer in search of new grazing areas. These days the Kashmir Government has adopted a policy of resettlement for the Gujar, and many now spend their winters close to the villages below the summer grazing pastures. For instance, the Gujar who graze their animals at Satlanjan in the Lidder Valley now settle in the villages just below Phalgam during the winter. Similarly, the shepherds from Sonamous take their buffalo to the villages in the lower Sindh Valley. The Gujar are easily identified by their turbans and the brightly coloured blankets that cover their shoulders. They are still considered to be outsiders and rarely intermarry with the Kashmiris.

The third group are the Bakharval, the goat herders who take their huge flocks to the higher, more remote, pastures during summer. The Bakharval are the 'cousin brothers' of the Gujar, and they have a lucrative business. Goat wool is sold at a high price as it is made into the famous Kashmir shawls. The Bakharvals still lead a semi-nomadic existence, driving their flocks to the highest pastures and sometimes on over the passes into Ladakh. As the winter approaches they return down valley and over the Pir Panjal passes back to the regions of Jammu, where they spend the winter months.

Essentially it is these shepherds who make it easier for us to trek in Kashmir. They assume the responsibility of reconstructing the bridges over the high flowing streams, and clear rock scree from the trails, so that we can follow in their footsteps.

Trekking Seasons
The trekking season, from mid-June to late October, although longer than the grazing season, is still dependent on the movement of the shepherds who clear the trails and reconstruct the bridges. It is possible to trek to the Kolahoi Glacier in May, although the upper Lidder Valley will be under snow. However, that is as far as you are likely to get. For pass crossings it is not advisable to plan an itinerary out of Phalgam until mid-June at the earliest, and in some seasons the passes can still be under snow in mid-July. July and August are normally good months for trekking, although there can occasionally be periods of heavy rainfall for up to three to four days at a time. September and October are ideal. Night time temperatures are still above freezing and the days are generally clear.

The first snow falls on the ridges in late October, usually during a bout of cold

weather, although the hardy trekker can still tackle pass crossings in early November, and Lidder Valley treks can be undertaken in most seasons as late as the middle of December.

Each month in Kashmir has its peculiar delights. In June the shepherds are establishing their camps for the season, and the first flowers are to be found at the margins of the snow melt. July is the month of mists and the first glimmer of summer and August is the month for the wildflowers. September sees the shepherds on the move again, and birch trees gaining their autumn hues which last until the end of October.

Fishing
If you have the tackle, then trout fishing is an added attraction while trekking in this region. Both brown and rainbow trout are stocked in the Lidder River below Aru and Chandanwadi, and also on the far side of Sonamarg in the Vishensar, Krishensar and Gangabal lakes. Permits are issued by the Fisheries Office at the Tourist Department and cost Rs100 per beat per day. For this you can catch a maximum of six fish per day. A fishing inspector is at hand on these sections to check permits and offer advice. Remember though, that 'Spinning is Sinning', and only fly fishing is permissible.

Trail Sanitation
Unfortunately the increased number of trekkers in these areas has exacted a toll, with the all-too-familiar problem of garbage and litter marring the main camping areas. There is increasing concern that campsites such as those at Aru, Lidderwat, and Gangabal will soon be completely spoilt.

Recently the local wildlife department introduced a levy of Rs 20 payable by all trekkers going past Aru in the Lidder Valley. How this money will be spent remains to be seen. One suggestion is that some of the tax be spent employing locals to clean up the more popular campsites at Lidderwat, Satlanjan and Seikwas. This could be put into practice with a minimum of delay, and continue until such time as sufficient ecological awareness is developed among both the Kashmiri and foreign trekkers. It is the latter group, however, which must take responsibility for much of the trail and campsite litter. Foreign groups introduced the dreaded plastic bag, tin can, tissue paper and other near-indestructible refuse, and it is up to all concerned to ensure that something constructive eventuates to remedy the situation.

PHALGAM
Getting Ready
From Phalgam ponies are readily available, and local guides are generally reliable. Rates start from about Rs 50 per day per horse, and are displayed at the tourist office and at the ponywallahs' stall. Remember to budget for a return journey for ponies and their handlers.

All provisions can be purchased in Phalgam, and although basic supplies such as rice, potatoes, and dhal are available at Aru, Lidderwat and on the Amarnath trail, these cannot be relied upon. Meat may also be purchased from the shepherds, however, it is normally sold 'by the sheep' and can work out expensive for a small party. Owing to the sensitivity of the Hindu pilgrims, alcohol should not be taken on the Amarnath trek.

Camping equipment in the old style, such as dressing tables and bathtubs, can be hired from the agencies in Phalgam. For tents, sleeping bags and other more useful items, it is best to enquire at some of the trekking lodges where gear is sometimes available.

Although these treks are undoubtedly popular, this is no excuse for being poorly prepared. Rivers, especially in late June and early July, must be crossed with care. I have heard of some very sad accidents that occurred because trekkers were ill-prepared. I have also witnessed some near accidents when individual trekkers and parties have crossed rivers without ropes or support.

Snow bridges are less hazardous than is generally thought. Wide cracks appear well before the ice is due to collapse, and these trails are abandoned by the shepherds long before they become dangerous.

Places to Stay
Accommodation in Phalgam varies from the deluxe hotels in the main bazaar to the popular alpine lodges that are situated along the banks of the Lidder, or in the forest on the far side of the West Lidder Valley. Many individual trekkers manage to organise themselves into groups while staying at one of these delightful lodges.

It is difficult to recommend a particular lodge as many have been built or converted in the last few seasons. *Kolahoi Cabin*, on the banks of the East Lidder River beyond the Phalgam Club, is one that has been mentioned, as have the relocated *Windrush* and *White House*, also on the far side of the same river. *Brown Palace* past Laripura village has also been popular since it was renovated some seasons ago. *Bentes Lodge* on the far side of the East Lidder is popular with many budget trekkers. Below Bentes, in the forest above the West Lidder, is the *Aksa Lodge*, the

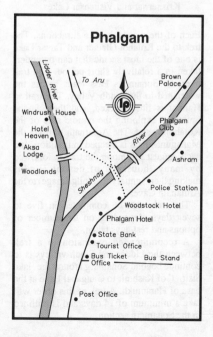

most popular and comfortable lodge in the vicinity of Phalgam, complete with classical music, good food and open fires and operating under the watchful eye of Mohammed Yasin. It is hoped that the management will not spoil the place with the new extensions.

Prices for rooms vary from lodge to lodge depending on the season. Basic rooms are from Rs 20 upwards, while rooms with all facilities tend to go from Rs 100 upwards.

Treks

The following routes are outlined in this section:

K1: From Phalgam to Lidderwat, Kolahoi Glacier and Tarsar Lake.
K2: From Phalgam to Sumbal via the Sonamous Pass.
K3: From Phalgam to Sonamarg via Harnag.
K4: From Phalgam to Amarnath via the Mahagunas Pass.
K5: From Sonamarg to Gangabal Lake via Krishensar and Vishensar Lakes

Each of these treks has its attractions. The trek to the Kolahoi Glacier and Tarsar Lake is one of the most scenic that can be undertaken in a relatively short period. The trek over the Sonamous Pass leads across the watershed to the Sindh Valley. The trail to Harnag is little trekked, and there is the option of exploring the remote side of the Kolahoi massif. The Amarnath trail via the Mahagunas Pass is steeped in tradition, and each August full moon the trail is followed by many thousands of devout Hindus making their annual *yatra* (pilgrimage) to the Armanath Cave.

The treks can be completed in five to seven days, depending on the number of options and rest days taken.

A recommended extension to a trek between the Lidder and Sindh valleys is to continue beyond Sonamarg around the 'lake district' of Kashmir to Gangabal Lake at the base of Haramukh. A trek of this order will take a minimum of 14 days and is outlined in the Sonamarg section.

K1: PHALGAM TO KOLAHOI GLACIER & TARSAR LAKE
Stage 1: Phalgam to Aru
(Average walking time 3 hours)
For the first day on the trail this is a convenient stage to check out your boots and blisters, particularly if you are setting out in the afternoon when the temperatures are by no means cool. The trail follows the jeep track along the West Lidder, well defined and well graded. After 5 or 6 km there are some impressive views back down the valley towards Phalgam and across to the snow-capped mountains which form the divide between the Lidder and Warvan valleys.

The village of Aru is situated at the confluence of the Nafran and Lidder rivers beside a huge open meadow. The village boasts a number of lodges and teahouses where food is available. Unfortunately the meadow in the immediate vicinity of Aru has been subject to a number of shanty developments that seem to be the hallmark of progress in the valley. It is recommended therefore to camp a few km on up the valley, in order to appreciate the true natural beauty of the surroundings.

Stage 2: Aru to Lidderwat
(Average walking time 3 hours)
Another short stage, so that you can easily reach Lidderwat in a few hours. From Aru the trail ascends the bridle track behind the village. The climb is quite steep in places until the trail reaches a small meadow. From here the track levels out through forest for 2 to 3 km, before reaching an alpine meadow that forms one of the most picturesque settings in Kashmir. The meadow is populated by Gujar and Kashmiri shepherds who are fully acquainted with trekkers. The well-marked trail gradually ascends the meadow before dropping down to the side of the Lidder River a few km before Lidderwat. Continue until you are past the confluence of the Lidder River and the river coming from Tarsar Lake, then cross the bridge that leads to Lidderwat.

In spite of the shanty lodges, the meadow retains much of its charm and beauty. For those going it alone and without a tent the lodges provide convenient shelter and food. The setup is similar to the lodges in Nepal. To complete the picture there is a *Government Rest House* situated on the far side of the meadow. Prices vary, with rooms from Rs 10 per night, and normally there is no scarcity of accommodation.

One could argue the ethics of supporting the illegally placed huts in the middle of this magnificent meadow. Obviously the shanty appearance detracts from the area's natural beauty and it would be ideal if the Kashmir tourist department relocated the buildings to the side of the main meadow. However, local enterprise should still be encouraged, and some incentive should be given (fixed camps perhaps) so that they can provide this service for trekkers.

Lidderwat can be used as a base for treks to the Kolahoi Glacier and Tarsar Lake. Both stages are quite long (up to 10 hours), and it is recommended that you camp higher, at Satlanjan for the Kolahoi Glacier trek, or at Seikwas for the Tarsar Lake trek. However, if that is not possible due to lack of tents or time, then an early start is imperative if you are to reach Kolahoi or Tarsar and return to Lidderwat before nightfall.

Stage 3: Lidderwat to Kolahoi Glacier & Return

(Average walking time 8-9 hours return)
The trail from Lidderwat continues along the right hand bank of the Lidder. Do not re-cross the bridge. From Lidderwat it is about 2 or 3 hours to Satlanjan. In the early part of the season the trail could be under snow and it is well worthwhile checking your footwear and finding a reliable stick to assist your balance. The trail is quite level by Himalayan standards, with a few ups and downs, until you reach the birch forests just below Satlanjan. The rock outcrops above are a perfect habitat for the brown bear, and they have been sighted wandering down to the water's edge at first light.

The Gujar village at Satlanjan is the most substantial in the Lidder Valley. The shepherds are familiar with the arrival of trekkers,

and the children lose little time in approaching for handouts. If you're camping at Satlanjan, there is an ideal spot on the meadow below the huts. From here you can explore the surrounding ridges later in the day, and continue to the Kolahoi base early the following morning.

From Satlanjan it is a further 3 hours to the base of the glacier. The trail continues across the meadow to the bend in the main valley, and from there you will appreciate the profile of the upper Lidder Valley. Essentially the trail ascends gradually across a series of small meadows set between moraine that extends to the snout of the glacier. Mt Kolahoi is situated high up on the left side as you continue up valley, its peak looming some 2500 metres above the valley floor. Note that the best views of the peak are from the last meadow before you reach the terminal moraine. However, to appreciate the character and size of the glacier it is necessary to continue over the terminal moraine for another couple of km. Watch closely for the rock cairns that mark the way through the boulders or you will waste energy when you can least afford it.

Stage 4: Lidderwat to Seikwas, Tarsar Lake & Return

(Average walking time 8-10 hours return)
From Lidderwat the trail ascends the steep hillside to the west of the meadow and continues up to the treeline. From here on the trek becomes easier, and after a few km opens out to a series of meadows that lead to Seikwas. After 4 or 5 km the trail crosses two gullies before winding below a rocky outcrop that can prove difficult for the pack horses early in the season. It is then a further 2 or 3 km to the confluence of the Lidder River and the river coming from Tarsar. The whole area is known as Seikwas.

The problem is then to cross and continue to Tarsar. In the early part of the season you may be able to cross the river by snowbridge, even lower down the valley, in which case the day's trek is considerably reduced. But by early summer (late June onwards) the chances are that you will have to ascend for

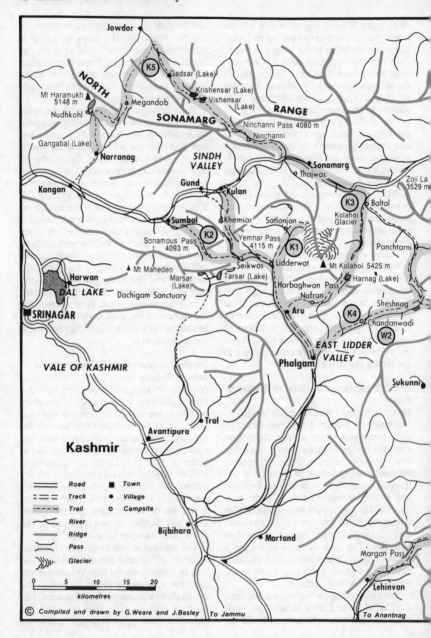

Kashmir

Symbol	Legend	Symbol	Legend
Road	■ Town
Track	● Village
Trail	○ Campsite
River	
Ridge	
Pass	
Glacier	

0   5   10   15   20
kilometres

© Compiled and drawn by G. Weare and J. Besley

Map labels:
Jowdor
K5
Gadsar (Lake)
Krishensar (Lake)
Vishensar (Lake)
NORTH
Mt Haramukh 5148 m
Megandob
SONAMARG
RANGE
Nudhkohl
Ninchanni Pass 4080 m
Ninchanni
Gangabal (Lake)
SINDH VALLEY
Sonamarg
Thajwas
Zoji La 3529 m
Narranag
Gund
Kangan
Kulan
K3
Baltal
Sumbal
Khemsar
Satlanjan
Kolahoi Glacier
K2
Yemhar Pass 4115 m
Panchtarni
Sonamous Pass 4093 m
K1
Mt Kolahoi 5425 m
Mt Mahedeo
Seikwas
Harnag (Lake)
Liderwat
Marsar (Lake)
Tarsar (Lake)
Harbaghwan Pass
Harwan
DAL LAKE
Dachigam Sanctuary
Nafran
Sheshnag
SRINAGAR
Aru
K4
Chandanwadi
W2
EAST LIDDER VALLEY
VALE OF KASHMIR
Phalgam
Sukunni
Tral
Avantipura
Bijbihara
Martand
Margan Pass
Lehinvan
To Jammu
To Anantnag

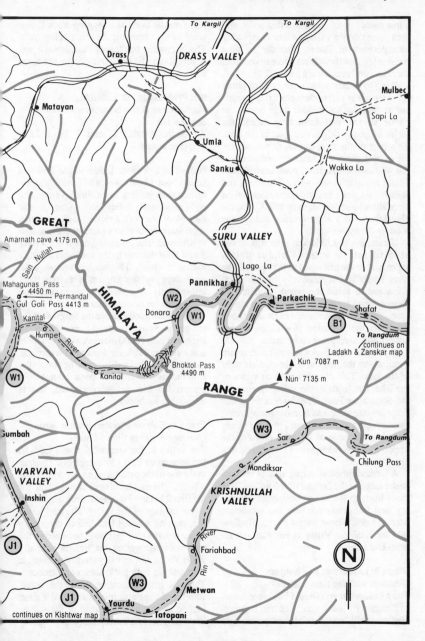

a few more km to a safe crossing point, and then return down valley before completing the approach to Tarsar. This can be time consuming, but there is no alternative. From the river confluence it is a further 2 to 3 hours walking to Tarsar, which can be hard going if the terrain is still under snow. It is important to head for the middle ridge beside the Tarsar stream, and from here ascend the series of grassy ridges that lead to the lake. This part of the trek can be tiring, but the views back down to Lidderwat and across to the well-defined Kolahoi peak compensate. Tarsar is a glacial lake about 3 km long and at its maximum 1 km wide, and enclosed on three sides by snow ridges up to 1000 metres above the water's edge; a perfect campsite as soon as the snows melt.

If camping at Lidderwat then it is advisable to return without undue delay, especially in the early part of the season. The river levels rise significantly by the afternoon and to avoid the worst of them you should aim at returning to Seikwas by lunchtime. You then have the rest of the afternoon to admire the profusion of wildflowers that appear after the spring snow melts.

If you started at Seikwas you could return by climbing the ridge to the immediate right of the lake. This affords excellent views of the lake, and leads to the valley en route to the Sonamous Pass. The descent from this ridge is quite steep and is under snow during the early part of the season. From the valley floor it is a couple of km back down to the upper Seikwas campsite to complete the circuit.

A further option is to trek around the lake to the ridge at the far end of the valley. This route leads to the upper Dachigam Sanctuary, and from the ridge you can appreciate Marsar Lake, whose waters eventually flow into the Kashmir Valley at Harwan, not far from Dal Lake.

Stage 5: Lidderwat to Phalgam
(Average walking time 5 hours)
From Lidderwat you should be able to return to Phalgam by lunch time. The trail is generally downhill, and it is always possible to

jump on the back of a logging truck if you want to save time on the stage below Aru. The last tourist bus leaves Phalgam at 4 pm, if you plan to be back in Srinagar the same day.

K2: PHALGAM TO SUMBAL
via Seikwas & the Sonamous Pass
Stages 1-3
As for the Kolahoi Glacier & Tarsar Lake trek (see page 60).

Note The trek from Lidderwat to Seikwas takes about 3 hours. From Seikwas there are three passes leading to the Sindh Valley. The right hand (east) valley leads to the Yemhar Pass (4350 metres), a moderate climb with a short steep descent to a camp at the meadow at Khemsar. The following day it is a further 3 or 4 hour descent to the roadhead at either Kulan or Gund. This trail is seldom used nowadays by the horsemen as the track immediately after the pass is exposed and dangerous for laden ponies.

The pass directly above the Seikwas camp involves another steady ascent to an unnamed pass (4200 metres), and from there it is a further 1½ hour descent to where this valley joins the valley coming from the Sonamous Pass. This pass is not recommended for the inexperienced, and is unsuitable for horses.

Stage 4: Seikwas to Sonamous camp
(Average walking time 5 hours)
The valley to the west of Seikwas leads to the Sonamous Pass (3960 metres). The trek to the top of the pass takes, on average, about 3 hours. The trail involves a steady climb for the first 2 km until it crosses the main stream to the far side of the valley. The trail levels out, passing a small lake before crossing a rather marshy trail that leads back across the valley. In late spring the trail is normally under snow, and an early start from camp is essential for both pack horses and trekkers. There is little indication as to the actual summit of the pass. It is in fact just a short incline as you near the head of the valley. From here there is a steep descent to a grassy

Top Left: Birdlife, Dal Lake, Srinagar (GW)
Top Right: Lotus, Dal Lake, Srinagar (GW)
Bottom Left: Lotus, Dal Lake, Srinagar (GW)
Bottom Right: Wildflowers, Himachal Pradesh (GW)

Top: Sunset above Seikwas camp, Kashmir (GW)
Bottom Left: Kanital Valley, Kashmir (GW)
Bottom Right: Trekkers approaching Seikwas, Kashmir (GW)

plateau, from where there is a bird's eye view of the Sonamous camp.

The next section is steep and difficult, particularly early in the season when the slopes are under snow. The mules are sometimes unloaded at this point, and the baggage rolled down the slopes. Early in the season it is essential for trekkers to have good boots, and a sturdy stick or an ice axe is also useful. It also helps if you feel confident in crossing relatively steep snow slopes. If you are not, then plan to cross the pass after mid-July. By then the snow will have melted and a trail will be cleared across the boulder fields down to the Sonamous camp.

Stage 5: Sonamous to Sumbal
(Average walking time 3-4 hours)
The final stage of this trek descends steeply to the Sindh Valley. It is not the easiest trail to follow, particularly through the forest, so some care should be taken to avoid any bush-bashing or backtracking.

Cross the Sonamous stream by the shepherd encampment, and follow the trail through the forest for a km until you cross a large side stream coming from the side valley. Here the trail descends below the small Gujar settlement, and then continues above the main river through the forest until after 4 or 5 km it descends steeply to a side stream. Cross the log bridge and continue down the trail, which is now just above main river.

After a km or so the trail crosses a substantial bridge over the main river. The trail passes through a Gujar village and follows the river bank until it recrosses the river a couple of km down the valley. The trail then widens, and continues to the outskirts of Sumbal village. Here the pony trail skirts the village fields, while the trekking trail cuts through rice and corn fields to the roadhead.

Getting Away At Sumbal there are a number of tea stalls where you can rest before catching the local bus. It will take 2 or 3 hours to return to Srinagar, and slightly less up the Sindh Valley road to Sonamarg.

K3: PHALGAM TO SONAMARG via Harnag Lake
Stage 1: Phalgam to Aru
(Average walking time 3 hours)
See Stage 1 of trek K1: Phalgam to Kolahoi Glacier (see page 60).

Stage 2: Aru to Nafran
(Average walking time 4 hours)
From Aru ascend the main meadow up the valley on the left bank of the Nafran stream. The trail splits frequently and you must be careful to remain in the main valley. By mid-June the Gujars have established a track which frequently fords the main nullah. The Gujar village at Arumin lies just below the Nafran meadow and provides an excellent campsite.

Stage 3: Nafran to Harnag
(Average walking time 4 hours)
The ascent to the Harbaghwan Pass (4200 metres) is quite steep. Early in the season an extensive snow field has to be crossed before you ascend a narrow gully to the pass. The trail involves a climb over boulders, and is very difficult for laden ponies. There is a short descent from the pass to Harnag Lake and it is advisable to camp towards the far end. Harnag Lake is sacred to the shepherds, and each spring a lamb is sacrificed at the water's edge to ensure good weather throughout the grazing season.

From this camp a day should be reserved to view the main buttress of the Kolahoi massif. It is then a matter of either returning to Phalgam, which can be done in a day, or continuing to the Sindh Valley.

Stage 4: Harnag to Baltal
(Average walking time 4 hours)
The shepherd trail descends from Harnag Lake on the right hand bank. During the early part of the season the trail relies heavily on residual snow bridges. Later in the season it is necessary to check with the shepherds at Harnag as to the state of the trail on to Baltal. Before reaching Baltal the trail meets the path coming down from the Amarnath Cave. It is advisable to camp here near the small

Gujar settlement rather than continuing to Baltal, which is close to the Indian army camp.

Stage 5: Baltal to Sonamarg
(Average walking time 3 hours)
Follow the track below the military encampment. You can either walk up to the road and hitch a ride to Sonamarg, or take the lower trail, following the Sindh River past the village of Sarbal. This route avoids the Srinagar-Kargil road until 3 km above Sonamarg.

The sprawling shanty village of Sonamarg has little to recommend it. Local buses leave from here to Srinagar throughout the day, with the last leaving for Srinagar at 4 pm. Supplies can be replenished here if you are continuing on another trek or if you're camping near the Thajwas Glacier, about 3 km below Sonamarg.

K4: PHALGAM TO AMARNATH CAVE
The trek to the Amarnath Cave is the most important in Kashmir. Each year on the August (*Shavan*) full moon about 20,000 Hindu pilgrims trek to the cave to view the ice statue which symbolises the presence of Shiva, the Hindu god of destruction.

There are many legends regarding the discovery of the cave, but little historical fact. In all probability it was discovered as shepherds wandered the valley in search of fresh grazing. Not only is it an ideal refuge for meditation but it is located at the head of one of the important tributaries of the Indus River. According to the legend, Lord Shiva related his theory of reincarnation to his consort Parvati in the cave on a full moon night. As if to substantiate the legend, a huge ice statue forms in the cave, and is said to wax and wane with the moon. The ice statue represents the *lingam*, a symbol of Shiva the source of creation, while the huge size of the cave is a symbol of Parvati and the vast womb of the universe.

For the wandering holy man (*sadhu*), the pilgrimage actually starts in Srinagar and takes a week to reach Phalgam, with rest stops at the temples at Bijihara and Martand en route. At Phalgam they join the main body of pilgrims that have driven directly from Srinagar, and prepare for the trek.

For some, the idea of walking with 20,000 Hindu pilgrims isn't exactly the ideal way to trek, as moving with such a large mass of people rather undermines any notion of isolation. On top of which you have to contend with all the associated hygiene problems. One alternative is to visit the cave before the August full moon: the trail is open by late June/early July and remains open until October. However, most people who have walked to the cave with me during the yatra (pilgrimage) have not regretted it, although most would not want to do it again. It is very much a once in a lifetime experience.

For those making their own arrangements, food can be purchased from the numerous tea stalls en route, and limited tent accommodation is available at the 'camp cities' that form each night to accommodate the pilgrims. It is necessary to stress the fact that drinking water from all the streams should be avoided, and a strict eye kept on all the baggage. Ponies are available for the trek. It is advisable to book your requirements in advance with the tourist office in Phalgam. Prices are significantly higher during this period and a packpony for the 5 day trek from Phalgam to the cave and return is approximately 50% more than the normal season rates. It is also possible to be carried to the cave by a dandy – a wooden platform supported by five or six bearers who charge around Rs 3000 for the round trip.

During the yatra, stages of the walk are carefully controlled by the authorities. The first stage of the trek is to Chandanwadi, the second to Sheshnag, the third over the Mahagunas Pass to Panchtarni, and then a final stage to the cave. Most pilgrims visit the cave and return to Sheshnag that day, walking back to Phalgam on the fifth day. There is an alternative approach from Sonamarg and Baltal; some pilgrims drive to Baltal and start very early the following morning for the cave. In this way they can get to Amarnath and back to Baltal in one very long day.

Stage 1: Phalgam to Chandanwadi
(Average walking time 4 hours)

The trail leaves Phalgam on a bitumen road, past the Shanker temple and along the East Lidder Valley. The trail is easy to follow, indeed it is suitable for jeeps as far as Chandanwadi. There are many obvious shortcuts on the route, and a number of tea stalls as this first stage always seems to be quite hot. The campsite is in a pleasant glade just before the main line of tea stalls.

Stage 2: Chandanwadi to Sheshnag
(Average walking time 5-6 hours)

From Chandanwadi the trail winds steeply for 500 metres to Pisu, on top of the ridge. From here, there are some commanding views back down valley to the mountains beyond Phalgam. During the main pilgrimage the tea stall owners do a thriving business, and keep you going on the long incline to the next main resting area at Wawajana. From here it is 2 to 3 km further to Sheshnag. The glacial lake here is set in remarkable surroundings, its waters reflecting the snow capped peaks of Vishnu, Shiva and Brahma. Rumour among pilgrims is that the lake is inhabited by a serpent of Loch Ness proportions, so it's advisable not to camp too close to the water's edge!

Stage 3: Sheshnag to Panchtarni
(Average walking time 6 hours)

The trail gradually ascends from Sheshnag with magnificent views of the mountains immediately above. The ascent towards the Mahagunas Pass winds up to a grassy plateau, and from there on to the pass it is a further hour's climb. Signs of encouragement amuse the weary: 'Just a hop and you're on the top'. The sign at the top of the pass states the height as 4580 metres. It is not a dramatic pass, but it is still no mean achievement for the pilgrims, many of whom have never been beyond the Indian plains. The descent to Panchtarni is quite long and tiring, but there are frequent flowered meadows to rest in and admire. The campsite can be seen from afar, and behind, on a further ridge, the bare, tree-

less mountainscape resembles the terrain on the far side of the Himalaya. There are more spacious camping sites upstream from the main camping area, and these are also a little cleaner.

Stage 4: Panchtarni to Amarnath Cave
(Average walking time 5 hours return)

The actual time to the cave will depend on whether you are going during the main pilgrimage. During the pilgrimage an early start is essential, with many of the pilgrims leaving well before first light. The pilgrims move more steadily and slowly than on the rest of the trek, as if in awe of their surroundings. After about an hour the trail enters the Amarnath Valley, descending to a permanent blackened snow bridge which fords the Amarvatti stream. The trail continues on this far bank to the base of the mountain, and from here it is a steep ascent up a series of concrete steps to the entrance to the cave.

It is not hard to imagine why the pilgrims believe this to be one of the most sacred places in the Himalaya. The cave is approximately 150 metres high and wide, and contains a natural ice lingam, the symbol of Shiva. The ice is formed by water trickling through the limestone roof, and the lingam is said to reach its maximum size during the full moon. Occasionally the ice does not form at all, and this is considered extremely inauspicious for the pilgrims. If you intend to enter the cave during the pilgrimage, be prepared for a long wait as only a limited number of pilgrims are allowed inside at any one time.

Most pilgrims return from Amarnath to Phalgam. However, if you are planning to continue to Baltal, return to the junction of the Panchtarni and Amarvatti valleys and turn down the valley. The trek to Baltal takes about 4 hours. The trail is subject to landslides, and should not be undertaken during and immediately after periods of heavy rainfall. Transport is possible from Baltal during the pilgrimage period, and buses will get you back to Srinagar that night. Alternatively, you can camp at Baltal overnight, and continue to Sonamarg at a more leisurely pace the following morning.

K5: SONAMARG TO GANGABAL LAKE via Vishensar & Krishensar Lakes

A trek in this region offers spectacular mountain scenery, beautiful flowered campsites and excellent fishing. It is the ideal extension for a trek between the Lidder and Sindh valleys, and can be undertaken from Sonamarg within one week. The trek can normally be completed from the end of June until the beginning of October. Trekkers must take all of their provisions with them, including fuel as wood is not readily available. Packponies are available at Sonamarg and from all reports their handlers are more obliging than their Phalgam counterparts. Rates are similar to those in Phalgam; about Rs 50 per horse per day, plus return to Sonamarg.

To reach Sonamarg takes about 4 hours by local bus from Srinagar. If time is not at a premium, a few days camping at Thajwas is recommended before undertaking the trek. There are a number of idyllic campsites which provide a convenient base from which to explore some of the hanging glaciers at the head of the valley.

Stage 1: Sonamarg to Nichanni
(Average walking time 5-6 hours)
Descend to the main road bridge over the Sindh River about 3 km below Sonamarg. Cross the bridge and follow the upper trail that leads away from the road. The trail is well defined, and leads to a number of Gujar settlements halfway up the hillside. If this is your first day out, take it easy; the going gets considerably steeper as you ascend. As you pass the Gujar settlement ensure that you keep to the trail that winds further up the hillside. There is then a tiring ascent for another hour until you reach the meadow of Shok Dharan. From here you will discover the real delights of trekking, with views back to the mountains behind the Thajwas Glacier, across to the main Himalaya and east to the mountains beyond the Zoji La.

It is possible to camp at this site beyond

the Gujar huts, but the water supply is strictly limited. It's a small spring line hardly sufficient for even a small group. From the meadow the trail leads along a small ridge through birch groves that are at their finest in the autumn. The trail descends to the valley floor and from here it is a further 2 or 3 km to the campsite. The trail ascends over a series of ridges which level by the side of the Nichanni stream. There are a number of excellent campsites, amid flowered meadows and bubbling streams.

Stage 2: Nichanni to Krishensar
(Average walking time 5 hours)
The ascent to the Nichanni Pass takes about 2 hours. Cross the Nichanni stream on one of the many snow bridges and continue climbing on the right-hand bank. The pass, at just under 4000 metres, is normally under snow until July, and some snow plodding will be necessary during the early part of the season. The pass is characterised by a gully cut between high rocky outcrops, hence the name Nichanni Bar which is frequently used on pre-1947 maps. From the top of the pass the views both back to Sonamarg and forward to the ridges beyond Vishensar are impressive. (The suffix *sar* means 'lake'.)

If time is not at a premium there is an option of climbing the gully to the immediate right of the pass. The climb is easy going over a snowfield and then over boulders. If you are fit enough, then continue for an hour or more until, if the weather is clear, you can see the distant peaks of the Karakoram. An ice axe is useful for crossing the steeper snow slopes.

The descent from the pass is steep at first, then across a series of grassy plateaus with the trail leading down the right hand side of the valley. It is necessary to cross the main stream, and wet boots are the order of the day unless you can jump the 10 metres or so to the far side. From here, follow the shepherd trails over to Vishensar Lake, taking care not to go too far down the valley. There is no shortage of campsites at the lake.

If you're spending a rest day here, contact the local fishing inspector who may oblige with the odd trout or two, providing you have the correct permit. A walk around the lake is also recommended. The largest trout can be seen in the clear waters on the far side of the lake, while the wildflowers on the banks enhance what is one of the most scenic campsites in Kashmir.

Stage 3: Krishensar to Gadsar Lake & Camp
(Average walking time 5-6 hours)
From Krishensar the trail leads past the higher Vishensar lake, before climbing the well-graded trail up the hillside to the pass. The climb looks quite formidable, but you should reach it in a couple of hours, even allowing for plenty of rest stops. From the pass it is possible to see Nanga Parbat. However an early start is necessary as by mid-morning the mist obscures the views. The descent from the pass is quite steep to Gadsar Lake, and from there it is a further 3 km on to the Gujar settlement.

This section of the trail attracts an exceptionally wide range of wildflowers, and days can be spent here identifying the numerous species. The normal campsite is below the Gujar settlement.

Stage 4: Gadsar Lake to Megandob
(Average walking time 4 hours)
Cross the Gadsar stream over the permanent snow bridge, and follow the trail up the Satsaran ridge – this is a steep climb for about an hour. The valley then opens out, and you may be fortunate to again glimpse Nanga Parbat. The trail is well defined to the lower (north) side of the Megandob Pass. As you approach the pass, cross to the right hand side of the valley, and follow the trail closely or you will be forced to do some unnecessary boulder hopping. The campsite lies in the sheltered valley at the north end of the pass. Magnificent misty views down to the Sindh Valley complement the site.

An alternative to following the direct route to Megandob is to divert down the Gadsar Valley for 4 or 5 km to the village of Jowdor. This is the only permanently populated village in the region, and it is completely cut off from Srinagar and the outside world during the winter. The village produces barley, potatoes, and fodder crops, and also a very coarse spun wool. It seems that some of the villagers may have originally migrated here from Gurais, a region several days walk down the valley. Many of the villagers have features similar to the Dardic peoples of Drass and other parts of Ladakh. It is interesting that the locals here have reported sightings of the rare Kashmir stag and the musk deer that roam the highest crags above the village. In late autumn the herds descend to the valleys above Jowdor, where they remain for the winter months.

From Jowdor the trail climbs steeply to Megandob, meeting the Satsaran trail just below the pass. Six hours should be allowed to complete this stage and continue on to Megandob.

Stage 5: Megandob to Gangabal Lake
(Average walking time 4-5 hours)
From Megandob, descend the main trail for about 1 km then turn up the hillside. Do not go any further down the valley. From here you follow the trail which winds up quite steeply for the first few km, until you reach a grassy plateau beneath the pass. Rest here before crossing the meadow and making the short, steep ascent. As you reach the pass the Haramukh massif comes into view, while below, the Nudhkohl Lake is often shrouded in early morning mist. At the head of the valley is the larger Gangabal Lake – an impressive lake by any standards – which

Shikara

flows into Nudhkohl Lake. Turning back, distant views can be had of the Kolahoi massif and the main Himalaya.

The descent to the lakeside is steep in sections, and it will take the best part of a couple of hours to get down to the camp. It is recommended that you camp at Nudhkohl Lake or further downstream. The lake is well known for its trout fishing, and even novices can catch enough to satisfy the appetite.

There is a proposal to dam Gangabal Lake for hydroelectricity, and the appalling structural remains of the first excavations scar the lake edge. However, it is still a beautiful walk around the lake's edge, and this can be completed in a couple of hours.

From Nudhkohl you can undertake a climb to the ridge south of the Haramukh massif, from where you can gain clear views across the Kashmir Valley. The Bakharval follow this trail in the autumn on their way back to cross the Pir Panjal Range.

It is not hard to understand why Haramukh was traditionally revered by the Hindus in the Kashmir Valley. Its impressive position on the northern reaches of the valley would have made it a natural attraction for the pilgrim. Indeed it is said that regular pilgrimages were made to the foot of the mountain and Gangabal Lake long before the Amarnath pilgrimage gained popularity.

Stage 6: Gangabal Lake to Narranag
(Average walking time 4-5 hours)
From Nudhkohl Lake the trail descends across the open meadow. The trail is easy to follow for the first few km as far as the Gujar encampment. It then skirts uphill, not down, through the forest. The trail remains on a high contour for several km until it reaches a small meadow with views overlooking the Sindh Valley. From here it is a steady descent through the forest. The trail twists and turns somewhat, but the descent to Narranag should take no more than a couple of hours. While descending, it is worthwhile appreciating why taking the trek in the reverse direction is not recommended: such a climb on the first day would be quite dispiriting.

At Narranag there are the ruins of some ancient Hindu temples dating from the 9th century. There is also a *Forest Rest House* and some good camping areas in the forest just up the valley. From Narranag it is a further 5 or 6 km to the village at Wangat, from where you can get a bus to Kangan, and from there on to Srinagar.

The Warvan Valley

Trekking from Kashmir to Ladakh
The Warvan Valley is an intermediate valley between the Pir Panjal Range and the main Himalaya. For trekkers, the valley links the trails from the Vale of Kashmir to the high Himalayan passes leading north towards Ladakh. The treks through the valley also have the advantage of providing a fascinating insight into Kashmiri village lifestyle, in an area not yet linked by roads.

Getting Ready
Basic food supplies can be purchased from the larger villages in the Warvan Valley. These cannot be relied upon however, and it is advisable to bring all supplies with you from Srinagar. Pack mule trains frequently ply the route out of Lehinvan but they are usually already contracted to the state authorities for the season. In practical terms it means that if you intend to trek to Ladakh you will either have to organise horses from Phalgam, or spend a few days in Lehinvan until a horse or two from a nearby village becomes available.

Treks
Three main treks are outlined in this section:

W1: From Lehinvan (in the Kashmir Valley) over the Margan Pass, then up valley to the Kanital Valley and the Bhoktol Pass to Pannikhar, in the Suru Valley, and Ladakh.

W2: From Phalgam over the Gul Gali, down valley to the Kanital Valley and over the Bhoktol Pass to Ladakh.

W3: From Lehinvan over the Margan Pass, down valley to the Krishnullah Valley and over the Chilung Pass to Rangdum and Ladakh.

Treks from Kashmir to Ladakh should not be attempted until mid-June at the earliest. The trails then remain open until mid-October, when snows once again block the main Himalayan passes. If you're undertaking a trek solely in the Warvan Valley, it is possible to cross the Margan Pass (the main pass above Lehinvan) in early May, although horses generally cannot cross until early June. Trekking the lower Warvan to Jammu can be undertaken up to December. Refer to the section on Jammu.

The most popular pass for trekking across the Himalaya, the Bhoktol Pass, is relatively low at 4420 metres. Even so, trekkers should be aware of the need to acclimatise properly, and an extra rest day or two, at a village or at one of the Bakharval encampments, is recommended before crossing the pass.

Accommodation is available in the Warvan Valley in the forest rest houses. These wooden bungalows were originally designed for the forest officers on their tours of duty. Facilities are basic, with string or wooden beds, the occasional chair and an open verandah on which to spend the late afternoon. The caretaker, or *chowkidar*, assigned to each rest house is normally very obliging, and it makes interesting reading to look through the register and discover what the major and his wife thought of the place in the summer of 1936.

Beyond the villages, shepherd huts can be used at the margins of the season, but from there on it is necessary to have a tent with you.

W1: LEHINVAN TO PANNIKHAR
via the Warvan Valley, Kanital Valley & Bhoktol Pass
Stage 1: Srinagar to Lehinvan & Camp
The drive from Srinagar to Lehinvan takes about 4 hours by taxi. If coming by local bus, allow all day. Firstly, catch the bus to Anantnag and then transfer to the local bus

stand for the bus to Lehinvan. This can take 5 or 6 hours, depending on the number of villagers, relatives, chickens etc which need to be offloaded, so don't be in a hurry to get far beyond Lehinvan that day.

There is a *Forest Rest House* at Lehinvan, just beyond the roadhead. Either camp there or continue through the forest for about 1½ hours to the open meadow and the tea stalls that mark the beginning of the climb to the Margan Pass. The trail is well defined through the forest and crosses the main stream a number of times. Do not divert to the jeep track as it will take you way above the easily graded shepherd trail.

Stage 2: Lehinvan to Margan Pass
(Average walking time 4 hours)
It is best to aim for a short second stage as the climb to the Margan Pass is quite tiring. Follow the trail that zig-zags up from the valley – there are plenty of rest stops for admiring the impressive views back down towards the Vale of Kashmir. During the early part of the season, there is constant movement of shepherds and their flocks, so take care to avoid any of the small rocks that are dislodged as the goats clamber over higher and rockier ledges on their way to the pass. A new shepherd trail has been constructed over the last few seasons that avoids the climb up to the cliff face just below the pass.

The Margan Pass is not a typical ridge-type pass. Instead it is about 5 km long, and slopes gently towards the Warvan Valley. A jeep trail over the pass is near to completion, but this can be avoided by following the well defined, if rather boggy, trail to the right hand side of the pass where there is a campsite. The pass is usually covered in wildflowers throughout the season. Views of Nun, Kun and the main Himalaya towards Kishtwar can be appreciated on a clear day.

Stage 3: Margan Pass to Warvan Valley
(Average walking time 4-5 hours)
The trek distance for this stage depends on where your party chooses to camp in the

Warvan Valley. It is recommended that the trek to the highest village at Sukkuni is completed over a couple of stages, with perhaps a rest day at one of the many magnificent campsites en route.

The trail across the Margan Pass climbs to meet the jeep trail shortly after the shelter hut in the middle of the valley. In the early morning the mountains are backlit and clearly profiled above the Warvan Valley. As the trail begins to descend, it becomes dusty with the roadworks. En route there are a couple of tea stalls before you head on down to the valley floor. The shepherd trail constantly switches back before reaching the *Forest Rest House* at Inshin, where you can

camp if you have come direct from Lehinvan that day. There is also an Octroi post here, where the shepherds and your horsemen pay a small fee for grazing the meadows in the higher reaches of the valley. (If you're doing trek K3, heading south-east towards the Krishnullah Valley then up to Chilung Pass, Inshin is where you turn down the Warvan Valley.)

The trail up the Warvan at this stage remains on the west bank, and there is no necessity to cross the bridge over the river to Inshin village. The villages in the Warvan are spaced out every few km on this section. The first main one at Choietramun is typical with an abundance of mothers and young children, and an enthusiastic school teacher waiting to show you around. These villages are cut off from Kashmir throughout the winter, and therefore tend to self-sufficiency. However this is certainly not the case just yet. The ponies laden with supplies from the Kashmir Valley are vital for keeping the villages going during the long winter days. These settlements are still generally unaffected by 'outside progress'.

The Kashmir villages, though untidy in details, are very picturesque. The cottages are two storied; in some parts they have mud walls, with a low sloping gable roof of thatch or of rough shingle; in others, where wood is more plentiful, they are entirely made of timber, made like a log hut. They are sure to have some rooms warm and cosy, to live in in winter time; and a balcony sheltered by the overhanging eaves makes a good sitting place in the summer. The lower storey of the cottages is used in winter for stabling the cattle; their heat sensibly warms the house, and partly counteracts the coldness of the season.
Drew, *Northern Barrier of India*, 1877.

That description, written over 100 years ago, is still applicable to the 20 to 30 rather poorly constructed farmhouses that compose a typical village in the Warvan Valley. Corn is still the staple crop, along with red barley for fodder. Simple watermills grind the corn, which is then stored in outbuildings for the winter. Rice from the government stores is, as we have seen, brought on horseback from

Srinagar. During the winter the villagers engage in coarse weaving, and some of the smocks and pullovers find their way into the Srinagar market.

There is no shortage of campsites in this area. One of the best is reached about 5 or 6 km up the valley from Inshin. Here the valley widens, and the trail drops to the same contour as the river. A couple of km beyond this point there is a large island to one side of the river, with a number of magnificent park-like campsites.

Stage 4: Camp to Sukunni

(Average walking time 4-5 hours)

From this island camp it is 4 or 5 km up the valley until you are opposite Basminah village. Cross the bridge here and continue on the opposite side of the valley. The pony trail cuts through the village of Rekinwas, and in the distance you can see Sukunni, the highest village in the valley. To reach Sukunni it is necessary to recross the main bridge above the village, and then head down to the *Forest Rest House* for the night. There is an alternative campsite about 1 km above the bridge and away from the main trail.

Stage 5: Sukunni to Humpet

(Average walking time 6 hours)

During your time at Sukunni check that the main snowbridge, or an alternative shepherd bridge, is in place to cross the Warvan River up valley.

If there is a bridge, then remain on the left hand bank and continue up valley for 4 or 5 km to the crossing. The trail to the bridge is quite tiring, with a number of ups and downs to cross the side streams. The snow bridge crossing is obvious, and the shepherd trail will clearly indicate the approach onto and off the bridge.

If the snow bridge is not in place, and the shepherds have not constructed an alternative, then recross the bridge above Sukunni and follow the trail on the far right hand bank. At places the ill-defined trail climbs steeply above the river. Above the snowbridge the trail is difficult for the horses to follow.

Residual snow banks remain until July, and it can take the best part of an hour or two to reach the confluence of the Warvan and the Kanital rivers. Sections of this trail will be under snow in the early part of the season which may involve more tiring climbs till you reach the confluence. Here you turn up the Kanital Valley through birch groves and past waterfalls until two short steep stages bring you out onto an open plateau and the summer grazing areas of the Bakharval shepherds.

The campsite at Humpet is beyond the shepherd encampment on the main valley floor. During the winter, birch trees are uprooted by avalanches, so you can build a modest campfire while appreciating the 6000 metre snow ridges of the main Himalaya. If a rest day is at hand, then it is worthwhile exploring the opposite valley. This includes some great climbs up the glacial valleys on the left hand side. However, watch the level of the Kanital River or you may be forced to swim it on the way back. It is very cold and rather puts a damper on the day, as the author will testify. Consult the shepherds beforehand as to the best crossing point.

If you take a rest day here you will find that the shepherds are keen to check out new arrivals, and are willing to offer goat's milk, curd, and corn chappatis in return for the odd Swiss army knife or two. Give the shepherds ample warning if you decide to visit their encampments, as the dogs are particularly fierce and will need to be chained.

It is particularly sad to note that here, and at the next campsite, many a trekker's camp has been broken into at night and items have been stolen. The chief culprits are not the shepherds at the nearby settlement but, apparently, those from the higher camps who have given the Bakharval a bad name. If you apprehend one of them, don't expect much help from the local authorities. Having reported a theft, the stolen items which I had recovered were impounded as evidence and sent to the police in Kishtwar. No less than six years later, the case is still pending – a less than encouraging note on the development of tourism in Kashmir.

Garry Weare

Stage 6: Humpet to Kanital

(Average walking time 3 hours)

Leaving Humpet, the trail follows the south bank of the river, and continues along the valley floor around to the Kanital campsite. The track crosses meadows which are covered in wild flowers during the summer months, while the glacial bed is rich in fossils. There is one side stream crossing en route, where the valley turns to the east. From here the Bhoktol Glacier and the main Himalaya come into view. There are a number of campsites to choose from, including one beside a waterfall on the last large open meadow before the moraine. Alternatively, you can trek further towards the glacier for about 2 or 3 km, and camp beside one of the smaller shepherd settlements. This will save time on the pass crossing the following morning.

Stage 7: Kanital to Bhoktol Pass & Donara

(Average walking time 8-9 hours)

From the camp, continue along the trail until you reach the last shepherd hut, and then make for the right hand side of the terminal moraine. Check the rock cairns as you commence your ascent through the boulders. There is, believe it or not, a trail for the horses to follow, and it should not take you more than an hour before the track descends from the boulders onto the centre of the glacial valley floor.

From here there is a gradual climb up the centre of the glacier. As you ascend the glacier avoid the obvious crevassed areas and move towards the right side of the valley. In the early part of the season even the crevasses on this side of the valley may be covered in snow, so a local guide is invaluable. The ascent is not particularly tiring, and within 3 hours of leaving camp you should be opposite a small defile that marks the top of the pass. From this point cross the glacier to the foot of the pass. There follows a short ascent to a grassy plateau, with views up the icefall leading to the Nun Kun massif. Then there is a further 150 metre climb to the pass, and you are in Ladakh.

From the pass there is an initial steep descent to the main glacier. Trek on down the glacier to where it meets a boulder trail on the left hand side of the valley. Here the track crosses the lateral moraine before winding down to the high pastures and the first possible campsite. The trail then cuts across the pastures to the shepherd camp at Donara, where there are campsites on either side of the river.

Stage 8: Donara to Pannikhar

(Average walking time 2-3 hours)

From Donara, follow the trail on the left hand side of the valley. The trail is well-defined, and en route you may pass some of the local village women collecting juniper for winter fuel. Midway down valley the peak of Nun is visible, and not long after the trail widens to a jeep track. From here it is a short distance to the road bridge and the road from Kargil. Cross the bridge to Pannikhar village. As with most campsites in Ladakh, a fee is payable, and Pannikhar is no exception. The best camping site is in the shady grove beside the river. Trekkers are warned to pitch their tents with care, as small children from the village delight in opening up irrigation canals and swamping the unwary. Ponies can be hired in Pannikhar, which is fortunate as the Kashmiris are seldom enthusiastic about continuing on with their horses to Ladakh.

From Pannikhar you can either descend the Suru Valley to Kargil, a drive by local bus or lorry of some 4 hours, or follow the trails further into Ladakh. Details of these are given in the Suru Valley section.

W2: PHALGAM TO PANNIKHAR
via Sheshnag, Gul Gali Pass, Kanital
Valley & Bhoktol Pass

The initial stages of this trek follow the Amarnath pilgrimage trail from Phalgam to Sheshnag before crossing the Gul Gali. From here you descend to the Bakharval encampment at Permandal, and the following day walk down the valley until it meets the trail coming from the village of Sukkuni. The stages are as follows.

Stage 1: Phalgam to Chandanwadi
Stage 2: Chandanwadi to Sheshnag
As for Stages 1 and 2 of the Phalgam to Amarnath trek, K4 in the Lidder & Sindh Valleys section (see page 66).

Stage 3: Sheshnag to Permandal
(Average walking time 5-6 hours)
From Sheshnag, ascend the rocky gully immediately beyond the lake. The climb takes about 2 or 3 hours to the pass at 4200 metres, from where the peaks of the main Himalaya can be appreciated for the first time. Early in the season, the ascent to the pass can be quite tiring in the soft snow, and from the pass there is an initially steep ascent before leading down the gully to the Sain Nullah and the upper Warvan Valley. Before reaching the valley floor, follow the trail to the left hand ridge of the gully, which takes you down to the Permandal campsite.

Stage 4: Permandal to Humpet
(Average walking time 5-6 hours)
The trail from the Permandal camp winds high above the valley floor through a series of shepherd encampments. The walk is shaded by birch groves, and affords good views up the Kanital Valley and the mountains beyond Humpet. From the viewpoint opposite Humpet the trail begins to descend, zig-zagging steeply down to the valley floor to a snow bridge over the river. Once across the snow bridge, the trail goes up the valley on the far bank, as per the description outlined in the previous section under Stage 5: Sukunni to Humpet.

Stages 5-7: Humpet to Pannikhar
The rest of this trek to Ladakh follows Stages 6, 7 and 8 of the previous trek, W1: Humpet to Kanital; Kanital to the Bhoktol Pass & Donara; Donara to Pannikhar.

W3: LEHINVAN TO LADAKH
via the Margan Pass, Warvan Valley, Krishnullah Valley, Chilung Pass & Rangdum
This challenging trek is an ideal alternative to the trek over the Bhoktol Pass. The trail goes through some beautiful valleys, and over a little-trekked pass to a point just below the Pentze La in the Zanskar. This pass has remained little-trekked because of logistic problems: it is not possible to pick up supplies of any kind for most of the route, and horses cannot cross the Chilung Pass. The ideal compromise is to take lightly laden horses as far as you can up the Krishnullah Valley, and then backpack the final few stages into Ladakh.

Stages 1-3: Lehinvan to Margan Pass & Inshin
The first three stages, to Inshin, are the same as Stages 1, 2 and 3 of trek W1 in this section (see page 71).

Stage 4: Inshin to Yourdu
(Average walking time 7 hours)
Cross the bridge at Inshin and follow the main mule trail down the valley. There is a clearing in the forest and a camping area halfway, just before the village of Hajikah (ideal as the end of a stage if you're coming the other way, from a camp on the Margan Pass). After about 4 or 5 hours trekking, the trail crosses to the opposite bank over the substantial bridge, and from there on to Yourdu takes about an hour or two.

Yourdu is the largest village in the upper Warvan Valley, and the bazaar is a meeting place for the Bakharval – a chance to buy bangles, jewellery and restock with supplies of flour, grain and basic essentials. Cross the bridge at Yourdu to the *Rest House*.

Otters have been seen at night, close to the bank of the river by the rest house. It is difficult to ascertain the number of otters in these waters, and it is a matter of speculation as to whether their habitat will be destroyed by the proposed dam, to be built immediately downstream at the village of Hanzal.

There have been significant developments in this region in the past decade or so. Education is one example, where the district authorities in Kishtwar have encouraged teachers from Srinagar to remain at one of the primary schools for a number of years. The classes usually begin in the spring, and continue until December, when the teachers return over the passes to Kashmir and home for the winter.

Stage 5: Yourdu to Tatopani
(Average walking time 4 hours)
From Yourdu, leave the Warvan Valley and follow the well-defined trail up the Rin Valley towards Tatopani. The trek passes through a series of picturesque villages which can be quite hot during the summer. There are a number of campsites at Tatopani, all within the vicinity of the hot springs which are well worth a visit. The hot springs are well maintained, with separate times for male and female bathers.

Logging activity here, as elsewhere in the Warvan district, is controlled by the forestry department. A re-afforestation programme is under way, but much wood is destroyed by spring avalanches and fire. Logging provides employment for many seasonal workers who come up from Jammu and the plains. To ensure selective felling, chutes are constructed high in the forest and the logs are then floated downstream to the roadhead at Kishtwar.

Stage 6: Tatopani to Metwan
(Average walking time 4 hours)
For backpackers, the route leads along a precipitous trail up and around the gorges beyond Tatopani. From here to the village of Metwan takes a few hours, so it is possible to trek from Yourdu to Metwan in one day.

For laden horses the stage is longer. The trail from Tatopani returns along the track to the last village, then commences the ascent up the hillside. The route is tiring and not well defined, but eventually returns back down to the main valley a few km beyond the gorges. From this point, the trail follows the valley on to Metwan.

The headman at Metwan is a lively, industrious character who still has a written testimony given to him by the French team which first climbed Nun in 1953.

Stage 7: Metwan to Fariahbad
(Average walking time 5 hours)
The trail up the valley from Metwan is cleared by the shepherds as they ascend to the higher pastures each spring. It is advisable to keep to the river trail, as the track forks on a number of occasions. A guide from Metwan would be useful if you're going it alone. The locals refer to the campsite where the Krishnullah meets the main valley as Fariahbad. However, some ground survey maps have confused the issue and use the same name to refer to a campsite higher up the Krishnullah Valley. From the camp it is possible to see the upper profile of Nun at the head of the valley.

Stage 8: Fariahbad to Mandiksar
(Average walking time 7 hours)
If the shepherd bridge is in position, cross the river here. If not, head up the valley to the first snow bridge and then return down the trail on the opposite bank. It is then necessary to ascend the main ridge to the north (left side) of the valley for about 500 metres. The laden horses will find this difficult in places, and on occasion will have to be reloaded. From the top of the ridge you gain the first uninterrupted views of the Himalaya. The trail continues past a number of shepherd encampments, and gradually ascends to a distinctive waterfall which marks the location of the next camp. The main Bakharval campsite at Mandiksar is about 2 or 3 km on from the waterfall.

In late summer the birch forest attracts both black and brown bears, and bharal also roam the upper grazing slopes above the camp.

Stage 9: Mandiksar to Sar
(Average walking time 6 hours)
You will need the assistance of the Bakharval to cross the main river valley at this point. The river gullies are fast flowing, and the ponies sink rapidly if they are not directed away from the insubstantial sandbar. You may need to unpack the horses completely,

especially in early summer when the water level is high.

The pony trail remains on the south bank for 3 km before a comparatively simple recrossing of the main nullah. There is an alternative route on the north bank, along the rocky exposed cliff section beyond Mandiksar, but it is not suitable for ponies. This route avoids the problem of river crossings, and meets the main pony trail further up the valley. The trail continues through encampments and grazing meadows to where the valley reaches a narrow gorge at Sar (incorrectly called Fariahbad on some maps). It is the highest shepherd encampment, and wood must be carried from Mandiksar.

Stage 10: Sar to High Camp
(Average walking time 4 hours)

Care must be taken at this stage to identify the correct side valley leading to the pass. This is particularly important as some maps completely omit one of the main glacial valleys immediately below Sar, which can cause untold confusion. Climb the ridge on the left-hand bank, and continue along the cliff trail for about 3 km. Packponies cannot complete this section.

Cross the main nullah either by the natural boulder bridge or, if you can find one, an appropriate crossing higher up, beyond the confluence of the two rivers. The easier trail up the left-hand side of the valley continues for 4 or 5 km. Camp here below the moraine and the upper glaciated section of the valley.

Stage 11: Chilung Pass to Rangdum
(Average walking time 10 hours to the pass, another 6 hours to the jeep track)
(Here I am indebted to friends who were with me on this trek over a decade ago, and also to a number of reports recently received – in particular from Rob Stevenson, Cheshire, UK)

The services of a local guide are invaluable on this stage, as the pass is by no means obvious. Ascend the Chilung Glacier on the left-hand side to the impressive cliffs and vertical glacier headwall. The pass is a small defile to the left (east) side of the glacier. Cross to the far side avoiding the ice seracs, then bear to the opposite side of the valley as you descend to the Lakong Glacier. From here the descent becomes easier, although it is necessary to remain on the right hand side of the glacial tributary. You can camp anywhere after the end of the glacial moraine. Once you reach the confluence with the Rangdum Valley, wander up the valley to a suitable crossing point north of Pentse La to reach the jeep road between Padum and Rangdum.

Jammu

The Dogra territories of Jammu extend fully into the Himalayan foothills, providing many interesting treks from the hill station of Kishtwar; north-west to Kashmir, east to Zanskar and south to Chamba.

The history of the Dogras – the hill dwellers of Jammu – can be traced back to the time of the Vedas. In these sacred texts, reference is made to the Vaishnu Devi Cave, set in the Siwalik Range north of Jammu. Pilgrims made their way across northern India to the cave, and it is likely that this trek predates the Amarnath pilgrimage. The journey to the cave involves considerably less hardship than crossing the high, snow-bound passes to Kashmir.

Rajah Jamboolachan's foundation of the present site of Jammu on the south bank of the Tawi River came far later, in the 9th century. Thereafter the Jammu Raj held court, providing the political nucleus of the hill people. Jammu was included on the journeys of the Moghuls en route over the Pir Panjal Pass to Kashmir.

Following the decline of the Moghuls, Rajah Ranjit Dev secured Jammu's independence. Jammu was established as a hill state on a par with Chamba and Kangra. The emergence of the Sikhs put a temporary hold on territorial expansion. By the 1830s ties between Jammu and the Sikh forces were beginning to loosen. The Dogras expanded their territory, but as the Sikhs held Kashmir, Ladakh was the logical alternative. Led by the army commander Zorawar Singh, the Dogras moved over the newly acquired lands of Kishtwar to the Warvan Valley, and over the Suru Valley to Ladakh. Negotiations with the Ladakhi king resulted in Ladakh becoming part of the Dogra Empire. The Dogra horizons expanded further, and by the early 1840s they had taken Baltistan. In 1842 they attempted to overrun western Tibet but the foray was unsuccessful, however, and Zorawar Singh was killed.

Yet the Dogras still maintained their presence in Ladakh and Baltistan and, for their assistance in remaining neutral in the Anglo-Sikh wars, the East India company granted them legitimate control over the vast region of Jammu, Ladakh, Baltistan and Kashmir. The agreement was ratified by the Treaty of Amritsar in 1846, and resulted in the Dogra ruler of Jammu, Gulab Singh, being named the Maharajah of this huge, but ill-defined, Himalayan kingdom. The British created the state, which survived intact for the next century, as part of the complex political buffer zone between the Indian Empire and the Russian Empire and Tibet.

Gulab Singh's wish was to establish Jammu as the religious centre of northern India – the Varanasi of the north. He commissioned the Raghunath temple, in the centre of the present city, which was completed by his son Ranbir Singh. Ranbir Singh in turn commissioned the Rambireswar temple, the largest Shiva temple in Northern India.

The Dogra tradition continued until the partition of India in 1947, when the then Maharajah of Kashmir, Hari Singh, was unable to retain his independence, and the state of Jammu & Kashmir was established.

The present heir to the Dogra title, Karan Singh, was the Indian Minister for Tourism in the early 1970s, and still played an active political role in the state.

JAMMU
Places to Stay

The main hotel area in the city of Jammu is around Vir Marg, in the city centre. The most popular hotel is the convenient, but rather run-down, *Tourist Reception Centre*, with singles and doubles from Rs 60 per room. If this is full, then it is likely that most of the other hotels in the vicinity will also be fully occupied. It is a good idea to find a place to stay as soon as you arrive as rooms are always at a premium, especially in May and June. At the railway station there are retiring rooms starting at about Rs 60 per double, or dorm beds for Rs 12.

Getting There & Away

Indian Airlines operate flights to Jammu from Delhi, Chandigarh and Srinagar. The flights out of Jammu are generally heavily booked, and if you don't have a confirmed seat prior to arriving, there is little point in waiting for one to turn up. The cost from Delhi to Jammu is US$74. There are a number of express trains from Delhi, departing in the evening and arriving at Jammu early the following morning. The costs are: Rs 567 air-con class, Rs 256 1st class, and Rs 78 2nd class. It is not necessary to spend time in Jammu if you don't wish to. The buses to Srinagar leave Jammu as soon as the train arrives, while a quick taxi or scooter transfer should see you reaching the town bus station in time to catch the bus to Kishtwar the same day.

TREKS OUT OF JAMMU

Vaishnu Devi

This important cave is dedicated to the three Hindu mother goddesses. Thousands of pilgrims visit the cave every year, particularly during the peak pilgrimage season between March and July. The cave is situated at 1700 metres. It is 30 metres long and is reached by crawling through a very narrow entrance. A small stream, the Chara Dunga, flows from under the image in the cave, and devotees pass through it to the shrine.

The origin of the pilgrimage is shrouded in mystery. According to legend, Vaishnu Devi usually stayed at a place called Adkunwari. It is said that the demon Bahairo wanted to marry her, and in trying to do so chased her from her resting place to the cave where she found refuge. During her flight she was able to kill the demon, so that nowadays pilgrims walking to the cave greet each other with a cry of *Jai Mataji* (Victory to the Mother Goddess).

To reach the cave you need to drive to the roadhead at Katra, some 48 km from Jammu, and from here it is an uphill trek for about 4 or 5 hours to the cave's entrance. The pilgrim

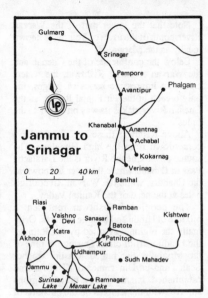

trail has been subject to considerable upgrading over the last few years. There are plenty of rest places as you undertake the climb, and it is recommended to start well before first light so as to escape the heat of the day.

There are regular and deluxe buses available for the 2 hour drive from Jammu to Katra. Taxis are also available from Jammu to Katra and return. At the base of the hill both horses and porters may be hired, should you wish to make a major expedition out of it.

Kishtwar

It is the region of Kishtwar that provides the most interesting trekking possibilities in the Jammu area. The town of Kishtwar is set on a plateau high above the confluence of the Chenab and Warvan rivers, and is noted for its saffron fields and its picturesque setting amidst a ring of snow-capped peaks.

Note that the lower part of the Warvan River, south of the town of Yourdu, is known locally as the Marwa.

Below the confluence of the Chenab and the Warvan rivers at Kishtwar, the waters create an impressive series of gorges, the only breach in the Pir Panjal Range, as the Chenab River makes its way on down to the Indus.

Above Kishtwar these two river valleys come down from the high Himalaya. The source of the Chenab River is the Baralacha Pass in Lahaul, where the river is known as the Chandra, while the Warvan River originates at the head of the Kanital Valley.

The people of Kishtwar represent a mixture of Hindu and Islamic cultures. Originally the region was ruled by the Rajputs, the Hindu warrior class. During the time of the Moghuls, the famed Muslim teacher Shah Fand-ud-Din came to Kishtwar and established Islam. Today both religions survive, with the temples on the outskirts of Kishtwar existing in harmony with the mosques in the centre of town.

Despite Kishtwar's closeness to Kashmir, it is still administered by Jammu. This situation can be traced back to the 1820s, when Zorowar Singh was appointed the first governor of Kishtwar, and the region was used as a base for the Dogra invasions of Ladakh, Baltistan and West Tibet.

Information
As yet there is no tourist office in Kishtwar, and no facilities for changing money. There are, however, prominent notices outside the State Bank of India building, forbidding the carrying of firearms inside the bank – intended more for the Bakharval shepherds than hordes of irate trekkers! You must therefore budget accordingly, and change your money before you leave Jammu or Srinagar.

Getting Ready
Supplies of kerosene, fresh vegetables, fruit, rice and biscuits are available in Kishtwar. However, it is worth bringing tinned food and luxury items like nuts and raisins, from Jammu or Srinagar.

Besides cooking excellent chicken curry, both chowkidars at the Kishtwar PWD Rest House are able to assist you with onward trekking arrangements. Porters and horses can be ordered with a day's notice so they can be ready at the appropriate roadhead. The cost of mules depends on where you are going. To Kashmir it would work out at about Rs 50 per mule per day, plus return, and you can double that for the approaches to the Umasi La or Chamba.

Prices in this region are generally very high, bordering sometimes on the extortionate, particularly if you do not have any local contacts.

Places to Stay
Accommodation in Kishtwar is still limited to the two *hotels* in the main bazaar – both very noisy and colourful – and the *PWD Rest House* 1 km away. The six rooms at the rest house cost Rs 50 each, and are well kept and maintained by the reliable chowkidars.

A tourist complex that will be able to accommodate larger groups visiting the area is still in the process of construction. The complex will include both private rooms and dormitory accommodation, a tourist information office and hopefully some facility to change money. Completion is scheduled for autumn 1990, but it is best to check with the tourist departments in either Jammu or Srinagar.

Getting There & Away
Kishtwar is still an isolated district of the state of Jammu & Kashmir. It takes nearly 15 hours to drive to Srinagar and more than 10 hours from Jammu. The road to Kishtwar leaves the Jammu-Srinagar highway at Batote, and is frequently subject to landslides and monsoonal cloudbursts that close the road for days at a time. The scheduled buses stop en route at Batote and again at Doda, the headquarters of the region, before arriving at Kishtwar in the late evening. A road has been constructed over the Sythen Pass, linking Kishtwar directly with the Kashmir Valley. It is open to jeeps and trucks for a few months each year (late July to

mid-September) and will eventually be upgraded for buses, cutting the travelling time between Kashmir and Kishtwar considerably. Proposals have also been made to start a Vayudoot air service from Srinagar to Kishtwar, which would make the whole region a lot more attractive for trekkers with limited time to spare.

Treks

The comparative isolation of Kishtwar has some advantages. It still attracts only a handful of trekkers each season, which means the trails to Kashmir, Chamba and the Zanskar are less trekked than elsewhere in the Kashmir and Ladakh region.

Three treks are outlined in this section:

J1: From Kishtwar to Lehinvan via the Warvan Valley.
J2: From Kishtwar to Chamba via the Sach Pass.
J3: From Kishtwar to Padum via the Umasi La

Kishtwar is subject to monsoon conditions, so the first few days of a trek in July and August may be a little wet. This should not deter trekkers from going on to the Kashmir Valley or the Zanskar, as the higher you trek up the valleys the less it is likely to rain. It's possible to start trekking out of Kishtwar in late May and early June, though you will still encounter snow on the passes of the Pir Panjal and the main Himalaya, including the Umasi La. The post monsoon period is particularly pleasant if you are continuing on a trek to Chamba or Lahaul, with conditions generally stable until the end of October.

J1: KISHTWAR TO LEHINVAN

The treks from Kishtwar to Kashmir follow two routes. One is via the Sythen Pass to Daksun and the other is via the Warvan Valley and the Margan Pass to Lehinvan. These days, with the road construction well advanced over the Sythen Pass, the route up the Warvan Valley is better, and is the one described here. If time is not at a premium there are many interesting detours, such as a

side trip up the Kiar and Kibbar valleys to the base camps of Sickle Moon and Brammah peaks. This can be undertaken either on the way to Kashmir, or as part of a round trip out of Kishtwar.

Stage 1: Kishtwar to Palmer & Ikhala

(Average walking time 6-7 hours)
From Kishtwar you can bus or walk to Palmer village. Buses leave Kishtwar at 7 am and take about 2 hours. The service is, however, irregular and is cancelled during times of heavy rainfall in the summer. As an alternative, the trail short-cuts down the Kishtwar plateau and up the ridge to Palmer, and takes about 4 or 5 hours.

Facilities at Palmer are limited to a few tea stalls and confined camping areas. It's therefore advisable to continue on for at least a few km along the road to Ikhala, to a convenient camp spot. It is possible to reach Ikhala in one day out of Kishtwar, providing you start early. The road to Ikhala is being extended, and this may soon be the only option. There is a *Forest Rest House* at Ikhala, immediately below the main trail, while the main village is further down the hillside.

Stage 2: Ikhala to Sundar & Sirshi

(Average walking time 6-7 hours)
This is a comparatively long stage. The trail winds through heavily forested gorge country, with little ground cleared for farming or grazing. The trail is shady and well defined, as the mule trains make their way with grain supplies to Sundar and Sirshi, and further up the valley.

The main valley widens into areas of terraced cultivation at the villages of Sirshi and Sundar. This is also the limit of the rice cultivation in the valley, and the limit of the monsoon. Higher up the valley the rice paddies give way to cornfields, which thrive on less rainfall. It is also the limit of the Hindu settlements; beyond here the villages are Muslim and simple shrines take the place of the village temple.

The trail climbs and falls as it crosses the Kiar and Kibar nullahs. There is a *Forest*

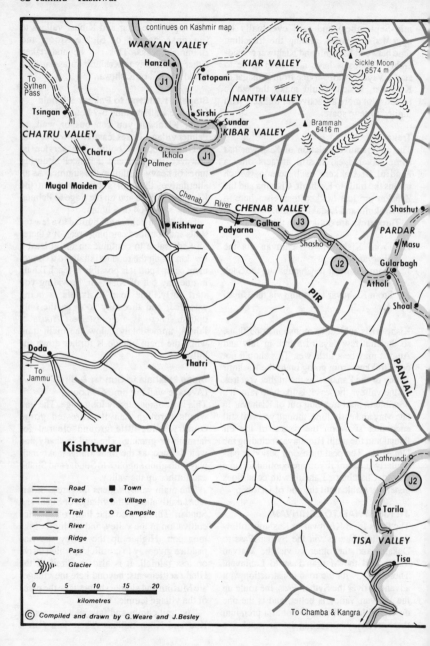

continues on Kashmir map

WARVAN VALLEY

Hanzal

KIAR VALLEY

Tatopani

Sickle Moon
6574 m

To
Sythen
Pass

NANTH VALLEY

Sirshi

Tsingan

Sundar

KIBAR VALLEY

Brammah
6416 m

CHATRU VALLEY

Chatru

Ikhala

Palmer

Mugal Maiden

Chenab   River   CHENAB VALLEY

Shashut

Kishtwar

Padyarna

Galhar

J3

PARDAR

Masu

Shasho

Gularbagh

J2

Atholi

PIR

Shoal

Doda

To
Jammu

Thatri

PANJAL

Kishtwar

Sathrundi

J2

	Road	■	Town
	Track	●	Village
	Trail	○	Campsite
	River		
	Ridge		
	Pass		
	Glacier		

Tarila

TISA VALLEY

0   5   10   15   20

kilometres

Tisa

© Compiled and drawn by G.Weare and J.Besley

To Chamba & Kangra

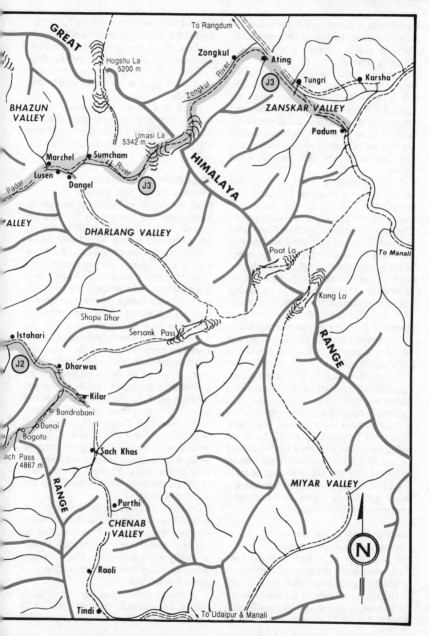

Rest House at Sirshi, half a km before the main bridge over the Marwa (Warvan) River. There is also a campsite just above the village graveyard.

If you're undertaking a trek up to the Brammah base camp, stop at Sundar. The trek in can be completed in two stages: the first going high above the gorge country, and the second descending back down to the valley floor as far as the base camp. Porters can be hired at Sundar, while horses cannot negotiate the narrow trails into the Kibar Valley.

If you're planning a trek to the Sickle Moon base camp, then leave the main trail at Sirshi. The trek route, like the one to Brammah, will take a couple of stages up the Kiar Valley. The first stage from Sirshi to the village of Tatopani, the highest settlement in the valley, takes about 5 hours. The village boasts hot springs, although not in such good condition as the springs en route to the Krishnullah Valley. There is an excellent campsite just beyond the village, with a plentiful supply of firewood. There have been reports of the snow leopard in crags above the village, and the local elders relate tales of outsiders attempting to poach for furs during the winter time.

Early in the season the trails from Tatopani are difficult for fully laden horses, but porters can be hired to carry supplies. The climb up through the forest, to the meadow at Sumbal, takes about 5 hours. The trail is ill-defined in places, particularly in the spring before the Bakharval herdsmen have had a chance to clear the trails. From Sumbal you must ford the Kiar Nullah in order to reach Sickle Moon base camp. Alternatively, you can continue higher to the terminal moraine of the Prue Glacier.

Stage 3: Sirshi to Hanzal
(Average walking time 4 hours)
This is a shorter stage, and the fit can leave Sirshi early in the morning and continue on to Yourdu, higher up the valley, the same day.

The main trail crosses the bridge below Sirshi village, and then continues through cultivated fields for a further few km before entering forest and gorge country. Just above the last farmsteads, the summit of Brammah can be seen on a clear day. At Hanzal village, the next main settlement, plans are underway to build a dam in the gorge in order to supply the main villages in the region with hydro-electricity.

There is a *Forest Rest House* beyond Hanzal, and there are some good camping areas 2 or 3 km further on, where the forest trail descends again to the main valley floor.

Stage 4: Hanzal to Yourdu
(Average walking time 4 hours)
From Hanzal, the trail continues through the forest gorge until it eventually broadens out at the rich farming settlements of Marwa/Yourdu district. This fertile region extends through some 5 or 6 km of the valley and is quite prosperous, complete with walnut and apple orchards. At Marwa there is a rural bank and a post office – but this is not the place to change travellers' cheques or post urgent letters. Cross the bridge at Yourdu to the *Forest Rest House*.

These villages were established in the late 18th and early 19th centuries, when the Afghans and Sikhs ruled the Kashmir Valley. The tax levied on the Kashmiri villages forced many to migrate over the passes and establish small farming communities in this area. The Sikh presence in the Kashmir Valley forced the Dogras to expand up the Warvan Valley, and new taxes were levied. Indeed, when the traveller Vigne visited the villages in the 1830s, he noted that there was a Dogra tax post at Yourdu – probably as a result of Zorawar Singh's forays up the valley to Ladakh.

Just below Yourdu, the Rin Nullah (which comes from the Krishnullah Valley) meets the main Warvan valley. Remember that the valley section between Yourdu and Kishtwar is locally referred to as the Marwa Valley, while the valley above Yourdu is referred to as the Warvan Valley.

If you're trekking to the Krishnullah Valley and Ladakh, the trail diverges at Yourdu. The stages of this trek are covered in Trek W3, in the Warvan Valley section (pages 76 and 77).

Stage 5: Yourdu to Inshin
(Average walking time 7 hours)
Note: This section of the trek is shown on the Kashmir map, page 63.

This is quite a long stage, following the trail beside the Warvan River. After leaving the bazaar at Yourdu, the trail continues along the west bank of the valley for about 6 or 7 km. You cross the main bridge and the trail continues on the opposite bank until the village of Inshin. En route there are a number of ideal camping spots, often frequented by Bakharvals during their seasonal migration. There is a *Forest Rest House* in Inshin, a convenient stop before the climb to the Margan Pass the following day.

If you are undertaking a trek over the Bhoktol Pass into Ladakh, then continue up the Warvan Valley. The stages are outlined in trek W1 in the Warvan Valley section (see pages 72 to 74).

Stage 6: Inshin to Lehinvan
(Average walking time 7 hours)
An early start is imperative on this stage, as the climb to the Margan Pass can become very warm by mid-morning. It also gets dusty because of the current roadworks, but the fine views down the Warvan Valley are ample compensation. Just before the pass there is a tea stall, and from here the climb is easier. The pass is about 4 km long, and is one of the main routes that the Bakharval follow during their migration to and from the Jammu foothills. On reaching the Kashmir end of the pass, the trail drops steeply to the alpine valley, with the small village of Lehinvan situated midway down the valley.

Getting Away Buses leave Lehinvan for Anantnag three times a day, and take 4 hours. The last bus leaves Lehinvan at 4 pm – just in time to miss the last connection to Srinagar, which is a further 2 hours down the highway. It is preferable, when all is considered, to camp or stay at the *Forest Rest House*

at Lehinvan overnight, and go on to Srinagar the following day.

J2: KISHTWAR TO TARILA & CHAMBA
The trek from Kishtwar to Chamba follows the Chenab Valley up as far as Atholi. From there, the trail to Chamba continues up the Chenab Valley to the headquarters of the Pangi district at Kilar, before heading south over the Sach Pass to Chamba.

Stage 1: Kishtwar to Camp
This stage is constantly being revised, as the construction of the road to Atholi extends up valley. Since 1985, funding from the Jammu & Kashmir government has upgraded the priority of the road, and it is estimated that it will reach Atholi in the next decade. Enquiries should be made in Kishtwar as to the extent of road building before you head off. The bus service up the valley has now continued well beyond the villages of Padyarna or Galhar, and tea stalls and rest stops will have been adjusted to suit the local trade. There are still many hundreds of mule trains carrying supplies into Atholi, so the trail should not be difficult to follow.

Hiring horses for these first few stages will be a problem, as the mule trains are fully contracted by the government. If you meet one of the local Gujars who lives in the villages between Kishtwar and the roadhead, then you may be able to make a deal. Otherwise, your first night's camp may be beside a dusty road with no sign of horsemen for the next day – not the best way to have to start a trek, particularly if time is at a premium.

There is a *Rest House* at Galhar, but otherwise the village has little to recommend it.

Stage 2: Camp to Atholi
Once beyond the roadhead, the trek through the gorge country is breathtaking. The trail winds high above the valley floor through luxuriant forest, with many tiring ups and downs, to cross the side valleys. Assuming that the road is constructed along the lower contours of the valley, the works will not spoil this delightful section of the trail. Well before reaching Atholi, the trail drops to the

valley floor, and from here on there are a number of campsites complete with firewood and water. The farming settlements of Kendal and Atholi support both Muslim and Hindu farmers, while on the far side of the river at Gularbagh there are Buddhist traders who migrated from the Zanskar Valley a few generations ago.

The town of Atholi is set on a small plateau above the confluence of the Pardar and Chenab rivers. It is the district headquarters, and there are both primary and middle schools, as well as a police station at the far end of the bazaar. Reliable supplies of biscuits and other basics can be purchased here, as the trail to Kishtwar remains open for most of the year. There is a campsite and a springline by the *Forest Rest House*, which is situated some way above the main trail when you first reach Atholi.

Until the 1830s, the Pardar district was an integral part of Chamba. In fact, during the period of 1820-25 the locals supported the Chamba forces in their invasion of the Zanskar. Allegiances changed a decade later. After invading Ladakh and the Zanskar, Zorawar Singh led his Dogra forces back over the Umasi La en route to Jammu. The Pardar people were suspicious of the Dogras, particularly when the small party of Dogra troops was left behind to 'facilitate communications' with Ladakh. The Pardar people killed the contingent of Dogras, and on hearing of this Zorawar Singh returned the following year (1836) and annexed the region to Jammu.

Both porters and horses are, again, very expensive here. The going rate for a horse is over Rs 100 per day. It is best to try to negotiate with some of the Buddhist pony handlers in Gularbagh. They are not much cheaper, but at least they are great fun to travel with.

At Atholi bridge the trails split. The main trail continues south-east up the Chenab Valley towards Chamba or Lahaul, while the trail north-east up the Pardar Valley goes to the Zanskar (see next section, page 88).

Stage 3: Atholi to Shoal
(Average walking time 3 hours)
A very easy stage, but given the absence of camping sites beyond Shoal there is little alternative. First, cross the main bridge at Atholi, and climb the trail on the opposite bank. The trail ascends gradually for 4 or 5 km before descending to Shoal village. The main trail cuts above Shoal to a convenient campsite next to the main side river, about 1 km beyond the village.

Stage 4: Shoal to Istahari
(Average walking time 6-7 hours)
From Shoal, the trail heads over to the next side valley before commencing a steep 500 metre climb that leads high above the valley floor. During the ascent there is a potential campsite, just above a beautiful waterfall. It is also an ideal place for a rest stop before the trail finally climbs to the ridge top. From here, there are spectacular views down valley, while the forested ridges on the far side of Kishtwar can be seen in the distance.

From the ridge the trail drops gently, skirting the village of Thari to a potential campsite. It is a further 2 hours to Istahari. Note that the main horse trail does not go down to the village at Thari. Istahari is the last main village in Jammu & Kashmir state, and from the *Rest House* you can distinguish the ridge line of the Shopu Dhar, which marks the border with Himachal Pradesh.

Stage 5: Istahari to Dharwas
(Average walking time 4-5 hours)
Leaving Istahari it is a long haul down to the Chenab River. The descent takes a couple of hours to the Shopu Nullah, where there is a seasonal camp of Nepalese workers who are working on a nearby logging project. The bridge over the Shopu Nullah is reconstructed each year, making the trail from Atholi to Kilar suitable for horses from mid-May onwards.

The trail continues, gradually ascending for a few km to a small cairn on the side of the trail. This marks the border between the states of Jammu & Kashmir and Himachal Pradesh. It is a further 2 hours on to Dharwas, and the trail passes many potential camp-sites, but there is a complete absence of water. The village at Dharwas is about 100 metres above the main trail. The climb to the village is worthwhile to see a small Hindu temple in the main square. This marks the springline which is the sole source of water supply to the village.

On the main trail below the village is the well-kept *Forest Rest House*. Here there is a signpost, dating back to the British adminis-tration, which sets out the trek stages on to Chamba and south up the Chenab Valley to Lahaul.

Stage 6: Dharwas to Kilar
(Average walking time 2-2½ hours)
A very easy stage. In the near future it will be possible to by-pass Kilar completely, by crossing the proposed road bridge over the Chenab, which will then link up directly with the jeep road under construction from Dunai and the Sach Pass.

Kilar is the headquarters of the Pangi dis-trict, and the government buildings are constructed in incongruous corrugated iron rather than the traditional wooden village styles. Camping areas are restricted to enclo-sures that have little to offer except for the passing horse trains. Basic supplies such as rice, flour and kerosene can be purchased in the summer season.

Stage 7: Kilar to Dunai
(Average walking time 2-2½ hours)
Assuming you leave Dharwas at a reason-able hour, it is possible to complete the stages from Dharwas to Dunai in one day. The trail from Kilar descends steeply to the gorge, and crosses the bridge over the Chenab River. There is then a steady haul before another frustrating descent to the Sach Nullah. While walking on this side of the valley it is easy to note how the hillside around Kilar is in dire need of a reafforestation programme.

On reaching the Sach Nullah, the trail meets the road that will eventually link the Pangi district with Chamba. The construc-tion has not developed as quickly as in other parts of the Chenab Valley, although it does provide an income for the large number of Nepalese workers who are employed by the contractors throughout the summer.

The teahouses at Bandrabani have

changed the area into something of a shanty village. There are also a number of campsites in the vicinity. The trail on to Dunai continues along the valley floor – over snow bridges during the early part of the season. Later on, it is a matter of choice as to whether to boulder-hop upstream after the snow-bridges have collapsed, or to follow the horse trail that eventually rejoins the valley floor at Dunai.

Dunai is just a small collection of tea stalls – three to be precise. It is the highest shelter for porters and villagers making their way over the Sach Pass, and a welcome stop for tea and snacks.

Stage 8: Dunai to Sach Pass & Sathrundi
(Average walking time 8-9 hours)
The trail from Dunai gradually ascends the main valley. The track is often over snow-bridges that remain in place for most of the season. The climb to the plateau of Bagoto takes about 2 to 2½ hours. Here there is a convenient campsite if you're coming direct from Kilar that day.

The climb to the pass is strenuous, and if it is under snow, then the going will be very slow. The trail ascends by a series of glacial steps until the base of the pass. The pass is not very obvious, just a small niche in the main ridge, complete with small cairns and prayer flags. The views fully compensate for the climb. To the north the main Himalaya can be seen, while to the south the forested ridges descend to the Ravi Valley, and across to the Dhaula Dhar.

The initial descent from the pass is steep to Sathrundi, where there is another teahouse 'complex' set beside a beautiful meadow. Here the road construction is in progress towards the pass, and by the time this edition is published it may be possible to get a lift in a jeep down the valley to Chamba.

Stage 9: Sathrundi to Tarila
(Average walking time 4 hours)
The trail from Sathrundi avoids the road construction coming from the far side of the upper Tisa Valley. The trail leads down past

a number of villages, the largest of which is Alwas. Further down, it becomes hot and humid, an indication of the altitude drop of over 2000 metres from Sathrundi.

Getting Away There is a roadhead at Tarila, but little else. From here there are three buses a day to Chamba, at 9 am, 1 and 4 pm. Double check these times with the villagers on the way, as you do not want to spend the night by the side of the road. The bus takes about 5 hours to reach Chamba, and the fare is about Rs 15. From Chamba it's a further 6 hour bus ride to Pathankot, or see the Himachal Pradesh chapter for other treks out of Chamba.

J3: KISHTWAR TO PADUM
The trek from Kishtwar to Padum, in the Zanskar Valley, can be completed in about 10 stages, depending on the time spent acclimatising in the Pardar Valley. Note that the Umasi La pass, shown on the map, is known as the Pardar La by the people from Atholi and Kishtwar. Umasi La is the Zanskari name.

This trek follows the the Chenab Valley up as far as Atholi, where it diverges from the Chamba trail. The trail to the Zanskar ascends the Pardar Valley and over the Umasi La to Padum.

Stages 1 & 2: Kishtwar to Atholi
These stages are as for the Kishtwar to Chamba trek, J2 (see pages 85 and 86).

Stage 3: Gularbagh to Shashut
(Average walking time 6-7 hours)
Cross the main bridge at Atholi to the village of Gularbagh. The small bazaar is populated by people of Ladakhi origin, traders who settled in the upper Pardar Valley. They own sufficient horses to transport most groups up towards the pass. They are canny dealers; after being engaged at inflated rates they lose little time in hiring a few more horses so they can trade with in-laws in the higher villages of the valley.

Just below Gularbagh, and directly opposite Atholi, there are some interesting Hindu carvings, and nearby there is an elaborately carved wooden temple similar to many found higher up in the Pardar Valley.

The trail up the valley initially crosses the Pardar River, and then winds up through the farming settlements high above the valley. There is a large logging operation about half way up to Shashut, and immediately beyond this there is an excellent campsite. Further up the valley, the trail crosses the river before a gradual climb to an alpine plateau just above Shashut village. Shashut has a teahouse and a small camping area beside the village temples. There is a *Forest Rest House*, 1 km further on.

Stage 4: Shashut to Marchel
(Average walking time 3 hours)
This is an easy stage to allow time for acclimatisation. The trail is well graded, ascending some 300 or 400 metres, with some beautiful views back down the valley and across to the range behind Atholi. Marchel lies at the confluence of the Bhazun Nullah and the Pardar Valley. It is the first village in the region that has a sizeable Buddhist community. Ladakhi farmers migrated to the upper Pardar Valley about five generations ago, and Marchel and the nearby village of Lusen support simple Buddhist monasteries which are periodically serviced by the Bardan Monastery in Zanskar. Other ties with the Zanskar are maintained, and marriages are arranged on both sides of the Himalaya.

There is a police checkpost at Marchel, but it's mainly to steer foreigners away from the Pardar sapphire mine on the far side of the mountain.

Horses are not able to cross the Umasi La, so porters can either be hired at Marchel, or booked to come up from Shashut. Their availability is governed by the harvest season, but generally you should budget for Rs 100 a day for seven days, including the return. If you are fit enough, then there is no reason why you should not continue on your own from Marchel. However, the trail over the Umasi La is not the easiest to follow,

especially in the earlier part of the season, and a guide-cum-porter is recommended.

Stage 5: Marchel to Sumcham & Camp
(Average walking time 5-6 hours)
The Umasi La trail turns north-east up the Bhuzas Nullah 2 to 3 km beyond Marchel. (If you continue up what appears to be the main valley, the Dharlang Nullah leads to the Sersank Pass and the Poat La). It is a further 3 or 4 km on to Sumcham, the last village before the pass.

From the village, the trail ascends through the terminal moraine and on to a plateau some 7 km in length. The area is grazed by the Bakharval shepherds during the summer. Midway across the plateau there is a birch grove, ideal for a sheltered camp spot, while the peak of Shivaling makes for an impressive backdrop.

The small hanging valley above the birch trees marks the route to the Hogshu La, a little-trekked glacial pass which leads to the upper Zanskar Valley.

Stage 6: Camp to Glacier Camp
(Average walking time 3-4 hours)
From here on, the stages depend on the state of fitness and acclimatisation of the group. The trail beyond the meadow ascends steeply to the left at the head of the valley. The steep climb goes above the treeline to a height of about 4000 metres. Here the glacial valley opens out. There is a small meadow with a stream coming from the glacier. It is the best campsite between here and the Zanskar, and affords some spectacular mountain views.

Stage 7: Glacier Camp to High Camp
(Average walking time 4-5 hours)
The trail ascends the main scree ridge to the left hand side of the valley. Keep a lookout for the cairns as the trail traverses the boulder fields. The initial climb is steep, before the trail eventually drops down to the main glacier floor. Follow the left hand side of the glacier up to the point where you are opposite the hanging glacier. Cross the main glacier here, and begin a very steep climb up the

boulder ridge to the left of the hanging glacier. The climb is hard going but the views reward this tiring stage. After ascending the ridge, there is an ideal, flat but rocky campsite beneath a huge cave outcrop. This is the normal resting stage before crossing the pass on the following day.

Stage 8: High Camp to Umasi La & Camp

(Average walking time 7 hours)

From the camp, climb the steep snow slopes to the left of the valley that lead onto a small glacier. The Umasi La at 5342 metres is at the head of this glacier. To reach the pass some care is necessary to avoid the crevasses that may be concealed early on in the season. Again, it is best to make an early start to avoid any tiring snow plodding. The time taken to reach the pass is about 2 or 3 hours, which includes plenty of time to admire the panorama of peaks that make this a really memorable stage.

The initial descent from the pass is down a very steep icy gully, and an ice axe or two would be an asset to any party. Once down the gully the trail meets the main glacial floor, and it is a further 3 or 4 km of easier walking down the glacier to the terminal moraine, and a sheltered campsite for the night.

Stage 9: Camp to Zongkul Monastery

(Average walking time 5-6 hours)

The trek continues down the valley across an extensive boulder field, before a short steep descent to the grassy ridges of the Zongkul Valley. The trail remains on the right hand side of the Mulung Tokpo until a natural rock bridge. Cross here, and continue down the valley to the monastery.

The Zongkul Monastery is situated high on the cliff side, with commanding views of the valley. According to legend, the monastery was founded by the sage Naropa in the 9th century. Nowadays it is serviced by half a dozen monks from Bardan Monastery.

Stage 10: Zongkul Monastery to Padum/Zanskar

(Average walking time 6-7 hours)

It is a further 3 or 4 km to the Zanskar Valley and the village of Ating. From Ating it is a short distance the down valley to the bridge at Tungri and the road into Padum. The trek from Tungri, past the monastery at Sani and on to Padum, takes 2 to 3 hours. Alternatively, you can hitch a lift if time is at a premium.

Ladakh

Ladakh – the land of high passes – is the trans-Himalayan zone which marks the boundary between the peaks of the western Himalaya and the vast Tibetan plateau. It is a region that naturally lends itself to exceptional treks which can still avoid roads for weeks at a time.

Since it opened up to tourism in 1974, Ladakh has been known as the 'Moonland', 'Little Tibet', and even 'the last Shangri La'. Whatever the description, Ladakh is one of the most remote regions of India. For the Ladakhis it consists of rugged and inhospitable terrain, tempered only in the depths of the valleys where the minimal rainfall has been diverted along irrigation canals. Here the barley fields and lines of poplar and willow trees contrast with the barren mountainscape. These fertile reaches support human habitation, where whitewashed settlements and monasteries perched on top of sugarloaf mountains add the essential character to this incredible landscape.

The Champa, the nomadic shepherds who roamed the Tibetan plateau, were the first inhabitants of Ladakh. Their horizons were restricted to the high windswept grazing areas, and it was not until the coming of the Mons, Buddhist missionaries from India, that settlements were established in the valleys. Later, the Dards from Gilgit wandered up the Indus Valley, and introduced irrigation in the upper reaches of the Indus.

In the 7th century the migration of the Tibetans from western Tibet, or Guge, slowly began to displace the Dards. These early rulers provided Ladakh with its first authentic history. Forts and palaces such as that of Shey were constructed, and the power of Ladakh, for the first time, stretched far beyond the Indus Valley.

By now the Buddhist scriptures had been fully translated and carried across the Himalaya. Much of this influence can be attributed to the Tantric sage Padmasambhava. During his travels in the 7th century he did much to popularise the fundamental Buddhist precepts, while at the same time undermining the animistic Bon-Po religion that had been central to the beliefs of the Tibetans. By the 11th century, the wandering Buddhist scholar Ringchen Brangpo had established 108 Buddhist monasteries throughout western Tibet and Ladakh. Many of the ancient sites in the Zanskar, such as at Lamayuru, Alchi, Wanla and Sani, date from this period.

The grand route up the Indus Valley followed many of these ancient sites. Travellers would come up the valley as far as Khalsi, and from there follow the trail to Temisgam, Likir and over the Rongdu La, to Bazgo, Nimmu, and finally Shey.

The highways to the east were also accessible. In the late 14th century the famous Tibetan pilgrim Tsong Khapa visited Ladakh, and popularised a new Buddhist order. The order was essentially a reformist sect which, under the first Dalai Lama, sought to qualify many of the elaborate rituals and practices that had become evident in Buddhist teaching. The Delgupta order, as it was known, gained popularity in Ladakh, and the monasteries at Thikse, Likir, and Spitok were founded in this period.

Ladakh, however, was still a divided kingdom. The lower kingdom was administered by the powers at Bazgo, while the upper kingdom was ruled from Shey. It was a situation that made the Ladakhis vulnerable to attacks from the combined Balti-Kashmir armies. It was the famous Ladakhi ruler Tashi Namgyal who was able to unite Ladakh. The Bazgo line of rulers established themselves at Leh, and built the upper fort, known as the Peak of Victory, to commemorate Ladakh's successful defence against invaders.

Ladakh was not to completely escape outside occupation. Tashi Namygal was killed by a raiding army from Kashgar, while in the early 16th century the kingdom was subject to the rule of Ali Mir, the ruler of Baltistan, and the Ladakhi King Jamyang Namygal was forced to marry one of the Mir's daughters.

During the reign of Singge Namgyal (1570-1642), the son of Jamyang Namgyal and the Balti princess, Ladakh's fortunes improved. The palace at Leh was constructed, while the royal family assisted monks from the Drukpa orders to establish the monasteries at Hemis and Stakna. Also of significance is the mosque at the far end of the Leh bazaar, which was commissioned by the Moghul Emperor Aurangzeb as a symbol of Ladakh's token affiliation with the vast Moghul Empire.

Ladakh's territories also expanded to include Guge, Zanskar and Spiti, as well as the Indus Valley. It was a situation that was to change as Ladakh was drawn into a war with the Tibetan-Mongol army under the 5th Dalai Lama. An appeal was sent to the Moghul Governor of Kashmir, which resulted in the Tibetans taking much of Guge, and leaving Ladakh's empire confined to the Indus Valley.

In spite of this setback, Ladakh was soon to regain some of its former territories, and re-entered a trading pact with Tibet. This situation continued until the 1830s, when the Ladakhi king was exiled to Stok by the armies of Zorawar Singh, the famous general of Gulab Singh who was destined to become the first maharajah of Kashmir.

Despite the changing fortunes of the Dogra army in Tibet, Ladakh became part of the maharajah's state in 1846, and remained so until independence in 1947. Since then, with the Chinese occupation of Tibet in the 1950s, Ladakh's connections with Tibet have been severed, while India's war with China in 1962 has further exacerbated the problem of Ladakh's sensitive borders. For this reason, Ladakh remained closed to outsiders until 1974.

Today the situation remains unsettled. While some of Ladakh's sensitive border regions, such as Rupshu, have been opened in the last few years, strategic factors can alter things at a moment's notice. Travelling plans will therefore have to remain flexible for some time to come.

Little Baltistan

The valleys of Suru, Drass, Wakka and Bodkarbu lie midway between the alpine valleys of Kashmir, and the fertile reaches of the Indus Valley and Buddhist Ladakh. The region is politically part of India, ethnically part of Baltistan, and geographically an integral part of Ladakh.

Geographically, there is little doubt that one has crossed the Himalayan watershed. The steep barren hills now stretch to the snowline. As the snows melt, the waters flow freely down into the heavily irrigated valleys. Here Tibetan-style settlements thrive. Whitewashed mud and stone houses contrast with deep-green barley fields. Mosques are the only sign that one has not yet entered Buddhist Ladakh.

When Arthur Neve wrote his book *Trekking in Kashmir, Ladakh and Baltistan* in 1911, he devoted one section to Kashmir, one to Ladakh and one to Baltistan. Since the 1947 Indo-Pakistan partition, the upper reaches of these valleys have become part of India. Being predominantly inhabited by Shi'ite Muslims, they are now culturally abandoned, midway between the Sunni sects of Kashmir and the Buddhist schools of Ladakh.

The earliest settlers of these isolated tributaries of the Indus were the Dards. According to the noted historian A H Franke, the Dards were already acquainted with the Buddhist teachings prevalent in north-west India, and had absorbed them into their culture some time before 500 AD. Later, as the Tibetan forces invaded Ladakh, much of the Dardic culture was abandoned, although isolated pockets of their heritage remain intact, notably at Drass.

The full cultural eclipse came far later, in the 15th century, shortly after the Kashmiris were converted to Islam. Most Dardic groups were also converted, including the people of

Drass. What remain today are Dardic groups distinct from the Baltis in both language and religion – the Dards are Sunni Muslims, and the Baltis are Shi'ite. To complete this cultural patchwork, there are some isolated Dardic communities, in the main Indus Valley below Khalse, which are still Buddhist.

In the Suru, Wakka and Bodkarbu valleys, the cultural similarities with Baltistan are more apparent. Trade links were also strong between Gilgit and Kargil, so the region's attention focused along the Indus Valley. Isolated Buddhist communities still remain at Mulbek in the Wakka Valley, and in the tiny kingdom of Heniskot in the upper Bodkarbu Valley.

The regions of Dardistan and Baltistan maintained a degree of independence from both the Moghul armies that held Kashmir, and the Mongol-Tibetan armies intent on taking Ladakh. In the 1830s, however, the Suru Valley was invaded by the army of Jammu's Dogra leader Zorawar Singh, who was intent on invading Ladakh. As a result of the Dogra forays, Ladakh and Baltistan came under the influence of Jammu, and in 1846 became an integral part of the maharajah's state of Jammu & Kashmir. A century later the region was divided, and the ceasefire line between Pakistan and India was drawn across the state of Jammu & Kashmir a few km north of Kargil. As a consequence, the politically sensitive regions down valley from Kargil are strictly no-go areas for foreigners.

KARGIL

To most, the region of Little Baltistan is nothing more than the town of Kargil, an overnight stop on the road between Srinagar and Leh. It is a place where you arrive hot, tired and dusty in the early evening, and leave at some ungodly hour the following morning. It is essentially a place of dingy hotels scattered along the main bazaar, and rows of trucks lining the outskirts of town. By 8 am each day, after the trucks and buses have left, taking their choking exhaust fumes with them, some sense of normality returns

to the bazaar. A day or two can be spent either exploring Kargil, or wandering up the Suru Valley for a glimpse of Nun and Kun and the main Himalayan range.

Kargil was, until quite recently, an important trading centre – not just for Srinagar and Leh, but to Gilgit and the lower Indus Valley. Before 1947, the route from Kargil to Leh went north down the valley to the confluence of the Drass and Indus rivers, and then south east, up and along the Indus Valley. These days, political factors necessitate following the road over the Namika La to the Bodkarbu Valley, and from there over the Fatu La, before descending to the Indus.

Getting Ready

The tourist office in Kargil has a limited supply of trekking equipment, mostly from previous climbing expeditions. The office is located near the tourist dak bungalow above the main bazaar. It is managed by Mr Kakpori, one of the most knowledgeable and helpful people in the district.

However, it is best to check with the tourist office in Srinagar as to the availability of gear. Fresh fruit and vegetables can be purchased in the market, but that's about it. If you are going on a trek to the Zanskar, it is advisable to bring most of your provisions from Srinagar. This includes kerosene, which is sometimes in short supply in the Kargil bazaar.

If you are staying in Kargil overnight there is a State Bank of India where you can change money, and also a post office.

Places to Stay

The Kargil bazaar is not exactly the best place to get a comfortable night's sleep, although there is no shortage of rooms, complete with string beds and bed bugs, for Rs 10 per night.

The *International*, below the main bazaar, and the *Crown Hotel*, near the bus stand, have better rooms from Rs 30 upwards. Rooms at the *Tourist Dak Bungalow*, above the bazaar, start at Rs 50 per night and present the best option if you are not worried

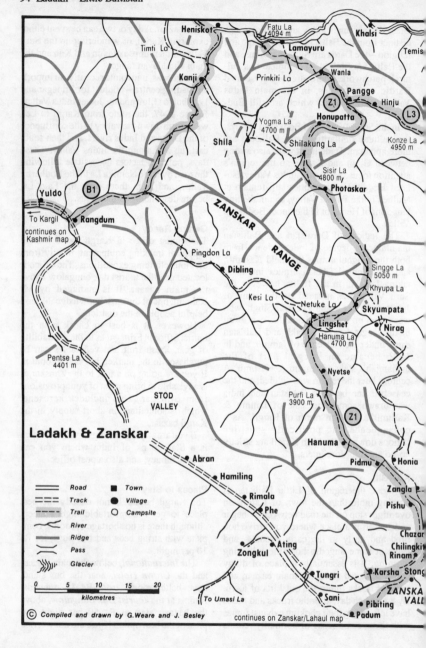

Ladakh & Zanskar

Heniskot
Fatu La 4094 m
Khalsi
Timti La
Lamayuru
Temis
Kanji
Prinkiti La
Wanla
Pangge
Hinju
Z1
L3
Yogma La 4700 m
Honupatta
Shila
Shilakung La
Konze La 4950 m
Sisir La 4800 m
Photaskar
Yuldo
B1
ZANSKAR
To Kargil
continues on Kashmir map
Rangdum
Pingdon La
RANGE
Dibling
Singge La 5050 m
Khyupa La
Kesi La
Netuke La
Skyumpata
Lingshet
Nirag
Hanuma La 4700 m
Pentse La 4401 m
Nyetse
STOD VALLEY
Purfi La 3900 m
Z1
Hanuma
Abran
Pidmu
Honia
Hamiling
Zangla
Rimala
Pishu
Phe
Chazar
Chilingkit
Ating
Rinam
Zongkul
Tungri
Karsha Stong
ZANSKA
VALL
Sani
Pibiting
To Umasi La
Padum
continues on Zanskar/Lahaul map

———— Road	■ Town
– – – – Track	● Village
– · – · Trail	○ Campsite
River	
Ridge	
Pass	
Glacier	

0 5 10 15 20
kilometres

© Compiled and drawn by G. Weare and J. Besley

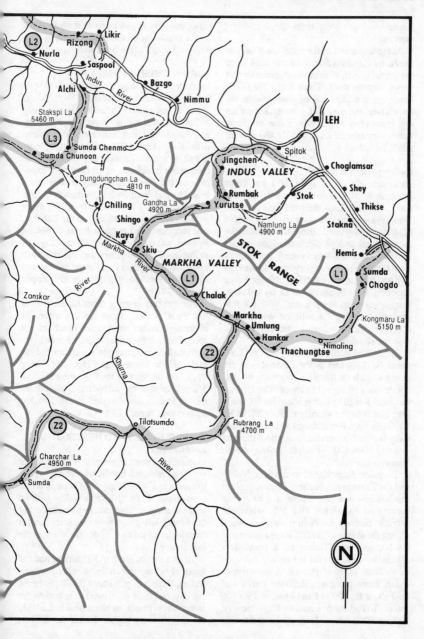

about waking up on time the following morning.

At the upper end of the hotel scale there is the *Hotel Caravan Sarai*, up the road from the tourist office, with its own generator and views over the town. There is also the *Highlands*, on the Suru Valley road beside the Suru River, and the *Zoji La*, on the same road and just below Highlands. Rates for these hotels vary around Rs 450 to Rs 480 with all meals included.

Getting There & Away

Although Kargil is only 200 km from Srinagar it takes a full day to drive from there. The Zoji La – the road pass over the Himalaya – is seldom clear until the middle of June, and even during the season the narrow road and precipitous edges restrict the traffic to a one-way system. The convoy from Drass to Sonamarg begins at 8 am every day, and the convoy travelling in the opposite direction, from Sonamarg to Drass and on to Kargil, leaves at about 2 pm. Within a few seasons the Zoji La will be widened to accommodate two-lane traffic, which will ease the situation.

The fare by A class bus over the Zoji La is about Rs 120, and is the same if you are going to Leh or Kargil – there are no discounts for getting off halfway. The B class bus from Kargil to Leh is about Rs 50, while jeep hire is in the vicinity of Rs 1200 to Rs 1400 one way. From Kargil to Leh there is a daily B class bus service throughout the year – convenient if you are going on to Lamayuru or Alchi.

Transport from Kargil to the Suru Valley and the Zanskar has become more regular in the last few seasons. There is a daily bus service to Pannikhar (Rs 10), while the service extends to Padum twice a week during the season. This fare is approximately Rs 100 one way. Trucks are a convenient alternative and the cost is roughly the same as the bus, more if you sit in the driver's cabin. Jeeps are available from Kargil and cost about Rs 400 to Pannikhar, and Rs 500 return. To Padum they cost Rs 4000 one way, and Rs 5000 return. Here again, the tourist office can give you an up-to-date assessment of the condition of the road, which is normally open to Padum by mid-July.

SURU & ZANSKAR VALLEYS

In many respects the introduction of the road has changed the character of the Suru Valley. When I first visited Pannikhar in the early 1970s, the road did not extend past Sanku, and the yak and mule trains would continue to the Kargil bazaar. The road was completed to Padum and the Zanskar in 1980, and since then many truckloads of tourists have experienced the best of the dusty road as they travel to and from Padum, with a few days in the Zanskar. For trekkers there are alternatives. For anyone trekking to the Zanskar, it is recommended to go as far as Rangdum by road, and then undertake the four day trek to Padum. This will afford the opportunity to appreciate the scenery on the Pentse La, and the whitewashed villages in the upper Zanskar Valley.

For trekkers coming from Kashmir over the Bhoktol Pass, there are a number of alternative routes that avoid much of the road. The trek over the Lago La is one highlight, before continuing to Rangdum and the high trails to Lamayuru or Heniskot. These stages are outlined in the following section, while details of the many trek possibilities out of Padum are detailed in the Zanskar section (see pages 113 to 120).

B1: SURU VALLEY TO HENISKOT & LAMAYURU

In Pannikhar you can either stay in one of the newly constructed hotels, or camp down by the river in a willow grove. If time is not at a premium, it is worthwhile walking down to the mosque at Namsuru, or just wandering the nearby villages, whose character has not been undermined by road development in the last decade.

Horses can be hired in Pannikhar, and are generally cheaper than those in the Kashmir Valley. Expect to pay about Rs 70 per horse per day, but there is no need to negotiate for return days. Prices, as elsewhere in Ladakh, are significantly higher during the harvest

Top: Jhelum River, Srinagar (GW)
Bottom Left: Flower seller, Nigin Lake, Srinagar (GW)
Bottom Right: Nigin Lake sunset, Srinagar (GW)

Top: Hot springs! Zanskar (GW)
Bottom Left: Upper Lidder Valley, Kashmir (GW)
Bottom Right: Horses approaching a pass, Kashmir (GW)

period. Basic supplies such as dried milk, rice and biscuits are available, but kerosene can be a problem. For supplies of fresh fruit and vegetables you will have to make an overnight trip to Kargil.

Note The first two stages of this trek are shown on the Kashmir map, page 63. The other stages are on the Ladakh & Zanskar map, page 94.

Stage 1: Pannikhar to Parkachik
(Average walking time 5 hours)

From Pannikhar, follow the metalled road for 3 km up the valley as if going to Rangdum, and then divert through the villages and cross the bridge over the Suru River. This links up with a road under construction on the far side of the valley. Follow the road down the valley for 1 km or so, and then turn off on the foot trail going uphill towards the dip in the ridge. This is the Lago La, which means 'pass of no consequence', but you won't think that when you're half way up it. It is a deceptive pass that takes the best part of 2 or 3 hours to climb.

The springline is about two thirds of the way up the hillside, although it is advisable to take boiled water with you from Pannikhar. As you reach the crest of the ridge you realise it is all worthwhile. The complete Nun Kun massif appears immediately in front of you. The climb is also rewarding in that this magnificent panorama cannot be seen from the road. It helps give the trekkers some sense of dignity the following day, when they are overtaken by a lorry load of tourists unaware of the views they have missed.

From the top of the pass the camping areas can be seen. These are rich green grazing areas for the local villages at Parkachik, and are fed by a series of springlines that are distant from the road. It is 300 metres down to the camp, and this takes about 30 minutes, it is quite steep, but there are many shortcuts. At the camp you may encounter some garbage left by less discriminate trekking parties. This is unfortunately a sign of things to come as you progress further into Ladakh.

Stage 2: Parkachik to Shafat
(Average walking time 6 hours)

This stage follows the jeep road for much of the way. The compensation is again the views of the main Himalaya, including the spectacular Parkachik Glacier which tumbles down to the water's edge just above Parkachik village.

The trek initially involves a gradual climb to the open grazing areas often referred to as the Lingti Plains. This takes on average about 3 hours. The Bakharval shepherds from Kashmir extend their migration to this area during the summer, something that the local villagers from Pannikhar and Parkachik dispute in terms of grazing rights. There have been instances of stealing from tents in this region, so it is worth ensuring that your overnight camp is properly guarded.

From the edge of the plains to Shafat takes a further 2 to 2½ hours. Here there are a number of camping sites situated opposite the valley that marks the expedition trail to the base of Nun peak. For those without tents, there is a huge rock cave in the boulder field, just beyond the Shafat grazing area. This is used by the Ladakhis for their horses and sheep, particularly at the margins of the season.

Stage 3: Shafat to Rangdum
(Average walking time 5 hours)

After the comparative drudgery of the previous day, this stage always seems a delight. Within a few hours of setting off you arrive at the village of Juldo. The mani walls (walls of prayer stones) and chortens (Tibetan stupas) that line the trail leave the trekker in no doubt that this is a Buddhist village. The monastery at Rangdum can be seen on top of the sugarloaf mountain at the head of the valley.

From Juldo there is a variety of short cuts on to Rangdum – that is if you have a sense of adventure and don't mind traversing the occasional bog. Compensations include the many wildflowers that bloom until mid-- September, such as edelweiss, delphinium, tansy, genfianella and moorcroftiana.

Although there are many campsites in the vicinity of the monastery, one alternative is to continue to the village of Tashi Tongtse, on the far side of Rangdum. The village is seldom visited by trekkers, and I have enjoyed many nights sharing the barley beer and joining the local women's dancing troupe. The villagers both here and at Juldo regard themselves as part of the Zanskar, in spite of their location to the north of the Pentse La. Marriages between these villagers and those of the Stod Valley in the Zanskar are common.

Many of the monks at Rangdum come from Tashi Tongtse and Juldo. The monastery was founded quite recently – about 200 years ago – and is affiliated to the Delgupta, the Dalai Lama's sect. The entrance fee to the monastery is Rs 10.

Stage 4: Rangdum to Kanji La Base Camp

(Average walking time 5-6 hours)

The trail to Kanji follows the valley behind Rangdum Monastery – the middle valley immediately before Tashi Tongtse. Which route you follow up the valley depends on the water level in the river. In the early part of the season it is easier to follow the trail on the right hand bank. Later in the season, when the water crossings are less of a hazard, it does not matter which side of the valley you follow. After ascending the valley for a few km there is a shepherd's hut on the right hand bank. From the hut there is a series of rather tiring ups and downs for several km, before reaching the base of the Kanji La.

The campsite is at the junction of the valley leading down from the Kanji La. This is a small rocky plateau about 50 metres above the water's edge, just beyond the narrow gorge leading to the Kanji La. To reach it necessitates crossing the main river, (a stream later in the season), which may require the use of ropes if the river is in flood. To reach the plateau, supplies will have to be offloaded from the horses as the trail is not suitable for laden animals. There is scarcely space for tents, and the horse handlers rarely spend a good night here, as they have to watch the horses in case they take off back down to the greener pastures of Rangdum.

Stage 5: Kanji La Base Camp to Kanji La & Camp

(Average walking time 7 hours)

An early start is imperative. The climb in the shade should give you sufficient reserves to reach the pass by mid-morning. From the camp, the trail leads up through a narrow gorge with the possibility of wet boots early on. As you climb higher, the valley opens out, and you can appreciate the dimensions of the Zanskar Range immediately behind you. There are no side streams en route to the pass, so water must be carried with you. Average time taken to the top of the pass is about 3 to 4 hours.

From the pass there are clear views back to the main Himalaya, while ahead lie the peaks of the Karakoram. Even better views are gained by climbing either of the side ridges for a few hundred metres.

Care is needed on the initial descent from the pass. The trail is down a steep gully, which is difficult under snow in the early part of the season. The trail then winds down and across a series of boulder fields, until it reaches a broad scree plateau. Cross the plateau and continue for several km, until the trail drops steeply to the main valley floor. The time taken from the pass is about 2 or 3 hours.

There is a campsite after this last steep descent, which is often used by trekkers coming from Kanji village. For fitter groups, the trail down through the gorge crosses the valley stream a number of times, until it reaches an open grazing area. The meadow is often frequented by yak herders from Kanji village, and there are a number of campsites in the vicinity.

Stage 6: Camp to Kanji Village

(Average walking time 2-3 hours)

If trekking from the lower camp, this stage can be completed in a few hours. Stay on the right hand side of the valley which winds and turns for several km. En route you will probably meet villagers from Kanji village, either with their flocks or tending the outlying barley fields. There is no need to cross the main river until you reach the gorge immediately above the village. Either camp here, or check out the option of camping in one of the enclosures in the vicinity of the village. A fee is payable, and it is essential that the horses do not stray into the barley fields, or you will face a stiff fine.

Kanji village is quite a prosperous settlement by Ladakhi standards, consisting of 20 or so families that farm the immediate area. Kanji village is also the trail junction. For parties going straight to the roadhead at Heniskot, the trail continues directly down through the gorge. The route to the Yogma La and on to Lamayuru follows the trail up the valley to the east of the village. (see the Kanji to Lamayura option outlined below.)

Stage 7: Kanji Village to Heniskot
(Average walking time 2-3 hours)
The trail down through the Kanji gorges has been considerably upgraded in the past few seasons. No longer are there the numerous river crossings lower down the gorges. Indeed, by the time this edition goes to print, the upgraded trail will probably be complete all the way from the roadhead to Kanji village. Assuming this to be the case, then there is more time to appreciate the gorge country, which is truly magnificent, on this final day of the trek.

The village of Heniskot is on the far side of the Kargil-Leh road, and is approached through a small gorge down valley from where the Kanji trail meets the road. The village is worth a visit if your schedule includes camping at the roadhead overnight.

If you're planning to reach Leh the same day, it is necessary to get to the roadhead early in order to meet the convoy that left Kargil en route to Leh earlier that morning. Alternatively, it is about an hour's drive from here over the Fatu La to Lamayuru.

Option: Kanji to Lamayuru via Yogma La
If trekking on from Kanji to Lamayuru, then it is advisable to continue past Kanji village (see Stage 7) and camp below the Yogma La.

The trek up the valley takes a couple of hours through the outlying fields and small settlements which are occupied by the villagers during the summer months. The climb the following morning to the Yogma La is deceptively easy, and affords good views of the immediate gorge country. The descent to the meadow below the pass takes a further 1½ hours. Camp here, or continue down to the Shilakung Gorges, a further 3 or 4 hours, with a steep descent in places.

The following stage, through the gorges, has some of the finest gorge scenery in Ladakh. Huge cliff faces often block out the sun for all but a few hours each day. Along the valley floor there are plenty of river crossings that can prove hazardous after a summer storm. The time to Shila village, at the head of the gorges, can therefore vary greatly. On average it takes 5 or 6 hours, with time the same day to visit Wanla village and monastery.

On the final stage, the trail leads up to the Prinkiti La. This is a hot stage once the sun hits the narrow gully. From the pass it is a further hour down to Lamayuru, with time for you to visit the monastery, before continuing by road to Leh the same day.

Leh & the Indus Valley

LEH
Leh, the capital of Ladakh, has long been a remote and fascinating outpost. Its situation in the upper Indus Valley made it an important crossroads for pilgrims and traders. Pilgrims continued from here along the Indus Valley to Mt Kalaish and Tibet, while traders would set off with their caravans over the Karakoram Pass to the markets of Yarkand, Kashgar and central Asia. Today, Leh is an important strategic centre for India. The large military presence is a reminder that the region of Ladakh is situated along India's sensitive borders with both Pakistan and China.

Despite this, the Leh bazaar still retains much of its character. There are no multistoried hotels, while Ladakh's physical isolation has deterred the huge influx of tourists that was predicted a decade ago. It's a very special place where the mind clears in the rarefied air, and you can discover a rich culture still coming to grips with the 20th century.

Leh is situated in a small fertile valley to the north of the Indus River. It has been the capital of Ladakh since the 15th century, when the upper kingdom of Shey united with the lower kingdom at Bazgo in order to preserve its independence from the invading armies of Kashmir and Baltistan. Soon after this, the Victory Fort at the top of Namgyal Hill was built to commemorate Ladakh's independence, and a century later the imposing nine-storey King's Palace was constructed for the Ladakhi royal family. In the 1830s the royal family was deposed by the Dogra armies, and exiled to Stok where their descendants still live today.

Leh's altitude is 3500 metres, so physical exercise should be taken at a very steady pace for the first few days. Ideally, your first climb should take you up to the now dilapidated King's Palace. It is proposed that the building may eventually be renovated to something of its former glory, complete with a museum. Going higher, the approach to the Victory Fort and Maitriya Temple affords fine views across the Indus Valley to the Stok mountains.

The outlying villages include Chandspar, about 2 km north of Leh, where there are important Buddhist carvings dating back to the 8th and 9th centuries when Ladakh was converted to Buddhism. Close by is the village of Shankar, the site of a modern monastery which serves much of the Leh Valley. The monastery is attended by some 15 to 20 monks from the monastery at Spitok. It seems surprising that Leh does not have a more impressive monastery; even the King's Monastery at the Palace is completely run down, and administered by a single monk seconded from Hemis.

Getting Ready

Trekking provisions and supplies must be purchased and carried from Leh, as tsampa, butter tea, and chang is about all you can get in the villages. Pack horses can be hired from the main villages such as at Stok, Hemis and Lamayuru, although you must allow a day or two for the horses to be brought down from the grazing pastures. Similarly with Alchi, Spitok or Likir, where horses may have to come from outlying villages several days away. Prices vary considerably; depending on the season you'll pay anything from Rs 50 to Rs 150 per horse per day.

As in Kashmir, the price for individual arrangements is generally much higher than it is in Nepal. There is no intense competition for work in Ladakh. Money has to be paid to induce people to leave their village for a week or more, as it may be necessary for them to pay someone to mind their fields while they are away.

Trek equipment is not generally available in Leh, so it is essential to bring your own tent, sleeping bag and clothing with you. It is possible to hire local 'parachute' tents for your Ladakhi crew.

If you are going it alone, a stove and tent are essential, as on some stages of the treks outlined there are no villages in which to shelter. Rope should be carried, particularly in July and August, even though bridges have been constructed over the worst river crossings in the Sumdo and Markha valleys.

Trekking Agents

The trekking agencies in Ladakh maintain a very low profile, unlike those in Kashmir. Agency signs hanging over windows in the main bazaar reveal simple offices with generally helpful staff. The Ladakhis have to some extent been overrun by Kashmiri operators, but there are exceptions. A few local agencies are run by well-educated Ladakhis who are extremely knowledgeable about their monasteries and culture. The tourist office, just off the main bazaar, has a full list of these and other agencies and is well worth visiting. Ladakhi assistants are on hand to provide the necessary introductions to a reliable cook, or a horse handler with whom you can negotiate.

Here some mention of the Artou Bookshop in Leh is also necessary. The Ladakhi staff here, besides having a comprehensive selection of books, are also helpful in giving trekking advice. If all else fails, a quick walk down to the Mandala Hotel will take you to Wangchuk Shamshu and Rigzin Jowa – two firm friends of the author – who are always pleased to talk without obligation about the delights of trekking.

Places to Stay

Ladakh was officially opened to tourism in 1974, and by 1980 there were over 50 guesthouses and hotels. Most are run by friendly Ladakhi families, and are often an extension of their own home. They are generally clean, simply appointed and constructed in typical two-storey whitewashed style.

Leh is not a big place, and you can walk around and check out a few hotels without having to hike for miles. You should be able to bargain for considerably less than the government rates outside the main season, which is from late July to August.

Rooms vary in price, depending on their size and location. In the old town, where accommodation is designed primarily to hold warmth in winter, the rooms are simply furnished and you'll get a bucket of water to wash with. In the mid-range, rooms will often have a view – usually of the snow-capped Stok Mountains – and have an attached bathroom with running water. The 'upmarket' rooms are simply furnished, although they will have blankets and a doona on the bed, and an attached bath with running water, most of the time!

The current rate for full board in the upmarket hotels is Rs 400 for a single and Rs 550 for a double. In B class hotels it's Rs 300 a single and Rs 400 a double, and for C class hotels and guesthouses, anywhere from Rs 40 to Rs 100, depending on the season and whether food is required.

Popular inexpensive accommodation includes the *Bimla Guest House*, just below the vegetable market by the turn-off opposite the Yaktail Hotel. The *Deluxe*, in the same vicinity, is from Rs 35 to Rs 85 per room. The *Kidar Palace View* in town also receives consistently good reports. There are a number of good guesthouses in the Chandspar area, including the *Asia*, *Eagle*, *Two Star* and the *Otsal*, which are all in the Rs 35 to Rs 85 price range. Closer to town, and directly above Leh, are the *Antelope* and the *Phunchoking* guesthouses.

In the middle range there is a wide choice. The *Umasi La*, *Rhi-Rhab* and *Snowview* hotels in Chandspa are all well run by local families. The *Himalaya*, above Leh, is also recommended, while in town there are the *Ibex*, *Bijoo* and *Yaktail* hotels. Rates in this category vary tremendously, depending on the season. Most have attached baths (some have hot water), and charge up to Rs 300/400 for singles/doubles with meals. These rates drop considerably in May and June, and from mid-September until the end of the season.

The upmarket hotels charge Rs 450/550 a single/double. Among the best are the *Lha Rhi Mo Hotel* and the *K-Sar* on Fort Rd, while the *Mandala* down the road is personally recommended by the author. Closer to town are the *Sengge Palace*, the *Galden Continental*, the *Lingzi* and the *Kangri*, while the *Shambala* is beyond Fort Rd, a couple of km from the Leh bazaar.

Getting There & Away

To/From Srinagar The journey from Srinagar to Leh by road vies for the title of the most demanding in the Himalaya. The 450 km drive is generally covered in two long days. The first is from the Kashmir Valley over the Zoji La to Kargil (see Little Baltistan section) The second day is from Kargil over the Fatu La to the Indus Valley and Leh. From the time you leave the alpine meadows at Sonamarg and wind over the passes, and on until you reach Leh, the drive never fails to keep the adrenalin going.

The 210 km drive from Kargil to Leh crosses cultural boundaries and travels over the outer rim of the Zanskar Range. The breathtaking scenery and the sheer size of the mountains are constant reminders that you are travelling through the trans-Himalayan zone.

The first Buddhist settlement is that of Mulbek in the upper Wakka Valley. At the side of the road is the famous Buddhist carving which dates back to the first century AD, when the first Buddhist monks trekked from Kashmir to Leh, and on to Tibet. From Mulbek, the road crosses the Namika La and descends to the Bodkarbu Valley where there is a Shi'ite Muslim village similar to the settlement of Kargil. The journey then continues past Heniskot to the Fatu La, the highest pass on the road at 4094 metres. The pass marks an outer rim of the Zanskar Range, from where you can appreciate the depth of the Indus gorges, and see the Ladakh Range in the background.

If you have the time, it is worthwhile leaving the road at the Fatu La and walking down the old pilgrim trail to Lamayura, past the ancient chortens and mani walls which date from the 10th century when the monastery was founded.

Later, Lamayuru was declared a holy site in which even criminals could seek sanctuary. For that reason it is known to Ladakhis as the Tharpa Ling, or the Place of Freedom. If you decide to stay here, there are a few small hotels in the vicinity of the monastery.

The road from Lamayuru drops nearly 1000 metres in the 25 km to Khalsi, and involves over 20 switchbacks. This must surely be a record for road building.

Beyond the village of Khalsi, the former Royal Highway followed the road to the village of Nurla, and then branched up the valley to Temisgam. From there the trail crossed the higher ridges to Likir and Bazgo. These days, the road follows the banks of the Indus, with the road hewn out of the mountainside as far as Saspool. From here you can get to Alchi on foot or by jeep.

From Saspool to Nimmu even the Indus gorges are too steep for modern roadbuilders, so the road climbs up over the Rongdu La to Bazgo. As you approach Bazgo it is not hard to see why it was of such strategic importance to the Ladakhis. It was here that the Ladakhi armies were able to repel the invading Balti forces for years at a time.

Nimmu is about 10 km further on, and it is here that the Zanskar River joins the Indus, and appears as the larger tributary. From here it is 40 km on to Leh. On the south side of the road the Stok Range can be seen, while to the north lies the Ladakh Range. Tucked into one of the sheltered side valleys is Leh.

The Srinagar to Leh highway is open for six months of the year, from mid-June until mid-October. During the winter and early spring the road between Leh and Kargil remains open for local traffic.

The A class bus is Rs 120 one way, and the B class is Rs 70. The deluxe buses are Rs 200, when available. They all leave from the tourist centre in Srinagar, where tickets can be purchased. Jeeps or taxis to Leh vary from Rs 3500 to Rs 4000 one way, depending on the time of the season. Trucks are a viable alternative, particularly later in the season. Prices are about the same as the bus.

When leaving Leh, allow time to book your return bus to Kashmir. During the season the delay can be up to a week. The problem is that the bus station staff do not know what buses are turning up from Kashmir until after they arrive. It is then a scramble for seats, which are at a premium. That is the situation in Leh, and this will continue for some seasons to come, particularly when flights are cancelled due to bad weather.

For those who want to make the journey at a more leisurely pace, there are plenty of places to stay en route. As well as the hotels in Kargil, there are government rest houses and tea stalls-cum-hotels at Drass, Bodkarbu, Lamayuru and Khalsi. Food and accommodation is basic; sleeping bags are necessary, as they are elsewhere in Ladakh.

There are regular Indian Airlines flights into Leh from Srinagar and Delhi, making Leh accessible to visitors throughout the year. The flights now arrive daily – twice a week from Delhi via Chandigarh, and five times a week from Srinagar. The services are heavily booked, and are sometimes cancelled in bad weather. The journey from Srinagar to Leh is a spectacular 25 minute flight, and is well worth taking at least one way. The cost is US$39 one way from Srinagar, and US$115 from Delhi.

To/From Manali The military road from Leh to Manali has been open for the past two seasons, although it is difficult to ascertain exactly what the current regulations permit. The bus from Leh takes two days to reach Manali, including a very long first day to Keylong in Lahaul, and an easier second day

Ladakhi spinning a prayer wheel

over the Rhotang Pass to the Kulu Valley. A number of fixed camps have been established to accommodate organised groups, as there is little else on the way after you leave the Indus Valley. The cost of the local bus is about Rs 100 one way. The problem is that the regulations do not at present permit tourists to take the bus. The only alternative is to hire a jeep from an authorised travel agent which is expensive – up to Rs 8000 one way.

Getting Around

Local buses (always crowded but never boring) leave from the bus station next to the polo ground, at irregular intervals, to most of the outlying villages and monasteries. These include daily services to Khalsi, Nimmu and Saspool, and also one service a day to Hemis that stops at all places en route. There are two services a day to Stok and Spitok. Those carrying all their trekking supplies should arrive early, as space on the roof is as limited as space inside the bus. Timetables are altered frequently, so it is best to enquire at the bus station the day before to find what is going on. Prices are cheap; for example, the bus to Hemis costs Rs 8, and to Stok Rs 4. For trips further afield, there are daily buses to Kargil for Rs 50. For Lamayuru, take the Kargil bus (Rs 25), while for Likir, the 'Khalsi Express' will drop you off at the roadhead for no less than Rs 8. Trucks are an alternative, although they prefer full-paying passengers going all the way to Kargil or Srinagar.

Jeeps or taxis are a convenient alternative. If you band together with others, the fare works out reasonably. It costs about Rs 350 to Hemis, Rs 400 to Alchi and Rs 1000 to Lamayuru. Jeeps are also a good way to cover some of the most important monasteries and palaces in one day. You can visit Shey, Thikse and Hemis for Rs 450 for the day, including waiting time. Although there are fixed rates for such outings, expect to bargain hard. A jeep to the airport will cost about Rs 30. Petrol is often in short supply.

Treks

Three treks are outlined in this section:

L1: From Spitok to Hemis via the Markha Valley.
L2: From Likir to Temisgam, north of the Indus Valley.
L3: From Lamayuru to Alchi.

Each of these treks provides an insight into Ladakhi culture beyond the Indus Valley. The Markha Valley trek reflects something of the kingdom of upper Ladakh, and includes the important monasteries at Spitok and Hemis, though at some point a visit to the Stok Palace should also be undertaken. The trek from Likir is easier, with time to appreciate the 'lower' kingdom of Ladakh, including the sites of Temisgam and Bazgo. The trek from Lamayuru to Alchi is a classic, and can be linked with the Markha Valley trek if you have two weeks to spare.

Acclimatisation is the most important consideration on these treks. The Stakspi La, above Alchi, is over 5000 metres; the Namlung La, above Stok, is around 4500 metres; and the Kongmaru La, two stages beyond Hemis, is at 5030 metres. Some time should therefore be spent in Leh, and the initial stages of the treks should be taken very slowly. Remember that Leh (3500 metres) is at the same altitude as Thyangboche in Nepal, the acclimatisation camp en route to Everest Base Camp.

The Markha Valley and Lamayuru treks are possible from early June onwards – as soon as the snow on the highest passes begins to melt. On the trek from Likir to Temisgam, the passes are far lower, and the trek can be completed throughout the year. July and August can be very pleasant, although the daytime temperatures may soar into the mid-20s. It is worth considering very early starts every day, to complete each trek stage by midday. Dehydration is a problem in this intensely dry area, and fluid levels must be maintained. River crossings still constitute a problem, although they are not as hazardous as in the Zanskar region. September is ideal, as the weather is settled, and in October the

days are generally clear, making this a good trekking month, providing you have sufficient warm clothing to endure any cold spells.

L1: SPITOK TO HEMIS VIA THE MARKHA VALLEY

There are two approaches to trek the Markha Valley. The first is via Spitok and Jingchen to the base of the Gandha La. The second is via Stok and the Namlung La. For those who are fit and well acclimatised, the Stok approach provides some breathtaking views of the Indus Valley as you approach the Namlung La. Normally one night is spent en route from Stok, camping in the gorges, and then it is over the pass to Rumbak for the second stage. The problem, as always, is acclimatisation. For the less experienced, the trek via Spitok and Jingchen is the better alternative.

Stage 1: Spitok to Rumbak
(Average walking time 6-7 hours)
It is a short drive from Leh to Spitok, below the airport. The Spitok Monastery here is one of the oldest in the upper Indus Valley, and was founded at the same time as Thikse and Likir. The monastery, like that at Thikse, is situated on top of a small hill with a commanding view up the valley. The positioning of this monastery indicates an historic change in the siting of monasteries in the Indus Valley which, up to the 15th century, were typically built in sheltered valleys, as at Alchi or Temisgam. The monasteries at Thikse and Spitok were not founded for strategic reasons, although in the ensuing centuries, when Ladakh entered into a period of further political turbulence, their position would have been considered an asset.

From the monastery cross the bridge over the Indus and, on the far bank, follow the trail that stretches across the barren and exposed flats. It is advisable to set off early. This stage is not particularly interesting, and it can become quite warm by midday. After 6 or 7 km, the Indus enters a tight gorge at its confluence with the Jingchen River. Follow the trail up the Jingchen Valley, which is lined with trees providing sufficient shade for rest stops. The main village at Jingchen consists of a few settlements with a number of camping stops in the vicinity. Either camp here, or continue for a few more km to the village of Rumbak.

Stage 2: Rumbak to Yurutse & Camp
(Average walking time 4-5 hours)
After visiting the village at Rumbak there is a steady ascent up the valley, following the well-marked trail that crosses the main stream before entering the side valley leading to the south. The whitewashed houses of Yurutse lie further up the valley. The large house here is owned by a very hospitable family whose supply of the local barley beer has curtailed many a day's trekking! For the less indulgent, there is a small campsite 2 or 3 km further up, which is complete with a small spring and inspiring views back across the snow ridges of the Stok Range.

Stage 3: Camp to Gandha La, Markha Valley & Skiu
(Average walking time 6-7 hours)
From the camp, it is a steady climb for an hour or so to the Gandha La. The pass has the usual array of prayer flags and cairns, and affords views that extend across the Zanskar Range to the south. From the pass, the village of Shingo can be seen a few km down the valley. The trail from the pass is well marked, and there is a good camping area above the village for those who are varying the trek stages described here. From the village, the trail enters a gorge lined with willows and colourful rose bushes, and continues on for 5 or 6 km until it reaches a number of small stupas which mark the confluence with the Markha Valley. Turn up the valley for 1 km or so, to the village of Skiu where there is a rather marshy campsite immediately below the main house.

If time is not at a premium then a rest day, with a walk down valley to the Zanskar River, is recommended. The walk passes the village of Kaya which has a village monastery and apricot groves. Combined with the

sight of villagers working in the fields during the long summer months, this will give you a feeling of being in Shangri La – but not for too much longer. The road which is being constructed up the Zanskar Valley from Nimmu is planned to reach the village in the next few years, and it is intended that this road will link all the villages in the Markha Valley during the 1990s.

While you're resting at the confluence of the Zanskar and Markha rivers, it is worth considering that the road is planned eventually to continue up the Zanskar gorges to the Zanskar Valley. This will be easier said than done. These gorges are some of the steepest anywhere in the Himalaya, as anyone who has rafted the river will appreciate.

Stage 4: Skiu to Markha
(Average walking time 7-8 hours)
This stage of about 17 km can be covered in one day's walk. The terrain along the valley is not demanding, though the trail crosses the Markha River a couple of times. The river crossings in the valley were a problem a decade ago, but nowadays, with the construction of bridges, the stage is more or less straightforward. There are a few ancient chortens along the trail, and a number of wolf pits used to trap wolves when they roam the valley during the winter months. Camping spots are available before reaching the village of Markha, should you decide to appreciate the valley at a more leisurely pace.

Markha is a substantial village, complete with a derelict fort on the hillside. Campsites are normally selected from the ample grazing flats just beyond the village, and a small charge of a few rupees is sometimes collected. The villagers are inquisitive and friendly, and there is a small village monastery just above the village – worth a visit if you can find the caretaker who holds the key.

Stage 5: Markha to Nimaling
(Average walking time 7-8 hours)
This is another long stage, but it can be split depending on the time available. The trail cuts across the river bed after leaving

Markha village. Opposite is the side valley which leads, via two passes, to the Zanskar Valley. A few km on from Markha is the settlement of Umlung, after which the valley broadens and the imposing peak of Kangyaze (6400 metres) dominates the horizon.

The village of Hankar is the highest village in the Markha Valley, and from there the trail ascends the side valley that leads to the Nimaling plains. The trail crosses the Nimaling stream just after Hankar, and from this point the climb is steady, and quite tiring due to the altitude. As the trail reaches the edge of the plains, the peak of Nimaling comes into view. It is important to note here that the trails begin to criss-cross the pastures, and the correct path is the one that leads up the valley and not towards the base of Kangyaze.

The Nimaling encampment consists of a number of summer camps where the villagers from Hankar and Markha graze their yaks and goats during the summer months. It should be borne in mind that inclement weather can build up quickly in this area, and a tent and warm clothing are necessary even during midsummer. I have known it to snow here in both July and August after some particularly fine, sunny spells.

There are many side trips that can be undertaken from the camp at Nimaling. The actual peak is not technically difficult but, as elsewhere in the Indian Himalaya, government regulations stipulate that no peak over 5000 metres can be undertaken without a permit and an accompanying liaison officer. Fines have been imposed in the last few years for climbing this peak and also the peaks behind Stok.

Stage 6: Nimaling to Kongmaru La & Chogdo Village

(Average walking time 6 hours)
From Nimaling, cross to the north side of the stream and start climbing up the well-defined trail to the pass. The climb should take 2 hours at the most. (If it has been snowing, get the shepherds to point out the general direction to you.) The pass is at the top of the ridge: there are no further climbs involved as is so often the case with Himalayan passes. From the pass there are clear views across to the Kangyaze, while to the north lies the Indus Valley and the Ladakh Range.

The initial descent is steep, down a series of zig-zags to a meagre campsite which is often used by parties trekking up from Hemis. From here the trail enters a gorge, and drops nearly 1000 metres to the highest village. The track may not always be in the best of condition, as flash floods wash away the hillside every few seasons. The resultant trail erosion illustrates clearly the delicate nature of the mountain terrain in Ladakh.

Chogdo is the first village you come to, and it is possible to camp there in the enclosure opposite the main cluster of houses.

Stage 7: Chogdo to Hemis

(Average walking time 4-5 hours)
The final stage of this trek follows the valley floor for 4 or 5 km to the village of Sumda. From here the trail improves until it meets the jeep track on the Leh-Manali road. Turn left (westwards) by the large chorten above Martselang village, and follow the rather dusty trail to Hemis. There is a camping ground just above the village, complete with a restaurant, and perhaps a beer. There is a camping charge of about Rs 10 per night.

MONASTERIES
Hemis

The monastery at Hemis is one of the most important in Ladakh. It is the principal monastery of the 'Red Hat' Drukpa order, and the head monk administers all the associated monasteries in the Ladakh and Zanskar regions. It was established in the 17th century under the patronage of Singge Namgyal, and since then has enjoyed the financial support of successive royal families. The monastery provides caretaker monks for the monasteries at Leh, Bazgo and Shey.

The former head monk of Hemis was detained in Tibet when it was taken over by the Chinese. He has recently been able to return to visit the monastery after a period of

20 years. In the meantime, a young monk from Dharamsala was appointed, and he has assumed jurisdiction over the monastery.

Each year the Hemis Festival attracts more than its share of visitors. It is held during the full moon in June, and is attended by monks and their families who have travelled throughout Ladakh and the Zanskar to be there. The highlight of the festival is a series of masked dances commemorating the deeds of the Buddhist figurehead Padmasambhava, the sage who introduced Tantric Buddhism to the Himalaya. Once every 11 years a huge tanka, one of the largest in the Tibetan world, is displayed on the walls of the Hemis courtyard. The next showing will be in 1991.

To fully appreciate the position of the monastery, and also to gain some insight into the meditative practices pursued by the monks, it is recommended to visit the Monks' Hermitage about an hour's climb behind the monastery.

The bus from Hemis to Leh departs around midday and takes about 2 hours. The bus stops at Thikse Monastery and Shey on the way, so these can be visited before returning to Leh.

Thikse

Thikse's site in the Indus Valley makes it one of the area's most imposing monasteries. It was founded in the 15th century, along with Likir and Spitok, as the monks from Tibet spread the word of the reformist 'Yellow Hat' school of Buddhism, which is associated with the Dalai Lama. The main monastery is situated on top of the hill, with the monks' quarters below. The library at Thikse is supposedly one of the best in the western Himalaya, and a multidenominational chapel has recently been constructed – proof indeed of the continuing vitality of Buddhism in Ladakh.

Shey

Shey was the former palace of the upper kingdom of Ladakh. Its foundation can be traced to the earliest history of Ladakh, while the inscriptions on the rocks below the palace date from the time when Buddhism was first introduced to the western Himalaya. The palace was occupied by members of the Ladakhi royal family until 1834, when they were exiled to Stok. Since then, many of the buildings have fallen into disrepair, and the clear lake at the base of the hill is now marshland.

In the last decade there has been some restoration of the Buddhist artefacts, including the two-storied Sakyamuni Buddha originally commissioned by Singge Namgyal.

Stok

To complete the upper Indus cultural circuit, the imposing palace of Stok is an hour's drive across the Indus from Leh. It was built during the 1840s to house the Ladakh royal family after they had been exiled by the Dogra army. The Rani (princess) of Stok has assumed responsibility for the maintenance and reconstruction of the Ladakh palaces in Stok, Leh and Shey. The exhibits at the Stok Museum include many of the important royal tankas, while the collection of headdresses are the most impressive in Ladakh. It is planned that the museum pieces will eventually be moved to the Leh Palace, when sufficient funds are available.

L2: LIKIR TO TEMISGAM

A trek over the low passes! This two-stage trek is an ideal introduction to Ladakh, combining comparatively easy trekking with a chance to visit the monasteries at Likir, Rizong, and Alchi. The trek follows the former trade route to the north of the Indus Valley, commencing at Likir and continuing across a series of small passes to the village of Temisgam a few km north of Nurla on the main highway. From here it is recommended that you drive back to Saspool and visit Alchi before returning to Leh.

As with so many developments in Ladakh, a jeep road is at present being constructed along the route, and within a few seasons the road will provide an alternative to the main highway. For now however, there are many points where you can avoid the construction,

and savour the natural Ladakhi countryside
for a couple of days. The trail has the added
bonus of being open practically throughout
the year. It is therefore an ideal alternative if
you arrive in Ladakh outside the normal
trekking season.

Horses can be hired at Likir or Temisgam.
The cost is approximately Rs 100 per horse
per day. If you're starting the trek from Likir,
catch the bus or jeep to the roadhead, stay
overnight in the monastery camping grounds
and make an early start the following
morning. As usual, supplies are limited along
the trail, and all food should be brought from
Leh. Part of this trek is off the northern edge
of the Ladakh & Zanskar map.

Likir

The monastery at Likir was founded at the
same time as those at Thikse and Stakna. It
is one of the most important Yellow Hat-
Delgupta monasteries in Ladakh, with many
of the remote Zanskar monasteries contrib-
uting towards its funds. The head monk at
Likir is a younger brother of the Dalai Lama,
although he is not in residence.

Likir's position has contributed towards
its importance in the Indus Valley. Its monks
act as caretakers to the nearby Alchi Monastery, while it serves many of the other smaller
monasteries in the area.

Stage 1: Likir to Yantang
(Average walking time 4-5 hours)
From the village, follow the jeep road
towards the first pass, the Pobe La. After
leaving the valley the terrain is quite barren,
devoid of shade and water. On the descent to
the settlement of Sumda you can appreciate
the views down the Indus Valley and across
to the villages of Saspool and Alchi.

From Sumda, cross the main stream and
ascend the small dry valley opposite. Most
of the passes on this route are not unduly
taxing, and can be completed in an hour or
so. The Chartse La is no exception, and from
here it is a gradual drop to the village of
Yantang – a small cluster of houses with a
camping area near the main stream in the
valley. The monastery of Rizong lies a few

km down the valley from Yantang, so it
possible to visit it as a side trip before continuing on the following morning.

Stage 2: Yantang to Temisgam
(Average walking time 5 hours)
From Yantang there is an hour's gradual
climb to the Sarmanchan La, then an equally
gradual descent to the main village of Hemis-
Shukpachu. The name is derived from the
small cedar grove on the far side of the
village – shukpa meaning cedar. The village
is the largest en route, with well-maintained
houses, ample barley fields, and bubbling
streams that could entice the less hurried to
camp for a day or two.

The trek continues with a gradual ascent
to a small pass that has no local name. From
there, the trail drops steeply to the valley
floor, then ascends just as steeply to another
pass, known locally as the Lago La – literally, a pass of no consequence. Tell that to
anyone who has been struggling up the trail
in the midday heat for the last hour! From the
pass, the zig-zags of the main highway from
Lamayuru can be seen, while the village of
Ang is visible shortly after you descend from
the pass. From Ang, the trail goes down the
valley a further 2 or 3 km to Temisgam. Rose
bushes are in abundance on the final stages
of this trek, while the apricot orchards and
rich barley fields contribute to the overall
prosperity of this fine Ladakhi village.

Getting Away From Temisgam there is a
daily bus service back to Leh. Alternatively
it is only 3 or 4 km down the valley to Nurla
on the main highway, from where there are
regular convoys back to Saspool and Leh.

An alternative to this short trek is to continue for a further stage, going north up the
valley to the village of Tea, and from there
over the Bongbang La to Khalsi, further
down the Indus Valley.

L3: LAMAYURU TO ALCHI
It is better to do this trek from Lamayuru – it
is a hell of a climb out of Alchi for the first
day and a half. The first pass, Stakspi La, is
over 5180 metres according to my altimeter.

Going from Lamayuru will give you some time for acclimatisation before crossing the first pass, Konkse La, at 4570 metres.

I first completed this trek coming from the direction of Alchi. The horseman from Saspool assured me that we would cross the pass with sufficient time to descend to the first village all in one day. Unfortunately he had not considered the feelings of his two horses and three donkeys, and we were all caught on top of the pass. The sight of the sunrise on the Ladakh Range was, however, sufficient compensation for a rather cold and windy night out.

Whether you're starting this trek from Lamayuru or Alchi, bring all your supplies with you, and allow a day or two to organise horses.

An ideal extension after the first four stages of this trek is to continue over the Dungdugchan La, to the village of Chiling and the Zanskar River. From there, it is a further stage to the confluence of the Zanskar and Markha rivers, and from there on to Markha and Hemis as per the Markha Valley trek, stages 4 to 7 (see page 105). Allow 10 to 12 days to complete this trek.

Lamayuru

The ideal way to approach Lamayuru is to follow the old caravan route that diverges from the Kargil-Leh road at the Fatu La. As you descend from the pass you can appreciate the impressive line of mani walls and chortens that lead down to the village.

Legend has it that the upper reaches of this valley were once filled by a vast lake. This was miraculously breached by the sage Naropa. The site of the breach was revered, and became the location of the monastery which was built in the 10th century. Whatever the legend, Lamayuru is one of the oldest monastic sites in Ladakh. One of the original temples is situated just beyond the main assembly hall and has been renovated. The monastery subscribes to one of the older Tibetan schools, the Kargyupa/Drukpa sect. For many of the outlying monasteries in the region the distinctions are technical – the monasteries at Wanla, Pangge and Khalsi,

although affiliated with Lamayuru, also have close cultural links with the main Drukpa monastery at Hemis.

Stage 1: Lamayuru to Hinju
(Average walking time 7 hours)
The camping area at Lamayuru is in the shady grove just below the monastery. From there the trail heads down the valley for 2 km before turning east towards the Prinkiti La. The climb to the pass (3506 metres) should take less than an hour. From the pass, the terrain towards the Konze La can be appreciated before you descend the narrow and rather dusty gully to the Shilakung Valley. From there you turn down the valley, past the village of Shila, to Wanla. You can spend some time at the monastery, which is believed to have been founded at the same time as Lamayuru.

The trek continues up the valley for 4 or 5 hours to the village of Pangge, where the trails diverge. The trail south to Padum continues on to Honupatta, while the trek to Alchi goes up the side valley to the small hamlet of Hinju.

Stage 2: Hinju to Konze La & Sumda Chunoon
(Average walking time 7 hours)
This is a strenuous second stage, and an intermediate camp or a rest day is recommended en route from Lamayuru.

The trek up the valley towards the pass is gradual to begin with, along a well-defined trail. The final few hundred metres to the pass are steep, with the pass normally under snow till mid-July. From the pass there are clear views across the Stok Range, and to the gorge country in the vicinity of the Zanskar River. The trail down to the open valley is easy to follow. (If you're coming in the opposite direction, be careful not to follow a stray track away from the pass.) Down to the main valley there are many campsites above the line of settlements referred to as Sumda Chunoon. There is a small, well-maintained monastery close to the village, while there are some large statues of the Maitriya

Buddha close to the site of a former monastery.

Stage 3: Sumda-Chunoon to Stakspi La Base Camp
(Average walking time 7 hours)

The time on this stage can be reduced if you don't get lost! Somehow the author took the trail that leads directly down the valley, staying close to the valley floor. This is the right way only to a point. I have since been reliably informed that rather than undertaking this bushbashing route, there is a higher trail above the thicket that makes the trek to the base of the Stakspi La much easier. I can only recommend a local guide from Sumda-Chunoon village to take you to the turn-off point that leads up valley to another substantial village known locally as Sumda-Chenmo. From here the trail is easier to follow to the campsite.

The monastery at Sumda Chenmo was founded at the same time as Alchi, and the assembly hall displays a similar variety of wall paintings and carvings. There is also an impressive statue of the Maitriya Buddha in the adjoining temple.

During the late autumn, herds of urial sheep make their way down from the meagre summer grazing pastures towards the shelter of the valley. For anyone interested in observing this migration, a trek from the middle to the end of October is recommended. During this time the author has also seen similar migrations, notably below the Rubrang La en route to the Zanskar, and also above Hankar village in the Markha Valley.

Option: From Sumda-Chunoon to the Markha Valley

From Sumda-Chunoon, head across the valley and up the opposite hillside to the Dungdungchan La. It is a long stage across the pass in one day, and an intermediate camp is advisable. From the pass, descend to the village of Chiling, where much of the copper-work for the Leh market is made.

From there you have the option of crossing the Zanskar River by pulley bridge and then going down the newly constructed jeep road to Nimmu. Alternatively you can continue up to the confluence of the Zanskar and Markha rivers, and then complete the trek to Markha and Hemis (see the Markha Valley trek, page 105).

Stage 4: Camp to Stakspi La & Alchi
(Average walking time 7-8 hours)

The climb to the pass is quite tiring, and an early start is recommended if you are to complete this stage in one day. The ascent should take between 2 and 3 hours, and from the pass there are wonderful views down the Indus Valley and across the snow-capped ridges of the Ladakh Range. From the pass, the trail descends quite steeply to a small grazing area and shepherds' shelter and a possible campsite. (This is useful if you're doing the trek from Alchi). From there it's a further 3 hours down to Alchi, where there is a regular campsite-cum-restaurant close to the monastery. It is a further 3 or 4 km along the jeep track to the Alchi bridge, and the main highway to Leh.

Alchi

The monastery complex at Alchi was founded in the 11th century, when the noted teacher Ringchen Zangpo was sent by a local Tibetan king to lay the foundations for Buddhist monasteries throughout Ladakh and the Zanskar. Due to its sheltered location, Alchi has remained intact to the present day.

Alchi's major interest stems from the fact that the Tibetans, being newly converted to Buddhism, did not have the artistic skills necessary to decorate the temples. Artists from Kashmir were therefore commissioned to complete the walls and entrances. These artists had been previously employed to decorate the Buddhist temples in the Vale of Kashmir, which have long been destroyed. Alchi therefore remains a significant example of the Indian-Buddhist styles which have long since disappeared from other sites in the west Himalaya.

For a complete survey of the Alchi temples, and a detailed history of the other monasteries in Ladakh, refer to Snellgrove & Skorupski's *Cultural History of Ladakh*, Vol 1.

The Zanskar Valley

The isolated region of Zanskar is composed of a number of small mountain-locked valleys to the south of Ladakh. The valleys are bounded to the north by the Zanskar Range, and to the south by the main Himalaya. To the east and west, high ridges linking the Himalaya and Zanskar mountains ensure that there is no easy link between the Zanskar and the outside world.

Zanskar essentially comprises the Stod Valley in the west, and the Lunak Valley in the east, which converge at Padum, the administrative centre of the region. The fertile region of Padum and its outlying villages and monasteries form the nucleus of the Zanskar. It is a small Himalayan kingdom by any standards. The valley is no more than 20 km wide at the most, while 50 km north of Padum the Zanskar River enters the impressive gorges of the Zanskar Range as it flows down to the Indus Valley.

The Zanskar's location on the lee side of the main Himalaya range ensures that it attracts considerably more snow than any other region of Ladakh. Snow can fall for over seven months of each year. Passes are often snowbound for more than half the year, and the winter temperatures of -20°C make it one of the coldest inhabited places in the world. In the depths of winter all the rivers freeze over. Even the fast-flowing Zanskar River freezes on the surface, and the Zanskaris walk on the ice to reach the Indus Valley near Nimmu – an otherwise inaccessible route.

Until a few years ago it took the villagers a week or more to reach the roadhead. However, in the last decade a jeep road linking Kargil and Padum has been constructed, creating direct access to Kashmir or the Indus Valley for three or four months a year. The Pentse La, the pass linking the valley from Kargil with the Zanskar, is generally clear of snow by early July. There have, however, been exceptions to this, and the author can recall at least two occasions when even up to early August the only access to the Zanskar was by foot. The road lifeline has taken its toll on the traditional culture of the Zanskar. Anyone searching for some long-lost Shangri La should look elsewhere. However, the yak and pony trains still make their way over the more remote passes to Lahaul, Kulu, Kashmir, and the Indus Valley.

Zanskar's uninterrupted Buddhist heritage has been principally due to its isolation. It can be traced back to a time when the Buddhist monks first made their way over the high passes from Kashmir. The monastery at Sani, founded in the 10th century, is an example of the earliest Buddhist influence. Indeed, legend has it that the sage Naropa meditated at the Sani chorten during his journeys through Ladakh. The original sites of such monasteries as Phugtal, Karsha and Lingshet may also be attributed to this period. In many respects, the development of the Buddhist orders in the Zanskar were the same as in other regions of Ladakh. The

Dalai Lama's order – the Delgupta – was established in the 15th century, and the well-preserved monasteries at Karsha, Lingshet and Mune date from this period. The King's order – the Drukpa – established its presence at Bardan and Zangla and 'colonised' the monastery at Sani in the 17th century.

Today, the Delgupta monasteries have established ties with Likir Monastery in the Indus Valley, while Bardan, Sani and Zangla have administrative and financial links with the monastery at Stakna, close to Leh.

The influence of Islam did not affect the Zanskar until the 19th century. The presence of Muslim families in Padum dates from the 1840s, when the Dogra forces made their way over the passes from Kishtwar, and established their presence both here and in Ladakh. The fort at Pipiting below Padum was built as a fitting testimony to the Dogra times, when the powers of royal families in both Zangla and Padum were reduced to the same nominal status as the royal families in Ladakh.

PADUM
Getting Ready

Trekking in the Zanskar is not easy. The trails are rough, the rivers often deep, and the passes are always high. This is not the place for inexperienced trekkers, and careful planning is a must for anyone visiting the region.

The development of the road from Kargil has made the region more accessible, and the increased number of visitors to the region has led to the establishment of many teahouses-cum-hotels in Padum, and in many of the villages near the main monasteries. Supplies can be purchased at a premium price. Kerosene, biscuits and other basics are generally available, but that's about it. There is a long way to go before the teahouse system in Zanskar is comparable to that in Nepal. It is therefore advisable to come to the Zanskar fairly self-sufficient, bringing your supplies from Kashmir, Kargil or Leh.

On arrival in Padum you are required to register with the tourist department. It is also worthwhile to detail the trek you intend to do; in the event of an accident this will help to get the administrative wheels moving, particularly if an evacuation is required.

Padum itself is not a particularly attractive place. Incongruous government buildings have been constructed, and the atmosphere is all that you would expect of a village that has been the roadhead for the Zanskar for the past decade or so. Vehicles are repaired, diesel drums are discarded, and much that is not used is disposed of here. Theft is also a problem, with tents being opened and pillaged a short distance from the police station.

The best campsite is a little way out of Padum, down the banks of the Tsarap River below the bridge. As always, check with the villagers in the fields as to where camping is permissible. Fees seem to rise after you have pitched your tent, so make a deal at the outset. The author sympathises with those who make deals and then find they are dealing with the wrong family, and later encounter yet another disgruntled landlord. Apart from this, there is a camp with a reasonable supply of water on the plains not far from the village centre, or you can stay in one of the many small teahouses-cum-hotels that are open during the season.

Prices for horses vary greatly throughout the season. Since the first edition of this book prices have at least doubled, and you must budget on paying at least Rs 100 per day for a relatively easy trek from July through to mid-August. During the harvest season, from the end of August onwards, the reduced availability of horses may entail a wait of many days and a price of between Rs 150 and Rs 200 per horse per day. Porters are sometimes an alternative, but again expensive in comparison to other regions of the Himalaya. If you're crossing the Umasi La you have no choice. Porters are asking up to Rs 1000 for the carry over the Umasi La as far as the highest village on the Kishtwar side – and they fully deserve it.

Getting There & Away

The drive from Kargil to Padum takes two days with an overnight stop, normally at Rangdum. For the last few seasons there has also been a regular local bus from Kargil to

Top Left & Right: Ascending to the Shingo La, from the south (RC)
Bottom Left: Ladakhi trader (GW)
Bottom Right: Near Rangdum Monastery, Zanskar (GW)

Top: Zanskari family, Photoksar (RC)
Bottom Left: Thikse Monastery, Ladakh (GW)
Bottom Right: Prayer flags at Leh, Ladakh (GW)

Padum two or three times a week during the season. The price is about Rs 100 one way. The buses are normally heavily booked, and getting a truck from the Kargil bazaar is an alternative. Prices are about the same as the bus. If you get a seat in the cabin it is likely to be a little more comfortable than sitting in the back. Whatever the choice, look forward to two very dusty days. The prospect of getting off and walking down the road from Pentse La is, I am sure, contemplated by most travellers who would like to appreciate the fine Himalayan views in a modicum of comfort.

Jeeps can also be hired from Kargil, but they are expensive. Expect to pay Rs 5000 one way, or Rs 6000 to 7000 if you're returning to Kargil within a few days.

Treks

Four treks are outlined in this section:

Z1: From Karsha to Lamayuru over the Singge La

Z2: From Padum to Leh via the Charchar La, Rubrang La and the Markha Valley

Z3: From Padum to Darcha via the Lunak Valley and Shingo La

Z4: From Padum to Manali via the Lunak Valley, Phirtse La and Baralacha

Note that the trek over the Umasi La to Kishtwar is included in the Kishtwar section of the Jammu chapter (Trek J3).

The three main treks in this section all go through some wilderness areas. On the trek from Zangla to Markha, for instance, you may see no-one for six days. The trails are often ill defined, and a local guide is highly recommended. The Zanskar area is no different from the rest of Ladakh when it comes to river crossings. In the late spring (May to June),water levels rise with the spring snow melt, and during the summer the occasional storm will change a fairly placid stream into a raging torrent. Schedules must therefore be flexible; take supplies for delays, and consider alternative routes in times of inclement weather.

It is interesting that the easiest summer

route out of the Zanskar – over the Pentse La – becomes the most difficult as soon as the first winter snows fall. The villagers then choose the alternative, and harder, trail to Markha and Leh over high passes which are not subject to heavy winter snow in early winter and late spring.

In the middle of winter an even simpler route is followed. From late January through to the end of February, the villagers walk on the frozen surface of the Zanskar River, straight down through the Zanskar gorges, a route that does not involve pass crossings or snowdrifts. A trek to Leh can then be completed in a week.

Z1: KARSHA TO LAMAYURU

This demanding trek crosses a series of high passes as it cuts across the grain of the Zanskar Range. As with the trail to Darcha, there are a number of small hotels in the villages, although it is still essential to bring some supplies, and at least a sleeping bag and tent to ensure a safe trek. A minimum of 10 days should be allowed to complete this trek.

Karsha

Karsha Monastery is the largest in the Zanskar region. It is situated on the hillside to the east of the Zanskar Valley, with commanding views of the entire valley and the main Himalaya to the south. The monastery attracts monks from many of the surrounding villages, and at any one time anything up to 100 monks may be in attendance. The monastery on this site was probably founded in the 10th century, while the main prayer hall and monks' quarters would have been built in the 14th century, the time that the Delgupta order was popularised in Ladakh.

Coming from Kargil, it is possible to drive straight to Karsha. Trekkers coming from Padum can now cross the new bridge over the Stod River instead of having to detour via Sani and Tungri.

Stage 1: Karsha to Pishu

(Average walking time 4-5 hours)

From Karsha the trail descends across the windy plains to the village of Rinam, and then follows the banks of the Zanskar River to Pishu. This is an easy first stage. It also allows time in the afternoon to cross the famous twig bridge of Zangla, and visit the monastery and palace grounds. There is a campsite below Pishu village on the open grazing grounds near the river.

Stage 2: Pishu to Hanuma
(Average walking time 4-5 hours)
Another level stage, with the trail frequently skirting the banks of the Zanskar. The village of Pidmu is about halfway, and there is a campsite down by the river below the village of Hanuma. Hanuma, Pishu and Pidmu on the west side of the river, together with Chazar and Honia on the other side, constitute the tiny kingdom of Zangla.

Stage 3: Hanuma to Nyetse
(Average walking time 5 hours)
A difficult stage for horses, which may have to be unloaded as the trail winds steadily up towards the Purfi La. From the pass there is a steep 500 metre descent down the juniper-covered hillside to the Jingchan Tokpo. Halfway down the hill there is a camping area and springline for parties coming in the opposite direction. The bridge over the Jingchan Tokpo marks the boundary between Zanskar and Ladakh. It also marks the start of a steady climb to the small shepherds' settlement of Nyetse. The settlement consists of a small system of shelters burrowed into the ground where, on more than one occasion, the author has been treated to ample supplies of goat curd, tsampa and salt tea.

The shepherds will point out the campsite, which is below their settlement at the end of the willow grove.

Stage 4: Nyetse to Hanuma La & Lingshet
(Average walking time 5-6 hours)
The trail from Nyetse gradually ascends the valley, which follows a tributary of the Jingchen Tokpo. River crossings can be a hazard here in July and August after heavy rains. The climb from camp to the pass (4800 metres) should take 3 to 4 hours. From the

pass there are clear views to the Singge La and the main Zanskar Range, while the sight of Lingshet Monastery can be appreciated in the valley below. The descent to Lingshet is quite steep by any standards, and it will take 2 or 3 hours to reach the village. There is a campsite complete with springline about 1 km before the monastery.

The monastery at Lingshet is set on the hillside with a commanding view over the valley. As at Karsha, the monastery was founded by the Delgupta order with its teachings brought from Tibet. There is, however, an older site further down the valley that may date back to the same time as Sani and Alchi, when Buddhism was first established in Ladakh.

There are normally 20 to 30 monks in attendance, while the monastery serves the outlying villages of Nirag, Yulchang and Skyumpata.

From Lingshet there is a trail across country to Rangdum. It crosses the Kesi La to the north of the Hanuma La, and then the Pingdon La, before passing the base of the Kanji La to Rangdum. In places the trail is hard for horses, and three days should be allowed to reach Rangdum.

Stage 5: Lingshet to Camp below the Singge La
(Average walking time 5-6 hours)
Although monks trek to Photaskar in one stage, this is not recommended for lesser trekking mortals. A midway camp is necessary, and the one below the Singge La, although not the most comfortable in Ladakh, is conveniently situated for an early climb to the pass the following day. The trail from Lingshet winds over the two minor passes, the Netuke La and Khyupa La, with plenty of ups and downs.

The settlement at Skyumpata lies between these passes. About 3 km before reaching camp, a trail diverges past the lone yak herder's camp at Yulchang, and continues down to the Zanskar River and the settlement at Nirag. From here on there is a rough trail, unsuitable for horses, that returns to Zangla.

At the base of the Singge La there is an

adequate, albeit rocky, campsite beside a springline, which eventually cascades down to the Zanskar River 1500 metres below.

Stage 6: Singge La to Photaskar
(Average walking time 5-6 hours)
The climb up the rather steep scree slope takes about 2 hours. Frozen waterfalls from the limestone cliffs form an impressive sight above the trail. The Singge La, literally the Lion Pass, is at 5100 metres and is the highest on the route to Lamayuru. Heavy snowfall on this pass precludes crossings in the winter and late spring. The route is not normally open to trekkers until the middle of June. From the pass you can appreciate the lie of the land across to the Sisir La beyond Photaskar.

From the pass, Photaskar can be reached in 3 or 4 hours with a choice of campsites in the vicinity of the village. The village supports two small monasteries that are serviced by monks from Lamayuru Monastery.

Stage 7: Photaskar to Sisir La & Honupatta
(Average walking time 6 hours)
From Photaskar it is a tiring haul to the Sisir La, although the views back to the Singge La and the main Zanskar Range are adequate compensation. From the pass other trek routes can be distinguished. The small pass at the head of the opposite valley marks the route to the Shilakung Valley, the Yogma La and Kanji village. The trail down to Honupatta can also be appreciated as it cuts across the barren ridge down to the valley floor. The time from the pass to the village is about 2 to 3 hours.

In late autumn, when the river levels are lower, it is also possible to descend directly from the village of Photaskar through the gorges of the Photang Valley direct to Pangge village. This shortcut bypasses the climb to the pass and Honupatta village, but must not be undertaken before first consulting the villagers at Photaskar.

Stage 8: Honupatta to Wanla
(Average walking time 5 hours)
From Honupatta the trail descends gradually for 3 or 4 km to the confluence of the Photang River. Here the trail enters a gorge where the trail construction has been considerably upgraded in the last few seasons. There are no river fords, except by bridge, before reaching the village of Pangge. Beyond here the trail gradually descends the valley, to the village and monastery at Wanla.

Stage 9: Wanla to Lamayuru
(Average walking time 3-4 hours)
From Wanla, follow the Shilakung Valley upstream for 2 km to the turnoff leading up the gorge to the Prinkiti La. The entrance is marked by prayer flags and small chortens. It is recommended to complete this gradual 2 hour ascent in the early morning while the narrow gully is still in the shade.

The descent to Lamayuru from the pass takes about 1 hour. The camping area is immediately below the village. There are a number of simple hotels in which to stay overnight while exploring the monastery.

Getting Away The following morning it is advisable to be at the roadhead by 7 or 8 am to meet the first of the truck and bus convoys going to Leh. If you are going to Kargil you can enjoy a sleep-in, as the vehicles do not normally arrive at Lamayuru until early afternoon.

Z2: PADUM TO LEH
This demanding trek crosses three passes at around 5000 metres. Between Zangla and the Markha Valley the trail winds through spectacular gorges and across windswept ridges, far beyond the limit of human habitation. It has become the natural reserve for various species of wild goat, sheep, bear and wolf. A naturalist could spend many weeks studying the wildlife; indeed, the area could appropriately be designated as a national park. A local guide is essential on this trek as the trails are by no means easy to follow. If you are doing the trek in July and August great care must be taken with the numerous river crossings.

Stage 1: Padum to Zangla
(Average walking time 7 hours)
This is quite a long but steady stage. With the construction of the road to Zangla much of this section is on the jeep trail, but there are compensations. From Padum the trail to Zangla crosses the main bridge over the Tsarap Chu and follows the well-graded track to Stongde, where there is an impressive monastery, affiliated with the orders at Karsha. The trail goes past the villages of Chilingkit and Chazar en route to Zangla.

The famous twig bridge of Zangla lies about 4 km above the town of Zangla. The original rope supports a span of over 40 metres across the swirling Zanskar River. Crossing it on windy days can be difficult, to say the least. Horses cannot take this route.

Ladakh and the Zanskar are famed for dogs, big and small, but nowhere are there as many per family as in Zangla. They include some corgi lookalikes that appear on the roof of one of the largest houses in the village. This is the house of the King of Zangla, a character well into his 70s who has been a delightful host to many a trekking party.

He is now a king in name only, but his ancestry can be traced to the time when the royal lineage was split. One side of the family ruled from Padum, and the other from Zangla. This continued until the invasion of Zorawar Singh. The King of Padum was killed during the forays of the Dogra army, while the King of Zangla was able to reach an accord, maintaining nominal rule over the nearby villages. The head monk at Spitok is related to this family, and also administers the Zangla Monastery which is situated on the cliff just beyond the village.

Stage 2: Zangla to Base of Charchar La
(Average walking time 3 hours)
Follow the trail beyond the chortens, up past the former fort high above the village. From here the trail follows the Zulung Valley upstream with many river crossings. There is a campsite after about 8 km that marks the junction of the main valley and a small valley coming from the north. There is a wooded grazing area with sufficient shade in which to spend a restful afternoon before crossing the pass on the following day.

Stage 3: Charchar La to Camp
(Average walking time 6 hours)
As with all trekking days in Ladakh, an early start is essential. The trail diverts from the main valley along a rough scree path for several km, then enters a large waterless side valley that marks the entrance to the pass. From here on, the trail ascends a series of glacial steps to the base of the pass. The final few hundred metres to the pass are hard going, but the views back to the main Himalaya are well worth the effort.

From the top of the pass (4950 metres) the trail drops steadily. If you are so inclined you can drop down to the valley floor and walk under one of the many permanent snow bridges. The time down to the first camp is about 2 hours.

Stage 4: Camp to Tilatsumdo
(Average walking time 6 hours)

Care must be taken when making the numerous river crossings on this stage. Six hours is the average autumn walking time to camp. In summer, when the water levels are higher, you may be forced to do this in two stages, walking only in the morning when the water levels are lower. There is no shortage of campsites, which are identified by thousands of sheep pellets. These are a legacy of the herds which the shepherds take this way in late autumn, en route to the Zanskar where they trade wool and meat for grain.

There are many wolf and bear droppings also, and it is not difficult to imagine that the stone caves on the hillsides would provide ideal shelter for brown bears throughout the summer.

One particular limestone cave, 5 km before camp, is of special importance because it contains a lingam, or phallic image, of Lord Shiva. Local tradition holds that barren women should touch this rock in order to establish their fertility.

Tilatsumdo is at the junction with the Khurna Valley, which comes in from the east. There is sufficient driftwood for a campfire, and to dry your boots for the following day.

Warning In some maps and guide books there is a trail marked down the Khurna River from Tilatsumdo to the Zanskar River and on to the confluence of the Markha Valley. This track is probably a late winter/early spring track that the locals follow after some sections of the ice on the Zanskar River begins to melt. There is no summer trail along the Zanskar River between the Khurna and Markha rivers.

Stage 5: Tilatsumdo to Camp at Base of Rubrang La
(Average walking time 5-6 hours)

The trail climbs alongside the Khurna River for 2 or 3 km, to the confluence with another side river coming from the north. Here the trail leaves the main valley, and climbs a series of rocky cliffs where the horses might need to be unloaded. The trail to the Rubrang La continues up the valley for a further 7 or 8 km, to a grassy camp at the base of the pass.

On these sections of the trek you may encounter the Champa nomads, who come from the eastern region of Ladakh. The Champa follow a nomadic lifestyle, very similar to that of the original inhabitants of Ladakh, living in tents made of yak hair and relying on the produce of their yaks, goats and sheep. To supplement their income they tend horses owned by the wealthier families from the Rupshu region. It is not uncommon to see them herding many hundreds of horses across these high grazing areas throughout the summer months.

Stage 6: Rubrang La to the Markha Valley
(Average walking time 6 hours)

The climb to the Rubrang La takes 2 hours. The trail ascends through a gully which opens out just below the pass. To the north are clear views of the Stok Range. There is a small springline 3 km below the pass, and a camping area that is convenient for parties coming from Markha, in the opposite direction. The trail descends into a series of impressive gorges that lead down to the confluence with the Markha River. Markha village is a further 2 km down the valley from there.

Stages 7 to 10: Markha to Leh

From Markha the trek to Leh can be completed in three or four stages. The options are either: continue down the Markha Valley, and then cross the Gandha La to the Indus Valley and Leh; or go up the valley to Nimaling, and cross the Kongmaru La to Hemis in the Indus Valley. Details of these stages are outlined in the Markha Valley trek in the Ladakh section (see pages 104 to 106).

Z3: PADUM TO DARCHA
via the Shingo La

This is the most popular trek in the Zanskar region. With the opening of the road to Padum the trail has become increasingly popular. This in turn has led to a number of teahouses and small hotels being constructed as far as the highest village at Kargyak. Thereafter, nothing is guaranteed. There may be a small teahouse at the higher camp before crossing the Shingo La, but it is not to be relied upon. The only way of checking is by word of mouth when you reach Padum, and by that time it could be too late to hire the tent and supplies you need. It is therefore recommended that you plan on being as self-sufficient as possible to ensure a successful trek. This trek is on the Zanskar/Lahaul map, page 137.

(The next section outlines a variation to this trek which crosses the less-trodden Phirtse La and leads to the Baralacha and Lahaul.)

Stage 1: Padum to Mune
(Average walking time 6 hours)
This stage is quite long if you're coming straight from Kargil. The first 10 km to Bardan are along a rather dusty jeep road. The Bardan Monastery is one of the most important in the valley. It is attached to the Drukpa order and has close ties with Hemis. The main assembly hall has been renovated in the last few years, while the huge prayer wheel is famed as one of the largest in Ladakh.

From Bardan, the trail continues alongside the Tsarap River for 4 or 5 km, then ascends to the plateau, with the village and monastery of Mune.

Stage 2: Mune to Purne
(Average walking time 8 hours)
This is another longish stage which could be shortened by visiting and camping at the village of Ichar en route. The main trail cuts across the Mune plateau, bypassing Reru village. However, for trekkers coming direct from Purne or Bardan, there are some excellent campsites on the outskirts of Reru.

After crossing the main tributary beyond Reru, there is a short climb then a gradual descent to the main valley. The trail reaches the river bank close to the village of Ichar, and from there it climbs and falls as it crosses a number of small side rivers. En route, the only village of note is that of Surle, which

has a limited camping area. From Surle, it is a further 3 or 4 km to the confluence of the Tsarap and Kargyak rivers, and the village of Purne.

Cross the bridge over the Kargyak River, and ascend the opposite bank to the main house, near which there are a number of campsites. Unfortunately, garbage has taken its toll. The camping areas are an example of the delicate Ladakhi environment not being able to accommodate the continual use and disposal of plastic bags, tin cans and the associated rubbish that careless groups leave behind.

Stage 3: Purne to Phugtal & Testa Village
(Average walking time, 4 hours return to Phugtal then 2 hours on to Testa)
From Purne the trail to Phugtal follows the right hand bank for several km before it reaches a makeshift bridge over the Tsarap River. From the bridge it is 2 or 3 km on to Phugtal Monastery.

The sight of the monastery clinging to the limestone cliffside never fails to impress. The main assembly hall is carved out of a huge cave, with the monks' quarters scattered down the hillside. Inside the monastery there is an inscription to the famous Hungarian explorer, Coso de Koros, one of the first Europeans to visit the Zanskar, and the first to translate the Buddhist texts from Ladakhi to English.

After returning to Purne there is ample time to continue 4 or 5 km on to the village of Testa. The trail remains in the gorge for several km before ascending to a large fertile plateau that supports a number of prosperous whitewashed villages. Testa is the first village you come to, with a delightful campsite off the main trail, close to the village. There is a camping fee of Rs 10 per tent.

Stage 4: Testa to Kargyak
(Average walking time 7 hours)
From Testa the trail is marked by a series of well-maintained chortens to the village of Karu. The trail is lined by substantial stone walls which protect the barley fields from

straying pack animals. This is a definite problem during the season, and can cause disputes between the villagers and the horse handlers of trekking parties. After Karu the trail descends back to the river bank, then crosses a bridge to the village of Tanze on the far bank. It is a further 4 to 5 km to the village of Kargyak, the highest in the valley. There is no shortage of campsites, and for those without a tent there are a number of houses in the village which will provide shelter and food for the night.

If time is not at a premium, an extra day can be spent wandering the valley opposite the village. On the map the valley extends into the main Himalaya, and there are a number of smaller settlements that make this an interesting day's option.

Stage 5: Kargyak to Base of Shingo La
(Average walking time 6-7 hours)
Remain on the same side of the valley as you continue up towards the impressive rock monolith known as Gumburanjan. After the rock face there are plenty of places to ford the upper reaches of the Kargyak River, then the trail heads across to the yak grazing pastures and shepherds' encampments that mark the route to the Shingo La.

There are a number of campsites to choose from, the most convenient being those on the highest pastures closest to the pass. For those without a tent, there are a number of small stone encampments that will shield you from the worst of the elements. Also enquire in Kargyak village as to whether there are other facilities, such as 'overnight' tea-houses.

Stage 6: Shingo La to Camp
(Average walking time 6-7 hours)
The climb to the pass is not hard by Himalayan standards, and can be completed in a couple of hours. This climb may take longer early in the season when the approach is under snow. The route follows the right hand side of the valley across a couple of side streams before ascending the main snow field. The walking conditions are generally firm, and the trail across the scree and snow

is well defined. A series of prayer flags marks the summit of the pass at 5090 metres. The pass is set beneath an impressive backdrop of 6000-metre snow-capped peaks that define both the main Himalaya and the Baralacha Range.

The descent should not present any real difficulties. The pass is well trodden, and the trail down the small glacier avoids the obvious crevassed areas. Once off the glacier and on to the right hand side of the valley, the trail descends past a series of shepherd huts to one of the many level, grassy campsites which are close to a small stream.

Stage 7: Camp to Darcha
(Average walking time 6-7 hours)
The descent is quite gradual until the last section where the trail meets the main valley floor. Until a few seasons ago it was essential to time your crossing of the river here with care. Nowadays, with the existence of a pulley system, and the planned construction of a bridge, there is no problem about getting your boots wet. Once across to the opposite bank, the trail crosses a number of side streams and boulder fields before recrossing the river over a permanent stone bridge. From there it is a few km down the valley to Darcha, and the confluence with the Bhaga Valley.

Getting Away At Darcha there are a number of tea stalls, and an adequate campsite. There is also a police checkpost where you will have to show your passport. The buses to Manali depart in the early morning, although it is recommended that you visit the monastery at Keylong before continuing on to the Kulu Valley.

Z4: PADUM TO MANALI
via the Phirtse La & Baralacha Pass
This trek is an ideal alternative to crossing the Shingo La. The route is the same as for the previous trek from Padum until the village of Tanze, just below Kargyak. Here the trails diverge, with the trail to the Phirtse La heading up a side gorge out of the

Kargyak Valley. An intermediary camp is necessary before crossing the pass.

Stages 1-3: Padum to Testa Village

As per Stages 1 to 3 of the previous trek, Z3. (see pages 117 and 118)

Stage 4: Testa to Tanze

As for Stage 4 of the previous trek, but stop near Tanze for the night.

Stage 5: Tanze to Base of Phirtse La
(Average walking time 7 hours)

Shortly after Tanze the trail to the Phirtse La heads up a side gorge that ascends steeply out of the Kargyak Valley. The climb is steep for nearly 500 metres until it opens out at the head of the gorge. A short walk back across the plateau will provide a bird's eye view down the Tsarap Valley to Purne. This is a particularly memorable sight if trekking from Lahaul. There is a good campsite a few km up the valley – in fact the best between Tanze and the pass. However, should time be at a premium, continue on up valley towards the base of the pass where there are a few restricted campsites.

Stage 6: Phirtse La to Camp
(Average walking time 7 hours)

The climb to the Phirtse La is short and steep, with the final ascent up a scree slope to the well-defined pass at 5450 metres. From the pass there are views across to the main Himalaya, while the climb up the small ridge to the north side of the pass will afford panoramic views across the Zanskar Range.

The descent from the pass crosses a series of scree slopes, and is steep in places down to Chunik Marpo. This is an ideal camp if you're coming from the opposite direction. The area is grazed by yak herders from the village of Kargyak during the summer months. It is the only settlement on this route between Tanze and Darcha. From the herders' camp, the trail follows a series of ridges before dropping into a narrow gorge to the main Lingti Valley. Continue down the valley to the first main tributary of the Lingti River, and camp for the night.

Stage 7: Camp to Kilang Sarai
(Average walking time 6-7 hours)

Cross the main tributary early in the morning. The high water level during the summer could present difficulties, but from September onwards this and the other side rivers are easier to negotiate. The trail cuts across juniper slopes and passes dilapidated mani walls before reaching the confluence of the Tsarap and Lingti valleys. The route then heads up the valley across extensive pastures that form the upper grazing limits of the Gaddi shepherds from Himachal Pradesh. A few km on, the military road from Leh crosses the valley at a point below the Kilang Sarai, where there is an adequate campsite. There is an army camp nearby, but the soldiers are friendly and glad to have a diversion from their duties.

Stage 8: Kilang Sarai to Baralacha
(Average walking time 3 hours)

From the camp, the trail follows a jeep track to the Baralacha. The steady climb is rewarded by impressive views of the peaks, many of which are over 6000 metres. The switchbacks on the road can also provide shortcuts until you reach the pass. The Baralacha is one of the most famous passes in the Himalaya. It is a double pass, at the convergence of the Tsarap Valley in the north, the Chandra Valley to the south, and the Bhaga Valley to the west. There is no shortage of campsites on the pass, with wildflowers and an impressive mountain backdrop.

Getting Away From the pass it is a double stage down the Bhaga Valley to Darcha. If the thought of trekking the road does not appeal, it should be easy to hitch a ride by truck to Darcha and the Kulu Valley.

An alternative is to continue trekking down the Chandra Valley to the lake at Chandratal. This creates two or three extra stages before joining the road coming over the Kunzun La from Spiti to Lahaul. This trek, Z7, is outlined in the Lahaul section (see page 139).

Himachal Pradesh

Himachal Pradesh is one of the youngest states in India. It comprises many of the hill kingdoms which had maintained a long history of independence until the 19th century. These included Kulu, Simla, Lahaul, Chamba and Kangra. Following the Treaty of Amritsar in 1846, the kingdoms were formally annexed to British India, and administered as part of the Punjab. It was a situation that continued after independence in 1947, until the Punjab was partitioned into the states of Punjab, Haryana and Himachal Pradesh in 1966. Himachal Pradesh was given formal recognition within the Indian Union in 1971.

Geographically, Himachal Pradesh extends from the Siwalik foothills across the intermediary ranges of the Dhaula Dhar and Pir Panjal, to the high peaks of the main Himalaya. It is drained by the headwaters of the Chandra, Ravi, and Beas rivers, which form a series of beautiful valleys that are seldom surpassed elsewhere in the Himalaya.

Himachal Pradesh has many attractions, including Simla, once the summer capital of British India and still one of India's most important hill stations. The state also contains the alpine Kulu Valley, with its flowered meadows, orchards and forests; Dharamsala, the home in exile for the Dalai Lama; and the less known yet equally attractive towns of Chamba and Dalhousie, which are ideal setting-off points for treks. Other attractions are Lahaul and Spiti, with a culture partly Buddhist and partly Hindu, which have historically close ties with both Ladakh and Tibet.

While Himachal Pradesh does not have the lakes and the houseboats of the Kashmir Valley, or the advantage of being beyond the monsoon region, the mountain trails are just as magnificent, and have the added bonus of being relatively under-trekked. With such attractions there are many outstanding trekking possibilities.

The treks out of the Kulu Valley are Himachal Pradesh's answer to Phalgam and the Lidder Valley. Treks out of Manali can be easily organised. It is a short drive to the roadhead to undertake treks to Beas Kund, the Malana Valley, the base of Deo Tibba, and over the Hampta Pass to Lahaul.

Lahaul, on the far side of the Pir Panjal, is cut off from the Kulu Valley for several months of the year. It is also beyond the influence of the Indian monsoon, allowing treks to continue through July and August when the rest of Himachal Pradesh is subject to the rains. One delightful trek is to the glacial lake at Chandratal and then on to the Baralacha. For those intent on trekking to the Zanskar, the region of Lahaul is a popular starting point.

To the west of the Kulu Valley, the regions of Chamba and Kangra both provide ideal alternatives. The historical town of Kangra has increased in popularity due to its proximity to the hill station of Dharamsala, the home of the Dalai Lama. From here, treks can be made over the snow-capped Dhaula Dhar to the Ravi Valley and Chamba, while from Chamba there are many possibilities to continue over the Pir Panjal passes to the Chandra Valley and Lahaul. As with the Kulu Valley, these trails come under the influence of the monsoon, making September and October ideal months to trek before the onset of the winter snows.

Many interesting day walks can be made out of Simla, while treks can be undertaken from the Sutlej Valley over to Kulu during the late spring and autumn, when other passes in Himachal Pradesh are under snow.

SIMLA

In the days before independence, Simla was the summer capital of India. Its temperate climate and alpine setting made it an ideal attraction for the British administration to escape the sultry heat of Calcutta or Delhi.

Simla was first surveyed in 1817 by the

Gerald brothers, two Scottish military officers on a tour of duty out of Calcutta. Immediately prior to this, Simla and the nearby hill states had been overrun by the Gurkhas. The local rajahs requested assistance from the British, which led to the Gurkha wars of 1814-15. The Simla hill states were annexed by the British, although Simla was later purchased from the local rajahs by separate agreement.

The first permanent house was built in 1822, and from that time on the town expanded rapidly as the British took advantage of the opportunity to escape the heat of the plains. They also lost little time in exploring the mountain trails across the Punjab Himalaya. Guidebooks written at the turn of the century detail the various trekking stages out of Simla to Kulu, Dharamsala and Leh, and it was not considered out of the ordinary to walk for months at a time, either on government service or for pleasure.

Following independence in 1947, Simla became the headquarters of the Punjab administration. In 1966 the Punjab was divided into the states of Punjab and Haryana, and Simla became the capital of the newly formed state of Himachal Pradesh.

Places to Stay

There is no shortage of accommodation in Simla; there are now over 100 hotels, mostly in the vicinity of the Mall and main bazaar. The Himachal Pradesh tourist offices, in the Mall and at the bus station, can assist you in finding a place during the peak domestic tourist seasons, from April to June and September/October.

Simla's two most famous hotels are *Cecils* and the *Grand*, both operated by the Oberoi chain. Other upmarket hotels include the *Woodville Palace*, about 1 km beyond the Mall. The Himachal Pradesh government *Holiday Home* is pushed hard by the government tourist office, but it lacks the charm and character of the Woodville Palace.

For peace and quiet, it is best to avoid the busy Mall and bazaar areas. If you are staying for more than a few days it would be

ideal to find a timber house or cottage similar to those in Manali. This, however, is easier said than done, as many concrete flats occupy Simla's finest vantage points, and have become summer homes for rich Indian tourists.

Getting There & Away

To get to Simla by rail involves a change from the broad gauge at Kalka, a town just north of Chandigarh. The narrow gauge trip to Simla takes nearly 6 hours. Add on 2 or more hours while changing trains at Kalka, plus the train trip from Delhi to Kalka, and you will find it much faster to take the bus. The train trip, however, is fun! The fare from Delhi to Simla is Rs 383 air-con class, Rs 175 1st class, and Rs 62 2nd class.

The deluxe bus from Delhi to Simla takes 8 to 10 hours and costs between Rs 100 and Rs 150. There are also deluxe and local bus services between Chandigarh and Simla. From Simla there are also regular buses to Manali (via Mandi) daily throughout the season. If you are continuing to Dharamsala, you must change local buses at Mandi. For Kashmir, it is faster to return to Chandigarh and get the night train to Jammu.

Vayudoot now have daily flights from Delhi to Simla. The cost is US$53, but they are heavily booked in the season. There is also a service from Kulu to Simla at US$16 − not that much more than the bus, but again, the flights are heavily booked.

Treks

There are many day walks in and around Simla. The Simla hills comprise Jakhu Hill, to the immediate west of the Mall, and Summer Hill and Prospect Hill to the east, where the ridge splits into two spurs. Following the bridle trails is no problem.

To climb Jakhu Hill, follow the trail behind the cathedral, up to the Jakhu temple. Dedicated to the monkey god Hanuman, the temple is at an altitude of 2455 metres, near the highest point of the Simla ridge. This spot is renowned for its fine views, especially at sunrise. The temple is a 45 minute walk from the Mall.

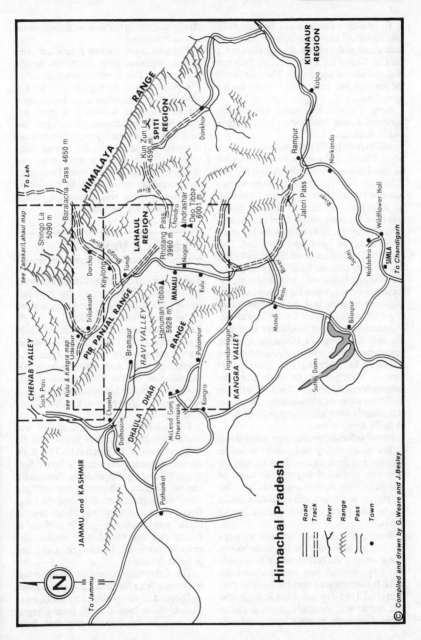

Himachal Pradesh

Road
Track
River
Range
Pass
Town

© Compiled and drawn by G. Weare and J. Besley

The walks to Prospect and Summer Hills take about half a day, and there are fine views back down to the plains. If you have time, a visit to Chadwick Falls, beyond Summer Hill, can also be undertaken. The falls are 67 metres high and are at their best during the monsoon.

Beyond Simla, day walks can also be undertaken from Wildflower Hall, Naldehra and Narkanda.

Wildflower Hall (2593 metres) is 13 km beyond Simla, and was the former residence of the Indian commander-in-chief, Lord Kitchener. The present huge mansion surrounded by pines is not the original one built for Kitchener. Naldehra, 23 km from Simla, was Lord Curzon's escape from the dispatch boxes of Simla. Narkanda is 64 km from Simla along the Tibet-Hindustan road. This is the road you take to reach the Sutlej Valley, and the treks on to the Kulu Valley. Spending a few days at Narkanda is recommended; the views are superb, while for trekkers, a climb to the nearby Hattu peak is a convenient way to get fit and acclimatise for the days ahead.

Accommodation at *Wildflower Hall* is at the hall itself, now a Himachal Pradesh government hotel, while both Narkanda and Naldehra have comfortable *Tourist Rest Houses*. Bookings can be made from the tourist offices in Delhi or Simla. Wildflower Hall costs about Rs 150 while the rest houses at Narkanda and Naldehra range from Rs 50 to Rs 70 for room only.

From Narkanda, the highway winds down to the Sutlej Valley and continues to the Kinnaur and Spiti regions. Both regions are presently restricted beyond the town of Rampur. However, there are plans to open up the regions to tourism, and up-to-date details can be confirmed with the tourist office in Simla.

Bearing this in mind, there are two treks that can be undertaken to the Kulu Valley. One route over the Jalori Pass has been made into a fair weather jeep and minibus road, while the second trail over the Bashleo Pass is an ideal 4 to 5 day trek out of Rampur. The trek has an additional advantage; it can be undertaken both in early spring (March/April), and also in late autumn through to the end of November.

The trail to the Bashleo Pass is not steep by Himalayan standards, and the pass height, 3600 metres, should not present difficulties. The ridge divides the regions of inner and outer Saraj, a subdivision of the Kulu administration. The walking stages are conveniently set between the villages, and the forest rest houses ensure that a tent is not essential. The pass is normally crossed on the third day, from where it is a further two stages to the Banjar-Largi road. From there you can either return to Simla by minibus, or continue to Largi, where there are regular buses to Kulu and Manali.

The Kulu Valley

The original name for the Kulu Valley was Kulantapith – 'the end of the habitable world'. It is a narrow alpine valley drained by the Beas River, and enclosed by the Pir Panjal to the north, the Barabhangal Range to the west, and the Parvati Range to the east. Within the confines of these ranges each mountain, stream and river confluence is sanctified to honour the numerous Hindu gods. It is therefore hardly surprising that the Kulu Valley is often referred to as the 'Valley of the Gods'.

For centuries, the Kulu Kingdom was restricted to the upper Beas Valley, with the original capital at Jagatsukh. The Kulu rajah's influence extended between Sultanpur (Kulu) and the Rhotang Pass, and it was not until the 15th century that the Kulu boundaries extended south beyond the Largi Gorge to Mandi. During the 17th century, the capital was transferred again from Nagar to Kulu, and the kingdom's boundaries extended north to Lahaul and Spiti, and east as far as the Sutlej.

The Kulu rajahs controlled the important trade route from the Indian plains to Ladakh and beyond. It was contested by both Sansar Chand, the influential rajah from Kangra, and later by the Sikhs during their brief period of power. After 1847, Kulu and the other hill states bordering the Punjab came under the British administration with its headquarters at Dharamsala.

The British appointed a district officer, and this in turn attracted a number of British families from Simla and beyond to settle in the valley. They followed the trails over the Jalori Pass or, if coming direct from the plains, via Kangra and the Dulchi Pass to the south-west of the Kulu Valley. The first road into the valley, up the Largi Gorge, was not completed until 1927. For many of the British settlers, this was the beginning of the end to the tranquil life in the valley, and many of the established families were on their way home before 1947.

The Kulu Valley today still retains much of its charm and beauty, and is a very welcome haven after that long bus ride from Delhi. The valley's size enhances its popularity; the bazaars at Kulu and Manali can be easily explored on foot, while the outlying villages of Jagatsukh, Nagar, and the nearby Parvatti Valley can be reached in an hour or two from Kulu or Manali.

Getting Ready

Most provisions for a trek can be bought in Kulu or Manali, and you should stock up on supplies if you are going on to Lahaul and the Zanskar.

Horses are in great demand in the region, and a local contact is necessary, particularly if you want to trek on to the Zanskar. The early winter snows have increased the reluctance to take horses across the Shingo La after the middle of September, so again plans must be made accordingly. Closer to the Kulu Valley, horses can still be at premium during the apple harvest period in September, and during the potato harvest that occurs during the following month in Lahaul. Horses will therefore cost something in the region of Rs 100 per horse per day, depending on where you are going.

Porters are an alternative, but they also can be hard to find. If trekking to the Malana Valley, or other districts where horses cannot go, it is advisable to contact one of the local

agencies in Manali who should be able to help. Allow Rs 100 per porter per day to cover costs, and food and clothing allowances. Guides and cooks can also be hired from the local agencies. The integrity of the staff is usually high, and there is little need to worry about whether you will be left alone in the back of beyond. In fact all the staff I have hired in Manali have been a delight to trek with.

Trekking Organisations

The number of trekking organisations in the Kulu Valley has increased over the last few seasons. It is likely that there will be a further increase with the opening of the Leh-Manali road, and if the political problems in Kashmir continue.

The Mountaineering Institute in Manali is a helpful intermediary, as is the tourist department in the main bazaar, which holds a list of all recognised agents. Iqbal Sharma and his agency can be recommended, as can Paddy's Treks, run by another colourful local character, Paddy Singh. Other local agencies such as International Trekkers have also been recommended. To locate any of these you have to ask further at the main bazaar, as office locations seem to change with the seasons!

Places to Stay

The Himachal Pradesh government has built a number of hotels in the last decade in both Kulu and Manali. Besides these, the normal retreat is to one of the many guesthouses, complete with verandah and open fireplace, and often surrounded by an orchard. It is a credit to the local authorities that they have attempted to limit the construction of unsightly buildings in the valley. In the vicinity of the main bazaar, cheaper basic accommodation is available for a few rupees a night.

In Kulu and Manali the government tourist offices seem, like the one in Simla, to strongly recommend the government-run hotels to the exclusion of all others. However there are many 'card wallahs' in Manali, both outside the tourist office and at the bus stand, to help expand the selection. Neither Kulu or Manali are large places, and a short walk around town should turn up something to your taste and pocket.

Rooms are more expensive from April to mid-June, and from September to mid-October, particularly during the Dussehra Festival time. Upmarket hotels and guesthouses are about Rs 400 per double for full board, but can be bargained down. In the middle range they are about Rs 150 per double, room only. There is a large choice of budget hotels from Rs 25 per room upwards. *Government Rest Houses* in outlying districts range from Rs 20 to Rs 80 for a room only. As in Srinagar and Leh, many hotels are family-run and it is difficult to recommend a specific place. They all have their attractions, and are ideal for a rest before undertaking a trek.

Getting There

There are daily bus services – deluxe, superdeluxe, and superdeluxe with video – from Delhi to Manali or Kulu. The service normally takes 18 hours (about the length of four to five Hindi movies) and costs in the vicinity of Rs 180 to Rs 250 per seat, depending on the facilities and the season.

The journey from Kashmir to Manali can be completed in two long days. The first day is by bus from Srinagar to Pathankot, and the second by bus that takes a further 15 hours to Manali.

From Dharamsala, there are regular bus services to Mandi, and from there on to Kulu and Manali. There is a nonstop bus service from Simla to Manali taking the road via Mandi, while the road from Simla to the Kulu Valley via the Jalori Pass can be undertaken by jeep or minibus.

From Kulu and Manali there are regular local bus services to the various trekking-off points. The bus fare is Rs 3 from Manali to Nagar, and Rs 2 from Manali to Jagatsukh. Taxis are a convenient alternative, particularly if you are sharing costs, and this can also considerably cut travelling time. The taxi fare is about Rs 100 one way to Nagar, and about Rs 70 to Jagatsukh. The fare from

Manali to the airport at Bhuntar, below Kulu, is set by the local authorities, and is now in the vicinity of Rs 200.

Vayudoot have a regular flight between Delhi and Kulu. The flights operate daily and cost US$67 one way. Book well in advance during the peak season. Flights are cancelled occasionally during the monsoon. A further flight operates to Simla. The cost is US$16, and again, the flights are heavily booked during the season.

Treks

The treks out of the Kulu Valley are a superb introduction to trekking in India. To spend a month based at one of the many lodges in Manali, trekking the surrounding valleys and passes, would be an ideal holiday. These treks are not too arduous and are comparatively easy to organise, while the rewards are many for anyone attracted to unspoilt alpine scenery beneath a backdrop of many impressive peaks.

Four treks are outlined in this section.

M1: From Manali to Beas Kund
M2: From Jagatsukh to Chandertal and Deo Tibba.
M3: From Nagar to Malana and the Parvati Valley.
M4: From Manali to Hampta Pass and Lahaul.

Although it is possible to trek from May onwards, heavy snow conditions are likely well into June and the onset of the monsoon. Therefore, you must be well-prepared to trek in the pre-monsoon season, particularly if you intend to go over some of the higher passes to Lahaul or the Barabanghal. However, the road over the Rhotang Pass, from the upper Beas Valley to Lahaul, is normally open to vehicles by mid-June.

If you have no alternative but to visit Kulu in July and August, then you will just have to put up with the rain. It doesn't rain all day during the monsoon, and in the late afternoon the clouds often clear, revealing dramatic views of the surrounding peaks. You will also be rewarded with an array of wildflowers on the alpine pastures above the treeline.

The post-monsoon period, from early September through to mid-October, is the most reliable season for trekking. Pass crossings can be made in relative comfort, and extended treks can be completed well before the onset of the winter snows. Late season treks can also be undertaken over the Dulchi Pass through to December, providing one of the few trekking opportunities in Himachal Pradesh at this time of year.

Most of the treks commence in the Kulu Valley at an elevation of no more than 2000 metres. It is therefore quite a climb up to some of the passes, and days should be reserved to adjust and acclimatise before going higher. You would certainly be going too high too quickly if you were to cross the Hampta Pass (4330 metres) after just a few days' trekking.

Rivers and streams can be a hazard in the early part of the season, from mid-June to late June, during the main snow melt. In the absence of snow bridges or newly constructed shepherd bridges, care must be taken with all crossings, and many must be negotiated by mid-morning.

Another local hazard is the bears, particularly the black bears that settle in the forest regions just above the cornfields throughout the season. Take extra care on the trails, especially if you are moving around at night. If in doubt, make as much noise as possible, and the bear should move off the trail.

M1: MANALI TO BEAS KUND

This is the most popular trek in the Kulu Valley. The stages outlined to Beas Kund are followed regularly by local trekking parties and the Mountaineering Institute, so you will never be in need of company. An extra day should be reserved for Beas Kund, with a climb to the Tentu La being one very attractive option.

Stage 1: Manali to Palachan & Dhundi
(Average walking time 3-4 hours)
There are regular buses from Manali to Palachan on the main road, from where there is a jeep road that goes to within a few km of Dhundi. This track up the Solang Valley will eventually be upgraded, as the plans to construct the tunnel under the Pir Panjal get underway. While this will undoubtedly ruin the tranquillity of the valley, the trek on to Beas Kund will still remain a worthwhile option.

A flash flood in the summer of 1988 brought a huge boulder slide down the valley, and the trail just below Dhundi still leaves much to be desired. Dhundi is situated at the confluence of the Solang Nullah and the side valley, the Seri Nullah that extends north to the foot of the Pir Panjal.

Stage 2: Dhundi to Beas Kund
(Average walking time 5-6 hours)
From Dhundi, the trail ascends through bush and low vegetation for 4 or 5 km to a base where the local Mountaineering Institute groups camp during the season. From here the climb becomes progressively steeper, over a series of moraine ridges. The trail is often ill-defined, and a guide is necessary to point out the occasional cairns that mark the way. Consult the Gaddi shepherds if in doubt.

The camp at Beas Kund is in a perfect alpine setting, complete with splendid views and enough options for side trips to make a few days of camping here worthwhile. The climb to the Tentu La, at the head of the valley, is particularly attractive and it is possible to get there and back to camp in one day. The ascent is quite steep, until you reach the small glacier which is not heavily crevassed.

The stage from Dhundi to Beas Kund can also be completed as a day trip – allow about 8 or 9 hours for the round trip.

Stage 3: Beas Kund to Palachan & Manali
(Average walking time 7-8 hours)
The return trek to Palachan and Manali can be completed in one day.

Getting There There are regular bus services from Palachan to Manali, although the

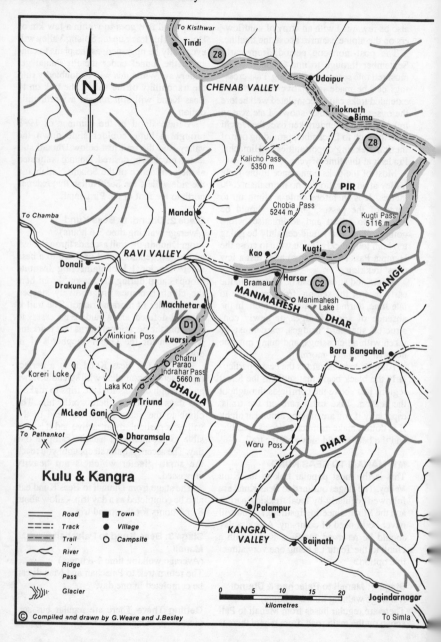

To Kisthwar

Tindi

Z8

CHENAB VALLEY

Udaipur

Triloknath

Bima

Z8

Kalicho Pass
5350 m

PIR

Chobia Pass
5244 m

Kugti Pass
5116 m

To Chamba

Manda

Kao

Kugti

C1

RAVI VALLEY

Harsar

Donali

Bramaur

C2

RANGE

Drakund

MANIMAHESH

Manimahesh
Lake

Machhetar

DHAR

D1

Minkiani Pass

Kuarsi

Bara Bangahal

Kareri Lake

Chatru
Parao
Indrahar Pass
5660 m

Laka Kot

DHAULA

Triund

McLeod Ganj

Dharamsala

Waru Pass

DHAR

To Pathankot

To Chamba

Palampur

Kulu & Kangra

KANGRA
VALLEY

Baijnath

Road	Town
Track	Village
Trail	Campsite
River	
Ridge	
Pass	
Glacier	

Jogindarnagar

0   5   10   15   20
kilometres

© *Compiled and drawn by G.Weare and J.Besley*

To Simla

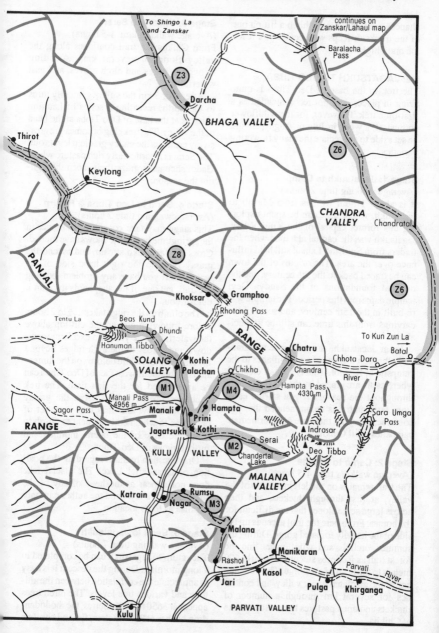

chances are that you will hitch a lift on one of the trucks or jeeps well before you reach the main highway.

M2: JAGATSUKH TO DEO TIBBA

The trek to the base of Deo Tibba is quite tiring in places, and not recommended as a first-time trek. However, for the wildflower enthusiast, a week in July or August should be set aside to appreciate the many flowering varieties.

Stage 1: Jagatsukh to Camp
(Average walking time 2 hours)

It is about 1 hour by bus from Manali to Jagatsukh, where time can be spent exploring this former capital of the Kulu Valley. Jagatsukh was the capital at a time when the traders from Spiti and Lahaul still held influence over the area. The origins of the town can be traced back to the 9th century, and the original foundations of the Sandya Devi temple date from this period. The temple was re-built in the 15th century, and some of the carvings from this time can still be appreciated.

From Jagatsukh, the trail ascends gradually through a series of small villages to the campsite at Khanol. This is a small clearing where cattle are grazed by the local villagers throughout the season. If you started early from Jagatsukh it is recommended that you continue, although there are no intermediate campsites until Chikha.

Stage 2: Camp to Chikha
(Average walking time 4-5 hours)

The trail remains on the left hand side of the valley, at first through thickets, and then across large scree slopes that are difficult for the horses. From here the trail ascends up the side of the heavily forested gorge. During the summer, orchids and wildflowers line the forest trail as it climbs steeply for nearly 600 metres to the head of the gorge. The trail then enters the glaciated upper valley, and continues for several km through a number of thickets and open pastures to the Gujar camp at Chikha.

Stage 3: Chikha to Serai
(Average walking time 4-5 hours)

From Chikha the trail continues along the valley floor for several km, ascending through pastures and birch groves, and past waterfalls.

After 4 or 5 km the valley gradually turns to the north, revealing a series of hanging glaciers at the base of Deo Tibba at the head of the valley. The trekking becomes progressively easier as the valley gradient levels out. The Serai is a particularly rich pasture where Gaddi shepherds graze their sheep throughout the season.

Stage 4: Serai to Deo Tibba & Return
(Average walking time 7 hours)

This stage may take considerably longer in the springtime before the snows have melted. Cross the Jagatsukh stream, and ascend the grassy ridge to the right hand side of the waterfall. If you have any problem locating the trail, get one of the shepherds to point it out for you.

The climb up the ridge takes 1½ to 2 hours before following around the clifftop above the waterfall. Here you gain excellent views down and across to the high ridges beyond the Kulu Valley, while before you the dimensions of the south-west face of Deo Tibba can be appreciated for the first time. The trek continues up the valley across the grassy slopes for a few km. It is then a matter of choice as to which embankment to climb to reach the edge of the lateral moraine and further views of Deo Tibba.

One question remains regarding the position of Chandertal Lake. The glacial lake does not appear at the head of any of the smaller side valleys, and the author can only surmise as to its location.

Stage 5: Serai to Jagatsukh
(Average walking time 7 hours)

The return to Jagatsukh can be completed in a long morning. During the descent it is easy to appreciate the correlation between the altitude and various tree levels. The birch trees appear at 3650 to 3700 metres, the rhododendron bushes at 3600 metres, firs and conifers at 3500 metres and, way down the valley, hollybush at 2150 metres.

Getting Away There is a regular local bus service from the market at Jagatsukh, so you should be able to return to Manali the same day.

M3: NAGAR TO MALANA & PARVATI VALLEY

This trek includes a visit to Malana village, an isolated community that has its own language, customs and laws, governed by a system of village elders. The village beliefs are determined by the God Jumla, said to be pre-Aryan and independent of the Hindu gods that rule the Kulu Valley. It is believed that the existence of this village is recorded in the Moghul annals, and until a generation ago it closely guarded its position against any intrusion from the outside world.

However, anyone who goes there looking for some long-lost idyllic village community will be disappointed. Malana's isolation has tended to create a degree of suspicion as far as outsiders are concerned. The village has an eerie atmosphere, devoid of the charm and friendliness of most mountain villages in the Kulu Valley.

Stage 1: Manali to Nagar & Camp

(Average walking time 2-3 hours)
This trek commences from the village of Nagar, which is about 2 hours by bus from Manali. The Nagar castle is steeped in legend and commands an imposing position looking across the Kulu Valley. Part of the castle has been converted into a comfortable *tourist bungalow*, and a day or two can be peacefully spent here. One of the main attractions is the Roerich Gallery, where samples of the work of the famous painter and philosopher Nicholas Roerich are displayed. His reputation as one of the avant-garde post-1917 Russian painters was enhanced during his stay in Kulu during the 1930s, when he made Nagar his home.

The location of the camp on this first stage depends on what time you set off from Nagar. The trail goes past Roerich's cottage

and along a main bridle trail for 1 km, then branches uphill to the village of Rumsu and the climb continues through forest. It's very pleasant and shady, but there are many side tracks, and it essential that you regularly check your bearings. After about 2 hours, there is an open meadow in which to camp, but there may be a shortage of water.

Stage 2: Camp to Below Chanderkani Pass

(Average walking time 5 hours)
The trail leading to the pass is frequently confused with other grazing trails, so a local guide is a worthwhile companion. The ascent is initially through forest, and later through huge rhododendron bushes, as you climb higher towards the treeline. Throughout the forest there are a number of meadows where you can rest and admire the views across the Kulu Valley. As the trail gradually ascends beyond the birch trees, the lie of the land towards the Chanderkani Pass can be appreciated. Several km below the pass there are a number of campsites to choose from, all of which afford even more breathtaking views – from the snow-capped Dhaula Dhar to the south, to Hanuman Tibba at the head of the Solang Valley and the Ghalpo peaks in Lahaul.

Stage 3: Across the Chanderkani Pass to Malana Village

(Average walking time 6-7 hours)
From the high camp the trail gradually ascends across the pastures before a short, steep, climb to the pass. This climb is harder at the beginning and the end of the season, when the pass and the upper meadows are under snow.

From the pass, a series of cairns marks the route along the ridge, with unsurpassed views of the upper Malana Valley and the 6000 metre peaks in the upper Tosh Valley, including White Sail. After completing the traverse, the trail heads above a rocky gully that descends steeply to Malana Village. The walk down to the village takes a couple of hours.

An alternative is to continue along the

upper valley, across a series of ridges that lead to the summer grazing pastures of the Gaddi. The trail, rocky in places, continues through birch groves then descends through thicker forest to the alpine meadows below. It has the added attraction of crossing a number of clearings that are frequented by the brown bears that roam these upper slopes. Our small party came face to face with a bear in mid-October, and it was only after a time that it retreated up the hillside. This incident ensured that the porters didn't stay too far behind for the rest of the day.

After camping in the alpine meadows, there is an option to continue up the valley and spend a few days camping in the vicinity of the Malana Glacier, before returning down to Malana village. This is highly rewarding if you have sufficient time and supplies.

Malana is not the most inviting village in the Himalaya, although the rules governing a visit are not as rigidly enforced as they were a decade ago. You are no longer required to take off your leather boots to walk through the village, but you must stick to the main trail and you must not touch the children, the walls or the Jumla temple. Failure to observe these rules can lead to a fine. Apparently the God Jumla is fond of money, although the purchase of a goat is the normal means of penance. You can take photographs and you can stay in the village dispensary, although there is a good campsite beyond the main settlement, about 100 metres from the second spring. The village itself comprises 50 or 60 houses, and is fairly self-sufficient, although there are plans to connect the village to the electricity grid. Until a few generations ago, the people intermarried only among their own community. Today the position has changed, and although the men tend to stay in Malana, the women sometimes marry into families in the Parvati Valley, or in Rumsu or Nagar.

Stage 4: Malana to Parvati Valley
(Average walking time 4-5 hours)
From Malana it is a steep descent for 800 metres to the valley floor. This trail is unsuitable for horses. It is then a fairly level walk through beautiful gorges, with the trail frequently crossing the river by either wooden or snow bridges. The first main village is at Rashol where the Malana River joins the Parvati River, and from here there is a steady

climb for the last few km to the road at Jari. From here there are frequent buses back to Kulu and Manali.

M4: MANALI TO HAMPTA PASS & LAHAUL
Although this trek is outlined in three stages, it is advisable to spend more time acclimatising before crossing the Hampta Pass. The trek affords some inspiring views down the Kulu Valley, and after crossing Hampta Pass there are options for continuing on an interesting circuit of Lahaul via Chandratal and the Baralacha. (Refer to the Lahaul section, page 138, for details.)

Stage 1: Manali to Sethen Village & Camp
(Average walking time 4-5 hours)
From Manali it is a short walk or drive to Prini village. From there, follow the main trail that leads across the ridges to Hampta village. In the village there is a tea stall selling biscuits and basics, good for a rest stop before continuing the climb through the well-defined forest trail to Sethen village. This village was established by settlers from Spiti and Kinnaur who made their way over to the Kulu Valley a few generations ago. There is an ideal campsite just above the village.

Stage 2: Sethen to Base of Hampta Pass
(Average walking time 4-5 hours)
From Sethen, the trail crosses the Hampta stream and heads up the narrow forested valley to the meadow at Chikha (3400 metres). The trail is well defined, steep in places, and there are many Gaddi camps if you need assistance. At Chikha there is an excellent campsite, although there is ample time to continue the gradual climb to a higher camp above the treeline. This camp is the Balu ka Ghera (the Den of Bears), some 2 hours on from Chikha, at the base of the Hampta Pass.

Stage 3: Hampta Pass to Chatru

(Average walking time 7 hours)

The 700 metre climb to the pass crosses a series of scree slopes that are under snow for half the season. The trek is quite gradual until the short steep climb just below the pass. Huge rock spires and boulders characterise the area, while there is a hanging glacier to the right of the pass. There is a well-formed cairn on the pass, and good views across to Deo Tibba and Indrasar.

The initial descent is very steep, and tough going for the horses, which may have to be unloaded at some stages. There is a choice of trails to follow. The easiest route down is on the right hand bank, and it is this trail that the horses take. However, there is a problem of recrossing the river, which by mid-morning is steadily rising as the snow melts off the Indrasar Glacier. The alternative is to stay on the left hand side of the valley for the entire walk down. There are some steep rocky sections which are good for goats, less so for trekkers.

From the bottom of the pass, cross the bridge over the Chandra River to Chatru, and catch a truck or bus as far as Khoksar. From Khoksar there are regular buses over the Rhotang Pass back to Manali.

Option An alternative is to continue the trek further into Lahaul. From the base of the Hampta Pass you cross the bridge to the far side of the Chandra River, then turn east. The trail skirts the Bhara Shigri Glacier, and crosses a number of swift side streams until you reach Batal. (See the Lahaul section, page 138, for details of the trek on to Chandratal.)

Lahaul

North of the Rhotang Pass, the geography of the Himalaya changes. From the alpine valleys of Kulu, the mountains of Lahaul appear bare and rugged, and the valleys devoid of forest and vegetation. It is a land which would have appeared to ancient trav-ellers as being beyond the habitable world. It is also the land that marks the southern influence of the Tibetan world.

Geographically, Lahaul is divided into two regions: upper Lahaul which consists of the Chandra and Bhaga valleys, and Lower Lahaul which comprises the land in the Chenab Valley below the confluence of the Chandra and Bhaga rivers. To the east of Lahaul are the sparsely populated valleys of Spiti and Kinnaur. The region is bounded by Ladakh to the north, Kulu to the south and Tibet to the east.

Lahaul's climate is similar to that of Ladakh. It is wedged between the main Himalaya Range to the north, and the peaks of the Pir Panjal Range to the south. It is the Pir Panjal that effectively blocks out much of the rain, particularly during the monsoon. The air is rarefied and clear on account of its elevation, which on average is well over 3000 metres. Cultivation is therefore restricted to the depths of the valleys, where irrigation schemes have been developed over the centuries. Like the Zanskar region of Ladakh, Lahaul is subject to heavy snow-storms in the early winter, which close the passes for many months of the year.

In many ways Lahaul's historical back-ground runs parallel with that of Ladakh. Accounts recall how sages crossed the Rhotang Pass and the Baralacha en route to Ladakh. In the 10th century, upper Lahaul was united with Spiti and the Zanskar as part of the vast Lahaul-West Tibet Kingdom, which is sometimes referred to as Guge. Ladakhi influence at this time stretched to the upper limits of the Kulu Valley, and for centuries the Kulu rajahs paid tribute to Leh.

Although political allegiances changed over the centuries, it was Ladakh's defeat by the Mongol-Tibetan armies in the 17th century that led to Lahaul being split into two regions. Upper Lahaul came under the influence of the Kulu rajah, while lower Lahaul, across to the district of Pangi, came under the influence of the courts of Chamba. Trade agreements evolved between Kulu and Ladakh, and Lahaul was considered neutral territory. Records have it that trade was conducted during the summer months in a series of camps on the vast Lingti Valley just beyond the Baralacha.

The Sikh forays into the Kulu Valley also extended into Lahaul, and for a time the entire territory came under the influence of Ranjit Singh. In 1847, Kulu and Lahaul came under the British administration as a division of the Kangra state. Spiti was linked to Ladakh at the time, and the newly formed maharajah's state of Jammu & Kashmir, but in the same year was exchanged for other territories and also administered by Kangra.

Under British administration, Lahaul's trails were upgraded, and bridges were constructed along the main trading highways that linked Lahaul and Kulu. Records recount how huge logs were hauled over the Rhotang Pass by upwards of 200 porters, while the system of *beggar*, or forced labour, was the only means that contractors had for improving the roads.

The Hakurs of Lahaul consolidated their positions during this era and secured many valuable trade agreements with Kulu and the towns to the south. To maintain these agreements many of the Hakurs set up bases in the Kulu Valley – a situation that has continued to the present day.

Lahaul is, however, still cut off from the Kulu Valley for many months of the year, though a tunnel under the Pir Panjal is being constructed. The tunnel is being built on the same lines as the Banihal Tunnel in Kashmir, and is due to be completed in the next decade. It will provide a lifeline for Lahaul throughout the year.

Getting Ready

Apart from the abundance of potatoes during the late autumn, there is rarely any surplus food in Lahaul. It is advisable to bring all provisions, including kerosene, with you from Manali. Some meat (goat or lamb) can be bought from the villages, as can biscuits and basics, but that's about it. Horses can be hired from the villages in the vicinity of Darcha if you are continuing on to the Zanskar, but most of the main contractors are fully engaged, and a few days must be reserved to make arrangements before you set off. Prices vary enormously during the season, particularly in midsummer when most horses are taken to the Zanskar. Budget for up to Rs 120 per horse per day if you're travelling in a small group. You may be fortunate enough to secure a better arrangement with horses returning to the Zanskar, but you would be foolish to plan for this occurrence.

Places to Stay

Along the roads there are a number of PWD or Forest Division *Rest Houses*, where you can normally stay without prior reservation. The chowkidar (caretaker) often lives in the nearby village, and is quite amenable to visitors. The rooms are simply furnished and cost somewhere in the vicinity of Rs 30 upwards for a room only. In a number of villages, such as Darcha, Udaipur and Khoksar, there are small hotels-cum-teahouses that are open for the season. Keylong is now the night halt for buses and jeeps going to and from Leh and the facilities are being upgraded at the moment (see next section). In all of these places you must bring your own sleeping bag.

Getting There & Away

The 3195 metre Rhotang Pass is the only road access into Lahaul and is normally open from mid-June until the end of October. Well-prepared trekkers and traders can, however, tackle the pass from late March until December, by ascending in the early morning before the snow softens. There have also been a number of enterprising ski touring groups that have crossed the pass in the springtime, and for those who are well-prepared this is an excellent way of exploring Lahaul out of season.

During the summer there are regular buses from Manali to Keylong and Darcha. Trucks are also a viable alternative, and it pays to enquire in the Manali bazaar. The tourist office operates a daily Rs 50 bus up to the pass during the season. It's mainly for domestic tourists to see the snow, but if time is at a premium it's a worthwhile excursion.

In the last decade roads have been developed through Lahaul. The most important has been the upgrading of the road over the Baralacha to Leh. Since 1989 tourists have been able to follow this route, providing their arrangements are made by a bona fide agent in either Leh or Manali. The cost of hiring a jeep one way to Leh is at present about Rs 7000, with an overnight stop at Keylong. There is also a regular bus service plying to and from Leh. The fare is about Rs 100 one way. Foreigners are not at the moment allowed to use this service, although the restrictions may be lifted by the time this edition is published.

Other road developments include the road down the Chandra Valley, which will eventually link up at the Sach Pass, and provide a connection to Chamba. The construction over the last few years has progressed rapidly down the valley, and it is estimated that the road will extend as far as the village of Kilar in the next few seasons. The days of trekking down the Chandra Valley are almost over, but other possibilities of exploring the Miyar Valley leading to the main Himalaya still remain.

A third development, still in its planning stage, is to extend the road leading to Spiti over the Kun Zun La up the Chandra Valley to Chandratal. Given this will be of zero benefit to Lahaul because there are no villages there, it would be nice to think that at least some parts of this magnificent region could be left beyond the infringement of trucks, buses and jeeps. The local agents in Manali need support here if this road is not to ruin one of the most beautiful lakes anywhere in the Himalaya.

Treks

With the development of roads into the region, Lahaul has become, to some extent, a transit point for trekkers from the Kulu Valley en route to the Zanskar and Ladakh. There are, however, some excellent opportunities to explore Lahaul away from the road.

Z5: Darcha to Kargyak via the Shingo La
Z6: Manali to Chandratal and Baralacha
Z7: Baralacha to Kargyak via the Phirste La
Z8: Down the Chenab Valley

Because it is outside the main influence of the Indian monsoon, Lahaul is an ideal alternative for trekking in July and August. The trekking season across the main Himalayan passes is from mid-June until mid-October. However, the trail down the Chenab Valley is normally suitable for trekkers by late May or early June – an ideal time to explore Lahaul before it becomes 'busy' for the season. To undertake a trek at this time of the year you must allow time to trek over the Rhotang Pass, which is not generally open to vehicles until mid-June.

Z5: DARCHA TO KARGYAK VIA SHINGO LA

From Manali it takes a full day by bus to reach Darcha, a small village at the confluence of the Bhaga River and the Zanskar-Sumdo Nullah. (The Zanskar-Sumdo Nullah is not to be confused with the main Zanskar River. Zanskar-Sumdo is a misnomer, as the river emanates from the south side of the Himalaya range, not from the Zanskar region). From Darcha it is possible to cross the Shingo La in three stages to the upper Zanskar Valley.

The first walking stage is to the confluence of the Zanskar-Sumdo Nullah and the Shingo Nullah (the Jhankar Sangpo), which is crossed by a flying fox pulley system, although a bridge is also being constructed. The second stage is to the base of the Shingo La, and the third over the pass to the shepherd camp at Lakong. Strong walkers could reach Kargyak, the highest village in the Zanskar, on the third stage.

You should have no problem in finding the route. The trail is well trekked by locals and groups during the season, and it is simply a matter of following the cairns. The glacial terrain below the pass is not heavily crevassed, although it would be advisable to wait for someone to indicate the way when

To Padum

Umasi La

GREAT

Marchel

Bardan

Shashut

Poat La

DHARLANG VALLEY

Kang La

Atholi

Shoal

continues on
Kishtwar map

Istahari

Sersank Pass

PIR

Dharwas

Kilar

Z8

Z8

PANJAL

Z8

Sach Pass

Sach Khas

To Chamba

RANGE

Purthi

Zanskar/Lahaul

Raoli

CHENAB
VALLEY

MIYAR VALLEY

Tindi

Road	Town
Track	Village
Trail	Campsite
River	
Ridge	
Pass	
Glacier	

Udaipur

Triloknath

0   5   10   15   20
kilometres

© Compiled and drawn by G.Weare and J.Besley

continues on Kulu & Kangra map

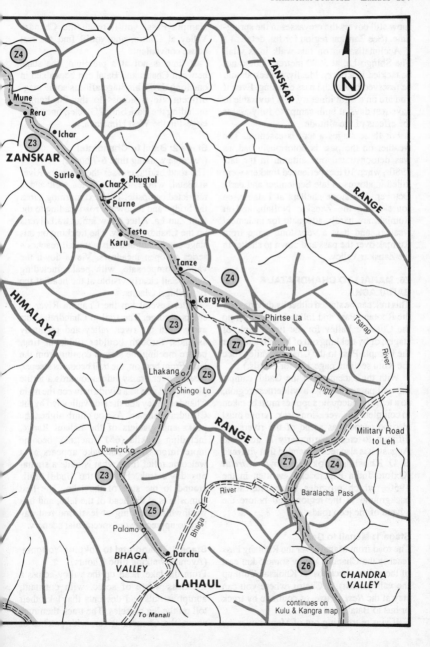

snow still covers the crevasses in the spring-time. (See Zanskar region for full details.)

Acclimatisation on this walk in is vital. The Shingo La, at 5090 metres, should not be tackled in a hurry. Ideally, a week should be reserved before the pass crossing. Even if you are on a tight itinerary, it is advisable to have rest days at both camps to fully assess the effects of the altitude.

For these stages a tent is essential. The weather on the pass is notoriously bad, as was demonstrated one autumn in the late 1980s, when 10 inexperienced trekkers were killed in storms in late September and early October. The stone shelters at Palamo, en route along the Zanskar Nullah, and at Rumjak, are hardly adequate for inclement weather, and it is a very long stage from Rumjak over the pass and down to shelter in the Zanskar Valley.

Z6: MANALI TO CHANDRATAL & BARALACHA

This trek can be started either by driving over the Rhotang Pass and following the road up the Chandra Valley for the first couple of stages; or by trekking out of Manali and over the Hampta Pass to the Chandra Valley (See the Kulu section, page 132 for details.)

With the exception of the Gaddi camps, the trail passes through a wilderness region, so a tent and adequate supplies must be taken to complete this week-long trek. A rope must also be carried, as some of the rivers are difficult to cross, particularly in July and August. It is also recommended that you read G D Khosla's book *Himalayan Circuit* (Oxford India Paperbacks), written in the 1950s, which provides some interesting background to the region well before the advent of the jeep roads.

Stage 1: Manali to Batal

The road from Manali over the Rhotang Pass reaches the Chandra Valley some 5 km east of the police checkpost at Khoksar. Turn up the valley (east) to Chatru, where you can stay at the *Rest House*, or continue by truck or bus to Batal.

If you're trekking out of Manali over the Hampta Pass, you'll reach the Chandra Valley at Chatru, and you'll find the rest house convenient.

If time is not at a premium, the stage between Chatru and Batal can be walked in one long day. This stage affords some magnificent views across to the Pir Panjal, including the Bara Shigri Glacier, one of the largest in the West Himalaya.

Stage 2: Batal to Chandratal

(Average walking time 6-7 hours)

The road bridge crosses the Chandra River at Batal, where there is a tea stall and a restricted campsite. The next morning, cross the bridge and follow the road leading to the Kun Zun La. After a few km, a trail diverts up the Chandra Valley. The trekking on this stage can be hot and dusty until it reaches a series of open meadows. Views down the valley compensate, with peaks including White Sail clearly visible at the head of the Bara Shigri Glacier.

After several km the Chandra River re-enters a gorge. The trail to Chandratal cuts away from the river valley and gradually ascends, through boulder fields at first, before meeting the stream coming from the lake. From here on, the trail becomes steeper, passing over grassy ridges towards a fertile plateau that acts as a divide between the main Chandra Valley and the side valley fed by the Chandratal stream. As you climb higher, the peaks and glaciers of the Lahaul Range, including Makila (6517 metres), become more impressive. The lake appears as a welcome relief from what is quite a strenuous day's trek. Follow the Gaddi trails around to the side of the lake. The best campsite is at the head of the lake, and it is worthwhile spending at least one rest day here to appreciate the spectacular scenery.

Stage 3: Chandratal to Tokping Yongma

(Average walking time 6 hours)

From the lake, head up the valley across a trackless waste of scree, with constant, abrupt ascents and descents that take their toll on the leg muscles. The track then runs above the Chandra River, with patches of wildflowers along the banks of the side streams, which provide welcome relief from the dun-coloured scenery. The camp beside the Tokping Yongma is the most suitable for the night.

Stage 4: Tokping Yongma to Tokping Gogma

(Average walking time 6-7 hours)

The time taken on this stage depends on the ease with which you cross the Tokping Yongma. Until early July the snow bridges should be in place, but from then to the end of August the river can be a problem. It is recommended that you seek the assistance of the local Gaddi to find the best crossing points. It is not advisable to attempt to cross on your own.

After the river crossing the trail is well defined, with a steady ascent through boulder landscape which offers little relief. After about 5 hours there is a raging side-stream, and care is needed to select the best crossing place. Ropes are again essential. There is a small campsite just beyond this side stream, or continue to the confluence of the next large side river, the Tokping Gogma.

Stage 5: Tokping Gogma to Baralacha

(Average walking time 4 hours)

Cross the side-river with care. Again, seek the help of the Gaddi if the water level is still high. From the river bank the trail climbs a steep scree slope before the country opens out. The trail is well defined by a series of rock cairns as it crosses the open meadows that lead gradually to the pass.

The Baralacha, at 5300 metres, is a double pass. It marks the divide between the main Himalaya and the Lahaul Range, and also between the Himalaya and the Baralacha Range which extends north to the Zanskar. The mountain ranges provide an impressive backdrop, and a night's camping here will afford some spectacular views.

Options The choice then is to either continue the trek on to the Zanskar by way of the Phirtse La, or trek down the Bhaga Valley, by two stages to Darcha and Keylong. If time

is at a premium, you can also hitch a ride by bus or truck coming from Leh, which will take you back to Keylong and the Kulu Valley in a day or so.

Z7: BARALACHA TO KARGYAK VIA PHIRTSE LA

This trek into the Zanskar is highly recommended either as an extension of the trek from Chandratal, (see the previous trek description, Z6) or as an alternative route for trekkers wishing to avoid the Shingo La. The route from the Baralacha La across the Phirste La to the upper Zanskar Valley takes a minimum of 4 to 5 days. Acclimatisation is the main concern, with Phirtse La at an altitude of 5450 metres.

The first stage is from the Baralacha, past the Kilong Serai, to the confluence of the main Tsarap River and the Lingti River.

The second day is a tougher stage, going up the Lingti Valley and turning off the side valley leading to the camp at Churnik Marpo. River crossings on this stage may force an additional camp.

From Churnik Marpo, it is a steady ascent to the Phirtse La, with a choice of camps on the far side of the pass. The best is one a few km before the steep descent into the Zanskar Valley.

From the camp, it is a matter of a couple of hours' walking until the trail joins the populated regions of the Zanskar Valley, just below the village of Kargyak.

A tent, and a rope for river crossings, are essential for this trek. This route is for the experienced trekker only. There are no villages en route, and the only people encountered are the shepherds grazing their yaks in the meadows around Churnik Marpo during the summer months.

Z8: DOWN THE CHENAB VALLEY TO CHAMBA OR KISHTWAR

The other trekking alternative in the region is to follow the Chenab Valley down to the district of Pangi, and then either cross the Sach Pass to Chamba, or continue on down the valley to Kishtwar.

Since the printing of the first edition of this

book, the roadworks have progressed rapidly down the valley from Lahaul, and within a few seasons the jeep road will be complete as far as Kilar – the main village in the Pangi district. Latest reports indicate that the roadworks are now well above Tindi village and going strong. From Kilar, construction of the road over the Sach Pass is well under way, to complete the road linking Lahaul and Chamba.

The alternative is to make your way down the Chenab Valley to the roadhead, and then continue down for a week or so to Kishtwar. The progress of the road from this end of the Chenab Valley is slower, and there are some delightful stages. (See the Kishtwar section, pages 85 to 87 for details.)

Kangra Valley

The picturesque Kangra Valley is situated between the snow-capped peaks of the Dhaula Dhar and the rolling Siwalik Hills. The valley extends from Mandi to Pathankot and, with Kashmir, is one of the most important valleys in the West Himalaya.

There is little to see in the ancient town of Kangra today, but it was once of considerable importance. Strategically, it was dominated by a fort which prompted the local saying 'he who holds the fort holds the hills', and was always fiercely contested by the rajahs of Kangra. Culturally, the famous temple of Bajreshwari Devi, in the heart of the town, possessed legendary wealth. The Mahmud of Ghanzi reputedly amassed a fortune in gold, silver and jewels after he raided the temples in 1009. Yet Kangra's position ensured that the temple was able to re-establish itself. So much so that, in the time of the early Moghuls, it was said that the temple was paved with plates of pure silver.

During the uncertainty of the Moghul period, many of the artists from Kangra fled to the hills. This led to the formation of the Kangra school of painting, and the technique of depicting in miniature many of the rajahs,

and the Hindu gods Vishnu and Shiva. Their inspiration and design, while Moghul in origin, were patronised in the various hill courts, and remained as a notable art form through to the 19th century.

With the decline of the Moghuls, many of the hill states were able to reassert their independence. In Kangra, the famous rajah, Sanser Chand sought to acquire a huge Himalayan kingdom, extending far beyond the boundaries of the Kangra Valley. The states of Chamba, Mandi and Kulu were attacked, and it was not until he came against the combined forces of the Gurkhas and the deposed rajahs that Sanser Chand retreated again to his fort. It was a colourful period in Kangra's history, before the Sikhs were able to assert their control over the Punjab Himalaya.

After the Treaty of Amritsar in 1846, the Kangra rulers hoped that they would gain some degree of autonomy from the British. This was not to be. The British established a new administration in the nearby foothills at Dharamsala in 1848. Kangra experienced an inevitable decline, and in the spring of 1905 even the fort was destroyed by an earthquake.

DHARAMSALA

Dharamsala was the district headquarters of the British administration of Kangra, Kulu and Lahaul until 1947. Testimony to this era is still in evidence, with the colonial buildings that remain in both Dharamsala and nearby McLeod Ganj. In 1863 the Viceroy of India, Lord Elgin, died in this area while on a tour of duty, and is buried in McLeod Ganj's Church of St John in the Wilderness. In those days the hill tracks would have been delightful on the four or five day walk from Simla to Dharamsala, and the two more days across the forested ridges of the Dhaula Dhar to Dalhousie.

Travel today is of a different nature, though driving is an ideal way to explore the foothills in the springtime before the onset of the trekking season, or after the passes have closed in late October. A drive from Simla to Manali and then on to Dharamsala, Dalhousie and

Chamba can be recommended. These days Dharamsala has an added attraction. Since the early 1960s it has been the residence of Tibet's government in exile, headed by the Dalai Lama. The Tibetan settlement at McLeod Ganj is the focus for the refugee camps that have been established in Himalayan regions as far apart as Ladakh, Kulu, Nepal and Darjeeling. The Dalai Lama has frequently visited these communities, and the major monasteries, in order to maintain Tibet's cultural traditions.

Getting Ready

Trekking supplies can be purchased in Dharamsala/McLeod Ganj. It is, however, imperative that you are fully equipped with tent, sleeping bag and other main supplies – Dhaula Dhar deserves as much respect as other mountain ranges in the Himalaya. You can enjoy the comforts of the rest houses, shepherd camps and rock caves, but you should still be equipped for inclement weather.

The Mountaineering Institute at McLeod Ganj is well worth a visit before you commence your trek. The institute is run by a keen and informative team who know the trails and passes of the Dhaula Dhar as well as the Gaddi shepherds. There are a number of maps available for inspection, and a three-dimensional model of the Dhaula Dhar, made by the institute's director.

Below the institute there is a local trekking agency, Yeti Trekking, that can provide a full range of trekking services, or just porters. Their rates are rather high, but here, as in other regions of Himachal Pradesh, you pay for what you get, and a charge of Rs 150 per day for porters may prove to be a sound investment.

It seems surprising that the local Tibetan community has not been tempted, like its counterpart in Nepal, to organise treks in the region. While this is not their homeland, one would have expected, after 30 years, at least a few agencies. Local porters are not in abundant supply and, if the institute or the local agencies cannot assist, it is suggested that you spread the word around the store at the head of the bazaar opposite the bus stand. Expect porters to carry a maximum of 15 kg, plus their food, and allow a day or so for them to get ready.

Places to Stay

Most travellers don't stay in Dharamsala itself, but up the hill in McLeod Ganj, close to the Dalai Lama's headquarters and the Tibetan community. The township has a happy atmosphere, full of energy, with the Tibetans engaged in shopping and trading in the main bazaar, and small shops selling Buddhist mementoes and pictures of the Dalai Lama. It is rather like Kathmandu in the late 1960s, with many Westerners seeking enlightenment.

For those on the path to enlightenment, there are many *viharas* (monasteries) and *ashrams* (retreats) situated high on the ridges, with commanding views over the Indian plains. For trekkers there are plenty of guesthouses and simple hotels. Finding a room in April and May is a problem, and it may take a bit of waiting to get a good room. However, no-one should feel an urgency to move on, and with room rates at about Rs 50 an extended stay is not likely to stretch the budget.

The only upmarket hotel, the *Hotel Bhagsu*, has rooms from Rs 120 upwards. The hotel is well positioned at the top end of the bazaar, but has little to recommend it unless you cherish the thought of listening to the screams of Indian families moving en masse from one meal to the next.

Down the hill, in Dharamsala, there is a better, government-run hotel, the *Dhaula Dhar*. Prices range upwards from Rs 150 per double, with excellent food. Its only failing is its position beside the bus stand – with all the associated mechanical sounds from 4 am onwards each morning.

Getting There & Away

Getting to Dharamsala or Kangra involves a 3 to 4 hour bus trip from Pathankot. Pathankot is connected by overnight train with Delhi, and was the railhead before the line was extended to Jammu in 1971. For train buffs, the narrow gauge train from Pathankot to Kangra runs four times a day and takes 4 hours. From Kangra, there are regular buses up the hill to Dharamsala.

From Kashmir, the journey takes two days. The first day is by road to Jammu, and the second day is to Pathankot, where you'll arrive with plenty of time to catch the connecting bus at the Himachal Pradesh bus stand. If you're trying to avoid the dubious delights of the monsoon, the only way is to share a taxi from Srinagar to Jammu, then take a bus to Pathankot and another from there to Dharamsala. The last bus to Dharamsala leaves Pathankot at 5 pm, so leave Srinagar early in the morning, to allow enough time for the 3 hour bus trip from Jammu to Pathankot.

If you're coming from Manali or Simla you need to change buses at Mandi. The bus takes about 4 hours from Manali to Mandi and 6 hours from Simla to Mandi. From Mandi it is another 6 hours on to Dharamsala. To visit Kangra it is best to stay in Dharamsala or McLeod Ganj and make a day trip. The bus takes about an hour.

Buses run frequently between Dharamsala and McLeod Ganj, but to keep fit a walk up the shorter hill trails is recommended. It is about 1 hour up the hill to McLeod Ganj, passing the Tibetan library and headquarters en route.

Treks

There are a dozen or more treks over the Dhaula Dhar, and you could spend a delightful season exploring them. I have outlined only one trek in this section, from McLeod Ganj over the Indrahar Pass to the Ravi Valley. This is the most convenient trek out of McLeod Ganj, and is also the easiest to organise, with the trail starting literally at the head of the bazaar.

Treks can be undertaken from the middle of June, providing you have prepared for the snow conditions you encounter as you climb towards the passes. By mid-July, and all through August the passes are free of snow, but the monsoon rains dampens trek possibilities. Early September through to mid-October is an ideal time

to trek, before the first of the winter snows block the passes.

The climb to any of the passes should not be underestimated. The average pass elevation is about 4500 metres, so extra days should be reserved for acclimatisation. The trails are not the easiest to follow, particularly when the gullies are under snow, and you may need the assistance of the shepherds if you do not have a local guide.

The Kangra and Chamba districts are the home of the Gaddi – the colourful Hindu shepherds who tend their flocks on the Dhaula Dhar and the Pir Panjal ranges throughout the summer months. Each spring, they bring their flocks from the Kangra foothills over the Dhaula Dhar to the Ravi Valley. From there they go higher across the Pir Panjal to the main Himalaya, and on to the rich grazing areas that stretch from the Lingti Valley, beyond the Baralacha, to the high ridges that mark the border between the states of Jammu & Kashmir and Himachal Pradesh.

The Gaddi can be distinguished by their wearing of a *chola* – a warm knee-length, woollen cloak which is tightened at the waist. They trace their origins back to the time when the first rajput settlers made their way to the Himalayan foothills, although it was not until the late Moghul period that some of the families chose to settle in Bramaur and Chamba. Today, the Gaddi migration, like that of the Bakharval shepherds in Kashmir, means they have to reconstruct bridges and clear the scree from the mountain trails. This annual task ensures their own safe passage over the passes, and is well appreciated by anyone undertaking a trek early in the season.

For a full account of the migration of the Gaddi shepherds, *Over the High Passes* by Christina Noble (Collins, London) is a valuable asset.

D1: MCLEOD GANJ TO CHAMBA VIA THE INDRAHAR PASS

This is the most popular trek over the Dhaula Dhar, crossing the Indrahar Pass (also known as the Laka Pass) at 4610 metres. The climb from Dharamsala is steep, and at least one rest day should be reserved before crossing the pass.

Stage 1: McLeod Ganj to Triund
(Average walking time 3-4 hours)

Turn left at the Mountaineering Institute and continue past the tea stall to the ridge known as Galu Devi, where there is a small temple. From here on the trail is well defined to Triund. An early start from McLeod Ganj is recommended, since the trail is south-facing and there is little in the way of shade, so it tends to become very warm by mid-morning and there are few, if any, springs to quench the thirst. The final few km up to the meadow are quite steep, but it is worth the effort for the views to the south, across the Beas Dam to the Indian plains, and to the north, where the snowy backdrop of the Dhaula Dhar predominates.

There is a comfortable *Rest House* at Triund, complete with an obliging caretaker. The rooms can be booked in advance from Dharamsala. There are some good camping spots, and no shortage of wood for a modest campfire, so this is an ideal place to spend a day or two out of McLeod Ganj.

Stage 2: Triund to Lahesh Cave
(Average walking time 4-5 hours)

The time taken on this stage will depend largely on fitness. The trail follows the ridge behind the prayer flags above the Gaddi encampment. If you have any doubts about the direction, ask the chowkidar at the rest house. The trail ascends gently, through oak and pine forests and across open meadows, to the shepherd encampment at Laka Kot. This is an ideal place to rest before beginning the ascent up through the scree to the right of the main gully that leads to the pass.

There is a tiring scramble for 200 to 300 metres to Lahesh Cave, a huge rock overhang, known as Lahesh Cave, that can serve as shelter for the night. There are a few level grassy ridges on which to pitch a tent, while water is supplied from a small stream in the main gully. The rock cave is distinguished by brown and black markings, and is big enough to house a large party of porters, trekkers and shepherds. Advance bookings cannot be made from Dharamsala. The porters can rely on a small supply of juniper wood for the night, while trekkers should bring kerosene stoves to cook with, or alternatively carry wood from Laka Got.

Stage 3: Lahesh Cave to Indrahar Pass & Chatru Parao
(Average walking time 6-7 hours)
The ridges of the Dhaula Dhar do not have easily defined passes. The pass is not immediately apparent from the camp, and a guide is essential if you are to conserve energy. In June the snow plod would be very tiring, while in September and October the rock scramble to the pass will take between 4 and 5 hours. At times you'll feel like giving up: one series of boulders follows another, and at this point nobody would deny the porters their modest payment. Do not underestimate the climb. The search for gullies and footholds over boulders, while by no means technical, is not the easiest introduction to trekking.

The trail remains on the left hand side of the main gully throughout, and it is only on the final few km that you actually traverse the ridge to the pass. The view is one of the finest in the Himalaya. To the south, the Indian plains stretch as far as the eye can see, and to the north the snow-capped ridges of the Pir Panjal provide an imposing backdrop. The peak of Mt Kailash can be seen to the east, and the depths of the Ravi Valley can be appreciated in the middle foreground.

The descent from the pass is initially very steep, down a gully strewn with loose boulders. The walking then levels out across a plateau marked with huge boulders which, when under a covering of snow, make the walking anything but easy. The trail down to the camp at Chatru Parao is often muddy and slippery, and very tiring at the end of what can be a long day. The camp consists of a few shepherd huts set in a meadow which offers both wood and water.

Stage 4: Chatru Parao to Kuarsi Village
(Average walking time 5-6 hours)
The trail follows the left hand side of the valley for the first few km. The trail is narrow, and no more than a goat track in places. Early in the season it would be worthwhile abandoning the trail altogether, and descending across the snow bridges on the main valley floor. After about 2 hours the trail crosses the valley on a permanent snow bridge, and then ascends steeply on the opposite bank to an open meadow. There is a springline here, and the meadow is an ideal spot for a rest. Continue down the right hand side of the valley, following a trail that's more suitable for goats than trekkers. The track peters out in places, and has plenty of ups and downs before you finally descend to Kuarsi village.

There is a campsite above the main springline in the village, or you could continue on for another 10 minutes to a secluded camp by the main river. The village itself typifies life in the upper Ravi Valley, and you can be assured of a friendly welcome.

Stage 5: Kuarsi Village to Machhetar
(Average walking time 6 hours)
Make an early start to tackle the climb out of the valley and over the ridge to the roadhead. After descending to the valley floor, the trek up the hillside – about 700 metres – can be very hot and demanding. The trail ascends through high grassland and forest to a springline about three-quarters of the way up the hillside. Thereafter the trail becomes easier, and traverses around to a well-defined pass marked with tridents and cairns.

The mountain views from the pass extend across the whole region. To the south the Dhaula Dhar is seen from a new angle. To the north-west the Sach Pass is visible over the Pir Panjal, while to the north-east there is the Manimahesh Range and the upper Ravi Valley. From the pass there is a steady descent for a couple of hours, through barley fields and forest, to the Ravi Valley. Just above the road there is a *Rest House* at Machhetar which charges Rs 12 per room, and it is recommended that you spend the night here before catching the bus to Chamba or Bramaur the following day.

Getting Away One note of advice about the bus. The first bus in the morning slips by at about 7.30. To say it is normally crowded would be an understatement, even by Indian standards. Be prepared to run behind the bus and climb onto the roof at a moment's notice.

Top: Dancers at Karsha Monastery, Zanskar (RC)
Bottom: Musicians at Karsha Monastery, Zanskar (RC)

Top: Indrahar Pass, Himachal Pradesh (GW)
Bottom: Chandratal Lake, Lahaul, Himachal Pradesh (GW)

This is no problem, except that in places the cliff overhangs the road with little or no room for baggage or passengers. It can be an eventful few hours until the village of Karamukh where many alight to take the side road to Bramaur. It is then a relatively pleasant 2 or 3 hour drive to Chamba.

Chamba

The Ravi Valley is bounded to the north by the Pir Panjal, to the south by the Dhaula Dhar, and to the east by the Bara Banghal Range. Chamba is perched on a plateau, overlooking the Ravi River where it turns south to forge its way through the Dhaula Dhar to the Indian plains. Founded in the 9th century, at about the same time as Jammu, Chamba has often been likened to a medieval town, remote in time and distance from the rest of India.

The Chamba state was historically referred to as the 'Middle Kingdom'. This title was derived mainly from its position between the Kangra Hills and the trans-Himalayan trails that lead through the Chandra Valley and on to Lahaul and Kashmir.

With the establishment of the capital at Chamba in the 9th century, the culture of the region flourished. Many of the temples date from this period, including the important Lakshmi temples close to the Rang Mahal. Since then Chamba has, with few exceptions, maintained an uninterrupted cultural tradition. The state paid only nominal tribute to the Moghuls, and its most famous rajah, Prithi Singh, saw to it that Chamba's borders extended far beyond the Ravi Valley. Later, Rajah Umed Singh was responsible for the Rang Mahal, 'The Palace of Colour', a fortress inspired by Moghul architecture. It was extended by his successors in the late 18th and early 19th centuries.

Following the Sikh wars, Gulab Singh from Jammu was granted all the country between the Ravi and the Indus rivers, and this included Chamba. A deputation was sent to Henry Lawrence in Calcutta, and it was agreed that the Chamba region, which at the time included the nearby Pangi Valley and lower Lahaul, would come under British administration.

In 1851 it was proposed to establish a sanatorium for Europeans somewhere in the Dhaula Dhar. A site near Chamba was chosen and a hill station, to be on a par with Simla, was founded by Lord Dalhousie in 1868. At this time Chamba, like the region of Lahaul and Kulu, had totally inadequate roads and forest trails. These were upgraded, trek stages defined, altitudes and spot heights determined and forest areas surveyed as PWD and forest departments moved up-country. Even today, the PWD and forest department rest houses are well maintained, and have signposts at their entrances outlining the stages to Kashmir or Lahaul prior to 1947.

Getting Ready

Supplies, provisions and kerosene should be bought in Chamba before continuing on to Bramaur. Generally, cooks and assistants must be brought with you from Kashmir or Kulu. Horses and porters may be hired at the roadhead, but allow a day or two for negotiations. This is particularly necessary at Tarila, at the base of the Sach Pass, where the mule trains are usually busy during the summer months, with contractors carrying supplies over to the Pangi District in the Chandra Valley. For crossing the Kugti Pass, porters are generally hired at Kugti village for about Rs 70 per day. The Director of the Mountaineering Institute in Bramaur can assist in this matter, and can also advise on local guides.

Places to Stay

Chamba For most, accommodation in Chamba is a choice between the *Akhand Chandi*, behind the Rang Mahal, and the new government hotel the *Iravati*, at the far end of the playing grounds. The rooms at the Akhand Chandi are from Rs 60 per room per night, and the staff are very helpful, although recent reports indicate that the hotel is soon to be turned into a video parlour. The government hotel is more expensive – in the vicinity of Rs 175 per night per double. It is possible to stay at the *Forest Rest House*, 2 km below Chamba, although permission must be received beforehand from the Forest Officer's Department. Double rooms are in the vicinity of Rs 40. In Bramaur there is a comfortable *PWD Rest House* which can be booked in advance from Chamba. There is also the Mountaineering Institute, whose director, by all accounts, is most obliging. Dormitory rooms are available at Rs 10 for those engaged in mountaineering or allied sports, which include trekking.

Dalhousie The availability of hotel rooms in Dalhousie varies with the seasons. It's a choice between the upmarket Indian hotels and the rather sad and dilapidated Raj-era guesthouses which have certainly seen better days. There are a number of large hotels, in various stages of antiquity, along the North Mall and clustered around Gandhi Chowk. Doubles are around Rs 150. The *Grand View Hotel* and the *Mountain View*, above the bus stand, have doubles for about Rs 250, while the *Aroma-N-Claire*, down near Sadar bazaar 2 km from the bus stand, with doubles from Rs 200 is recommended. Alternatively, accommodation can be found at the *Government Circuit House* and at the *Tourist Bungalow*. Bookings need to be made in advance for these, but there is a helpful government tourist office two minutes from the bus station.

The *Government Bungalows*, at nearby Khajjiar, are a convenient alternative at Rs 150 per double. There is also a *Youth Hostel* across the meadow, with beds from Rs 10.

Getting There & Away

To get from Delhi to Chamba, take the train to Pathankot, and you are then faced with a 6 hour bus ride the rest of the way.

From Dharamsala, Chamba is quite close as the crow flies, but the trip still involves a long day. The direct super-express from Chamba to Dharamsala goes first to Dalhousie, then across country, arriving in Dharamsala in the late afternoon. Alternatively, there are buses which go via Pathankot and take around the same time.

From Kashmir, Simla and Kulu it is also necessary to go via Pathankot. It's a tiring journey, which is why Chamba has remained off the tourist map for so long.

There are two roads out of Chamba. One is to Tarila; a 6 hour drive through some marvellous hillside scenery to the foot of the Sach Pass. The bus costs Rs 20. The other road goes up the Ravi Valley. Bramaur is a short diversion off this main road, 65 km from Chamba. The journey takes about 4 hours and costs about Rs 15. Jeeps can be hired from Chamba if you are growing tired of the crowded Himachal Pradesh buses, but they are considerably more expensive – in the vicinity of Rs 500 one way.

Treks

The treks over the Pir Panjal between Bramaur and Lahaul cross some of the most remote territory of the Pir Panjal. The difficulty of getting to Bramaur deters all but the most enthusiastic trekker, leaving the trails comparatively undertrekked. There are some superb possibilities, not only crossing the passes to Lahaul, but also going up the Ravi Valley and over to the Kulu Valley. A third alternative is to trek over the Dhaula Dhar from McLeod Ganj/Dharamsala. (See the Kangra Valley section, page 142.)

The trek over the Sach Pass, to Chamba via Tarila, is outlined in the Kishtwar section, page 85.

An outline of the passes from Lahaul is given in this section. (See the Kulu & Kangra map.)

Treks out of the Ravi Valley can be undertaken from early June onwards, although most of the passes are quite heavily snowbound until July. The exception is the Sach Pass, which is crossed by the locals from early May onwards.

Chamba does come under the influence of the monsoon, but the rainfall is not as heavy as in Dharamsala and the Kangra Valley. It is possible therefore to commence a trek during the summer here, particularly if you are going on further to Lahaul or the Zanskar region. As with other regions of Himachal Pradesh, the ideal trekking season is in September and October, before the onset of the winter snows.

C1: BRAMAUR TO THE CHANDRA VALLEY

There are three main passes over the Pir Panjal to Lahaul – the Kalicho, the Chobia and the Kugti. They are all around 5000 metres, and involve quite tough trekking, particularly in the immediate vicinity of the passes.

The most popular of the three passes is the Kugti, which can be approached in three or four stages out of Bramaur, depending on the fitness of the group and the time of the year. The first stage includes a short drive by jeep to the village of Harsar, and then on along the Budhil Valley to the village of Kugti. Here a rest day may be in order for organising porters and savouring the rich variety of Hindu legends that abound in this valley.

The ascent out of Kugti is steep at first, to the famous Kailung temple, and then more gradual, through forest to the alpine encampments frequented by the Gaddis. The climb involves criss-crossing trails leading to the various grazing areas, and it is advisable to rely on your local porter or guide for assistance. Make camp on the highest of these grazing areas, which are particularly attractive in August when the wildflowers are in full bloom.

From the highest camp, the trail cuts across extensive moraine, and traverses a small glacier that leads to just below the pass. There is then a steep climb for the last

hundred metres or so to the pass. The descent is by no means easy. The moraine on the far north side is encrusted in ice, making the trail slippery and quite dangerous and good boots are the order of the day. After a long traverse beneath the pass, the terrain drops steeply, and an intermediate camp is necessary.

The following day there is a steady descent to the Chandra Valley and the villages of Lahaul. After crossing the Chandra River, a few days can be spent exploring the villages and temples of Lahaul, before catching a bus or truck over the Rhotang Pass to the Kulu Valley.

C2: TO MANIMAHESH LAKE

Another recommended option is to trek to the Manimahesh Lake at the base of Mt Kailash, the highest mountain of a subsidiary range between the Dhaula Dhar and the Pir Panjal. The trek is popular among Hindu pilgrims, who climb to the lake each August to revere this resting place of Lord Shiva.

On the first day, leave Bramaur early by local jeep (cost Rs 15) to the village of Harsar. From here, the pilgrims' trail follows the Manimahesh stream, ascending about 1000 metres to the pilgrims' hut at Dancho. This stage can be hot and tiring as there is little shade en route.

On the second day the pilgrims ascend 2000 metres direct to the Manimahesh Lake at 3950 metres. It is possible to return to the Dancho camp the same day, and on the third day return to Harsar and Bramaur. Check the local jeep timings. There are only basic pilgrim huts en route, so it is better to take your own tent, particularly as the weather can be quite wet, particularly in August.

Uttar Pradesh

Uttar Pradesh is India's most populous state, and geographically one of the most diverse. Most of the state comprises the flat Ganges plain, but the northern corner, to the west of Nepal, extends into the Himalaya. This region, with some of India's highest mountains, is known as the Garhwal.

From the northern plains of India, the Garhwal Himalaya provides an immediate and stunning panorama. These peaks, situated at the headwaters of the Ganges, would have provided inspiration from the time of the early Aryan settlers. Pilgrimages would have been undertaken to the various sources of the Ganges tributaries, and places such as Yamunotri, Gangotri, Kedarnath and Badrinath are still visited by many thousands of devotees each year.

Gangotri is recognised as the source of the Ganges, though the actual source is at nearby Gaumukh, where it emerges from the glaciers at the base of the Bhagirathi peaks. Yamunotri is the source of the Yamuna, a principle tributary of the Ganges. Kedarnath is recognised as one of the divine resting places of Lord Shiva, while Badrinath is assigned to Vishnu.

The Garhwal, with its deep valleys, gorges and high mountain ridges, is naturally conducive to autonomous mountain kingdoms. Many of the kingdoms maintained their independence by establishing a *garh*, or fortress, in a strategic position to protect themselves from both their immediate neighbours and invading armies from north-west India. Even during the Moghul period, the region was only partially unified.

This position was to change in the early 19th century. The local rajahs were overrun by the armies of the Gurkhas, who had extended their kingdom from Nepal across to the Sutlej. The Gurkha ambitions, together with the formidable Sikh armies in the Punjab, were of great concern to the British. The East India Company thought it essential to maintain a neutral Himalayan territory between these two powers in order to protect their own trade interests. When the local rajahs asked the British to intervene, the East India Army was involved in a number of wars with the Gurkhas that resulted in the Treaty of Sagauli in 1815. This treaty brought Nepal's western border back to the Kali River, its present day border with India.

As a result of the treaty, the British gained the districts of Almora, Nainital, Kumaon and Dehra Dun, and the eastern district of the Garhwal. The western districts were restored to the local rajah, who established his capital at Tehri – now known as Tehri Garhwal. Hill stations were built to accommodate the British, notably at Dehra Dun, Mussorie, Almora, Nainital and Ranikhet. To complete the picture, Simla was also established at the same time – becoming the summer capital of India in 1864.

The British districts in the Garhwal were initially administered by the Residency of Bengal, then became part of the North-West Frontier Province, and after that part of the United Provinces. Finally, after Indian independence, the entire region became part of the state of Uttar Pradesh.

It was during the British rule, in the later part of the 19th century, that the hill trails of the Garhwal were improved. The region became more accessible, not only for the PWD and forest departments, but also for the Indian pilgrim, as many of the popular pilgrimage trails were upgraded. Yet many of these trails were constructed through deep and inaccessible gorges, where the occasional summer storm would wash away complete sections at a time. It is only recently that the main mountain trails have been made into roads, and the trekking times to the places of pilgrimage have been considerably reduced. Gangotri, for example, can now be reached by road. It is only one stage from the roadhead to Kedarnath and Yamunotri, and you can drive all the way to Badrinath. Pilgrims now gain greater merit by going higher

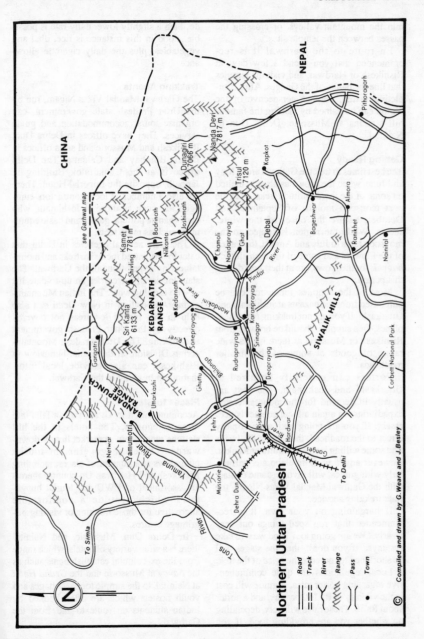

Northern Uttar Pradesh

Road
Track
River
Range
Pass
Town

Compiled and drawn by G. Weare and J. Besley

CHINA

NEPAL

Pithoragarh

Nanda Devi
7817 m

Dunagiri
7066 m

Trisul
7120 m

Kapkot

see Garhwal map

Kamet
7781 m

Badrinath

Almora

Shivling

Nilkanta

Joshimath

Bageshwar

Ranikhet

Sri Kanta
6133 m

KEDARNATH
RANGE

Kedarnath

Chamoli

Nandaprayag

Ghat

Debal

River

Nainital

Pindar

Gangotri

Mandakini River

Soneprayag

Ghat

Karanprayag

SIWALIK HILLS

BANDARPUNCH
RANGE

Uttarkashi

River

Ghuttu

Bhilangu

Rudraprayag

Srinagar

Corbett National Park

Netwar

Yamunotri

Tehri

Deoprayag

Yamuna River

Mussoorie

Rishikesh

Hardwar

Ganges River

Dehra Dun

To Delhi

Tons River

To Simla

into the mountain valleys, or crossing the passes between the temple sites.

En route to the Garhwal it is recommended that you spend a few days at Rishikesh or Hardwar, and visit the temples that line the banks of the Ganges. After completing a trek, another perspective of the region can be gained by visiting the famous hill stations at Mussorie, Dehra Dun or Nainital.

Getting Ready

The best times to trek the Garhwal are in May and June, when the snow has already melted on some of the lower altitude treks, or in the post monsoon months of September and October, before the onset of the winter snows. While the region is subject to the monsoon rains in July and August, the Valley of the Flowers and some of the high altitude *bugyals*, or meadows, are at their best during this period.

Most of the supplies for a trek can be purchased from the bazaars at Joshimath and Uttarkashi. If you are not trekking from these places, then supplies should be brought from Rishikesh or Mussorie as there isn't a wide range of goods at some of the smaller roadheads.

Porters can generally be hired at Uttarkashi and Joshimath. The best are usually in demand for the mountaineering expeditions, so again a local contact is necessary. If you are going with a small party direct to the roadhead, then you will always find some willing hands at Ghuttu or Kapkot. However anything more elaborate, particularly with guides, will involve some contact with the Garhwal Mandal Vikas Nigam, the state trekking service.

If bargaining on your own, it is recommended that you spell things out very clearly. 'We are going to ..., and we will take six days.' If you don't, then the stages will be shortened to increase the price of the trek.

Local regulations are quite comprehensive regarding porter rates. A guide will cost in the vicinity of Rs 100 per day, and a porter about Rs 50. These rates will vary, depending on whether you are providing food. If you

do, then a slightly lower daily rate is possible. Food in this instance is rice, dhal and vegetables, plus the daily cigarette allowance.

Trekking Agents

The Garhwal Mandal Vikas Nigam, run by the Uttar Pradesh state government, can organise tours, accommodation and guide services. They have offices in Dehra Dun, Rishikesh and Mussorie and sales offices in Delhi, Bombay and Calcutta. The Delhi office is at the Chandralok Building in Janpath, opposite the Imperial Hotel. There are also a number of local contractors-cum-agencies, such as those at Joshimath, who can organise porters, guides and basic equipment such as mess tents.

There are several agencies in Delhi that cater for organised inclusive treks and mountaineering expeditions in the Garhwal. The state tourist office carries an up-to-date list of who is doing what. The Indian Mountaineering Association in New Delhi can also help in this regard for areas not covered directly by the Uttar Pradesh government undertaking. The Uttar Pradesh Mountaineering Division, at the tourist bungalow in Rishikesh, can also provide local information on trekking in the Garhwal.

Places to Stay

Accommodation in Uttar Pradesh falls into three categories. The hotels in the hill stations range from upmarket luxury downwards. There are government tourist bungalows at a number of places, including Rishikesh and Hardwar. Up-country there's an assortment of PWD and tourist bungalows which provide a comfortable alternative for those trekking or visiting pilgrimage centres.

In Dehra Dun, Mussorie, and Nainital there is a wide variety of hotels, which range from the ex-colonial establishments such as the *Savoy* at Mussorie and the *Grand Hotel* at Nainital, to the simple tourist cottages and youth hostels which are often booked by Indian students en route to and from the Garhwal.

At Hardwar and Rishikesh there are the Uttar Pradesh state government *Tourist Bungalows* with rooms only for about Rs 40. The *Tourist Bungalow* at Rishikesh, about 8 km from the bus station, is particularly recommended. Food is available there and you can relax in the pleasant garden. The *Tourist Bungalow* at Hardwar is less conveniently situated, across the river from the main part of town. There are many hotels nearer the station, and of course the railway retiring rooms, providing you have a reservation.

In the mountain districts, apart from the locally run hotels, there is a comprehensive network of government-run places. There are *PWD Rest Houses* and *Tourist Bungalows* at Deoprayag, Rudraprayag and Karanprayag. At Joshimath, Badrinath, Soneprayag and Kedarnath there are *Tourist Bungalows* and *PWD Inspection Bungalows*. At Uttarkashi and Hanumanchatti, below Yamunotri, there are *Tourist Bungalows* and *Forest Rest Houses*. At Gangotri there is a *Forest Rest House* and a *Tourist Rest House* and at Yamunotri, a *Forest Rest House*.

Accommodation can be booked at Uttarkashi for Gangotri, at Mussorie for Yamunotri, at Joshimath for Badrinath and at Soneprayag for Kedarnath.

Further into the mountains there is a comprehensive system of *Forest Rest Houses* and chattris (pilgrims' rest houses), but after setting off from the roadhead a tent is an invaluable asset on whatever trek you undertake.

Getting There & Away

From Delhi there are regular bus services to Hardwar and Rishikesh, leaving from the interstate bus terminal. There are also frequent bus services to Dehra Dun, Mussorie, Nainital, Almora and Ranikhet. Deluxe buses are also operated by the Uttar Pradesh government, and bookings can be made at their offices in Janpath, New Delhi, or through one of the many private operators whose boards are displayed at the corner of Janpath and Connaught Place.

Train reservations from Delhi to Hardwar,

Rishikesh and Dehra Dun are always tight, so the tourist quota is the best alternative. Prices from Delhi to Dehra Dun are Rs 335 air-con class, Rs 148 1st class, and Rs 57 2nd class. To Rishikesh they are Rs 302 air-con, Rs 140 1st class, and Rs 42 2nd class.

Vayudoot run a daily flight from Delhi to Dehra Dun. The cost is US$40. Bookings are heavy, particularly in the pre-monsoon season.

To get you to the trek-off points, there are regular buses from Rishikesh to Uttarkashi for treks out of Gangotri, to Soneprayag for treks from Kedarnath and to Joshimath for treks from Badrinath.

From Rishikesh there are frequent buses to Dehra Dun, and from Dehra Dun there are daily bus services to Simla and other places in Himachal Pradesh.

Treks

The following treks have been selected for ease of arrangements, and would suit a first-time trekker to the Garhwal region. Many seasons could be spent researching the remote trails, and it is hoped that in future editions some of the longer and more challenging treks will also be included.

To assist in undertaking the following treks, there are details of the best times of the year to do the trek, the condition of the trails, the availability of porters and supplies and a description of the main pilgrimage centres such as Yamunotri, Gangotri, Kedarnath and Badrinath.

For a well-illustrated guide to the region, *Garhwal Himalaya* by Gurmeet & Elizabeth Thukel is highly recommended, while the local state trekking service, Garhwal Mandel Vikram Niwas, has also produced an informative guide.

Har-ki-Dun Valley

A trek up the Har-ki-Dun Valley can be undertaken from late spring through to November. The valley is a principal tributary of the Tons River and its villages are inhabited throughout the year. To reach the valley does not entail crossing any high passes so you can visit the villages even during the winter months, although a trek up to Har-ki-Dun and the higher meadows beyond the valley would not be possible.

The villages in the valley are linked by well-defined bridle trails, though this valley, like so many of the other inhabited valleys in Kashmir and Himachal Pradesh, will be linked by road in the next decade or so.

From all reports, the villagers are very hospitable, while a series of PWD Rest Houses means that it is not necessary to take a tent. Basic food supplies can also be purchased, although if you are planning to trek above the highest village at Osla, then both a tent and additional food supplies must be carried. The trail up to the summer pastures and glaciers at the base of the impressive Swargarohni peaks is well defined, although here as elsewhere a local guide can be a valuable asset for fully exploring the region.

From Dehra Dun or Mussorie it is a 7 hour drive by bus to the main village of Netwar. The cost is Rs 50 to Rs 60. Porters are available here for about Rs 45 per day plus food. There is a jeep trail to the next major village of Sunkiri. From here, the stage to the village at Talukar can be completed in 4 or 5 hours with a simple *Forest Rest House* for overnight accommodation. From the village of Talukar it is a further stage to Osla, the highest village in the valley, where biscuits and other basics can be purchased during the summer months.

Once past Osla, the trek up to the meadow of Har-ki-Dun can be completed in 5 to 6 hours. There is a *Tourist Rest House* under construction there, and a couple of days can be spent trekking in the vicinity of the Jamudar Glacier, and admiring the alpine backdrop of the Swargarohri peaks. The return trek to the roadhead can be completed in two stages, making this a worthwhile one-week trek without the need to cross high snowbound passes.

G1: HAR-KI-DUN TO YAMUNOTRI

An extension of the trek up the Har-ki-Dun Valley is to continue over the Majhakanda Pass to the pilgrim centre at Yamunotri. The trek can be undertaken as soon as the snows begin to melt in late June or early July. For those interested in wildflowers, the trek can also be completed during the monsoon, through July and August. As with all treks in the Garhwal region, the post-monsoon period from September to early October is an ideal time for completing this walk. Note that only the last stage of this trek is shown on the Garhwal map.

The trail is followed by villagers crossing from the Har-ki-Dun Valley to Yamunotri, and by the Gujar shepherds who graze their buffalo and sheep on the alpine meadows during the summer months. The trail, however, is not easy to locate, especially in the forest and through the boulder field just below the pass, so a local guide or porter from Osla is recommended. There is little in the way of accommdation, apart from some basic stone shelters, so it is essential to carry a tent as well as supplies.

The trek can be completed in five stages. The first two ascend through the forest to the meadows and camp below the pass, the third stage is over the pass, and there are a further two down to Yamunotri and the roadhead at Hanumanchatti. From here, it is a day's drive back to Dehra Dun, from where you can return to Delhi.

The trek commences from the village of Osla, two stages up from the roadhead at Netwar. From here, the trail ascends out of the main valley to one of the forest meadows where the Gujar camp during the season. There are plenty of intermediate campsites to choose from, and no shortage of water. The climb to the higher camp beneath the pass takes another full day, and provides good views of the Bandapunch Range. There is a rock shelter on the upper edge of the meadow where villagers from Osla spend the night.

The pass crossing on the following day is, by all accounts, strenuous. The trail is hard to follow at times, particularly early in the season when the snow on the boulders is melting. There are, however, magnificent views from the pass, before you descend over moraine to the camp site.

The trail on the fourth day is particularly steep – described by a trekker going the opposite way as 'a hands and knees job'. (On account of either the incline, or the fitness of the trekker). On reaching the treeline, the trail again follows a steep forest path to the camp at Damni.

From Damni the trail is more gradual, down to the Yamuna Valley and the temples at Yamunotri. You can spend some time here before trekking the last few hours down the pilgrim trail to the roadhead at Hanumanchatti.

G2: HANUMANCHATTI TO YAMUNOTRI & RETURN

Yamunotri is the source of the Yamuna River. The main temple is on the left bank of the river, and is dedicated to the goddess Yamunotri. Just below the temple there are hot springs where the water emerges from the ground at boiling point. This is a popular place for the pilgrims to cook their food after returning from the temple. To reach Yamunotri from Hanumanchatti takes about 5 or 6 hours, and it is normal to stay overnight at one of the pilgrim shelters, and return to the roadhead the following day. It would be ambitious to complete the trek in one day.

Gangotri Area

From Delhi it takes two or three days by bus to reach the source of the Ganges River. The first to Rishikesh or Mussorie, and the second to Gangotri. From Rishikesh it takes between 5 and 7 hours (Rs 45) to reach Uttarkashi, where you can stay overnight if you're hiring porters or guides for your trek. From Uttarkashi to Gangotri takes a further 4 or 5 hours (Rs 30), depending on the condition of the road, which is subject to landslides during the summer.

Gangotri, at 3140 metres, is situated at the junction of the Kedar Gorge and the Bhagirathi River, which is the main tributary of the Ganges. The Bhagirathi River at this point flows in a north-west direction, giving the town its name – Gangotri means 'Ganges turned north'. Many pilgrims visit the temple of Gangotri, which is dedicated to the goddess Ganga. The shrine of Bhagirathi was built in the early 19th century by the Gurkha commander in the Garhwal, Anan Singh Thaypa. The temple remains open from May until October, when the priests take the temple offerings back to Uttarkashi.

Treks

Three treks are outlined in this section, including the trek to Dodital out of Uttakashi. These treks can be completed in a few days and do not require complex logistics. Each of the treks is a return walk, so excess gear can be left behind at the roadhead.

Porters are available at Uttarkashi and Gangotri for Rs 45 to Rs 50. Basic supplies can be purchased, preferably from Uttarkashi, while a tent is essential as the region is renowned for sudden changes of weather during the summer.

The treks can be completed from mid-June onwards but, as always, anticipate some snow plodding in the early part of the season. The monsoon clouds form by early July and remain to the end of August. From this time on, through September to mid-October, the weather is more settled and it is an ideal time to trek.

G3: TO GAUMUKH & GANGOTRI GLACIER

The first stage beyond Gangotri is to Bhujbasa, which is a convenient place for an overnight camp. The path to Bhujbasa is along a well-defined bridle track which cuts up through the pine forest to the alpine plateau at 3800 metres. The 11 km climb takes about 4 to 5 hours and gains about 300 metres in altitude.

There is a *Forest Rest House* at Chirbasa, midway between Gangotri and Bhujbasa, and many tea stalls along the route. At Bhujbasa there is an *ashram* where both

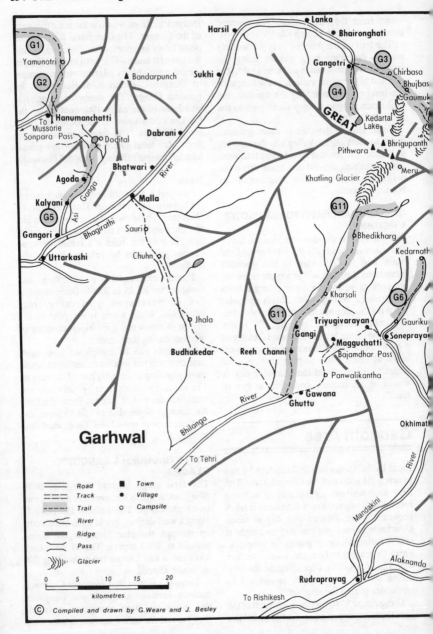

Garhwal

Road
Track
Trail
River
Ridge
Pass
Glacier

Town
Village
Campsite

0   5   10   15   20
kilometres

© Compiled and drawn by G.Weare and J. Besley

G1 Yamunotri
G2
Bandarpunch
Harsil
Lanka
Bhaironghati
Gangotri G3
Chirbasa
Bhujbas
Gaumukh
G4
GREAT
Kedartal Lake
Bhrigupanth
Pithwara
Meru
Khatling Glacier
Sukhi
To Mussorie
Sonpara Pass
Hanumanchatti
Dodital
Dabrani
River Ganga
Bhatwari
Agoda
Kalyani
Asi Ganga
Malla
Sauri
Chuhn
Bhagirathi
Gangori
Uttarkashi
G5
G11
Bhedikharg
Kedarnath
Kharsali
G11
Triyugivarayan
Gangi
Magguchatti
Bajamdhar Pass
Reeh Channi
Panwalikantha
Jhala
Budhakedar
Gawana
Ghuttu
Bhilanga River
To Tehri
Gaurikund
Sonepraya
G6
Okhimath
Mandakini River
Rudraprayag
Alaknanda
To Rishikesh

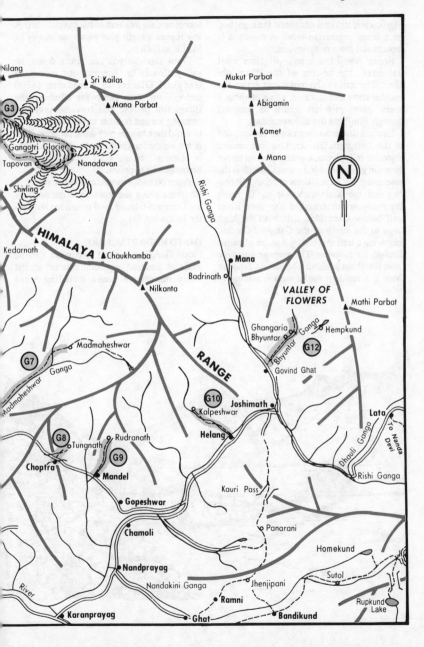

pilgrims and trekkers can spend the night and get a basic vegetarian meal. A donation is appreciated from nonpilgrims.

From Bhujbasa many pilgrims visit Gaumukh, the source of the Bhagirathi River. The trail to Gaumukh cuts across the boulder scree and moraine, a trek of about 3 hours. Most pilgrims return to Gangotri through Bhujbasa the following day.

Beyond Bhujbasa the trek can be extended to the Gangotri Glacier. One convenient objective is Tapovan, a grassy plateau above the main glacier at 4463 metres, which is the base camp for expeditions climbing Shivaling and the Kedarnath Range. To reach Tapovan you must cross the Bhagirathi River well below Gaumukh. Climb to the high ridge to the south of the Gangotri Glacier, following a trail marked by a series of cairns through the moraine. The average trek time from Bhujbasa is about 5 hours. At Tapovan there is a resident sadhu who is willing to

accommodate trekkers in his cave/shelter. A few rupees a night plus your own supply of food is sufficient.

From Tapovan you can return down the valley directly to Gangotri, or traverse the Gangotri Glacier to Nanadavan (4500 metres), the base camp for climbing the Bhagirathi peaks. The traverse involves crossing ice and boulder terrain, so take care to avoid the obvious crevassed sections. This is not for the inexperienced trekker. A guide is essential, as are your own tent, stove, kerosene and supplies.

From Nanadavan you can return direct to Bhujbasa along the moraine to the north of the Gangotri Glacier, and return to Gangotri the following day.

G4: TO KEDARTAL LAKE
From Gangotri a short excursion can be made to Kedartal, a glacial lake set amidst many impressive peaks including Meru

(6672 metres), Pithwara (6904 metres) and Bhrigupanth (6772 metres). The trek is quite strenuous in places, and the need for acclimatisation should also be borne in mind, as Kedartal is situated at 4500 metres.

The trek follows the Kedar Gorge along a trail that is used by shepherds from June onwards. The trail ascends through forest to the camp at Bhoj Kharak, a meadow just above the treeline. This stage takes about 5 hours to complete.

From Bhoj Kharak it is a further 5 hour climb through the open meadows to a higher camp – Kedar Kharak. The camp is distinguished by a number of shepherd camps – an Arcadian setting during the summer months.

From Kedar Kharak, the trek across boulders to the edge of Kedartal can be tiring, but the views to Bhrigunpanth and Thalesgar peaks compensate. The return from Kedar Kharak to the roadhead can be completed in one stage.

G5: KALYANI TO DODITAL

The trek to Dodital can be completed in three stages, although it is recommended that you take sufficient food and supplies to spend a few days appreciating the natural beauty in the vicinity of the lake.

From Uttarkashi, follow the Gangotri road for about 5 km, until you reach Gangori, where you may able to hitch a ride in a truck to the roadhead at Kalyani. From Kalyani, the trek ascends through the forest, quite steeply in places, to the *Forest Rest House* at Agoda. This stage takes about 3 to 4 hours.

The following day the trail is well marked, but again steep in places, to the *Forest Rest House* at Dodital. The time taken on this stage is about 5 or 6 hours. There is a resident caretaker at the Forest Rest House during the season, and some basic food supplies may be available.

There is an extension to this trek which involves three further stages to Yamunotri. The first involves ascending to a high camp in the meadows beneath the Sonpara Pass (3953 metres). The second stage is crossing the pass, with superb views of Bandarpunch, then descending to the treeline to camp. The third stage involves a steep descent through the forest to Hanumanchatti and Yamunotri.

Panch Kedar & the Kedarnath Region

The Kedarnath region is drained by the Mandakini River, one of the main tributaries of the Alaknanda, and the Bhilanga River, one of the major tributaries of the Bhagirathi. It is characterised by deep gorges and huge glaciers south of the main Himalaya, including the Khatling Glacier.

Kedarnath is the most sacred site in this central region of the Garhwal. It is dedicated to Shiva and is one of the *Panch Kedar*, the five sites that devout Hindus should visit during their time in the region. The sites of the Panch Kedar are places where Shiva is said to have rested, and comprise Kedarnath, Madmaheshwar, Tungnath, Rudranath and Kalpeshwar. Today, each is no more than a day or so from the nearest roadhead, and the pilgrimage can be completed in a week or so.

G6: TO KEDARNATH

Kedarnath is a day's walk from the roadhead at Gaurikund. Pilgrims normally drive from Rishikesh to Soneprayag, 5 km below Gaurikund. The state authorities establish a tent colony at Gaurikund during the season. The temple is open by the last week of April and remains open until the Diwali festival, normally in mid-October. The shrine at Kedarnath also commemorates the sage Shankaracharya, who died here. He is credited with revitalising Hindu philosophy during the 8th century, and his travels across the Himalaya are well documented.

The trail to Kedarnath is well defined along the banks of the Mandakini River. At the village of Rambara the trail steepens until it reaches the next main resting place at Garurchatti. Here the Kedar Valley opens out to reveal some magnificent views of the Himalaya. Several day trips can be made out of Kedarnath. These include a 10 km walk to

Chararadi Tal, where some of Gandhi's ashes were scattered in 1948.

G7: TO MADMAHESHWAR

The trek to Madmaheshwar is the most strenuous of the Panch Kedar treks. From the roadhead at Okhimath, the winter residence of the priests of Kerdarnath, the trail follows the Madmaheshwar Ganga for 30 km up to the site, which is at 3289 metres. There is a *PWD Bungalow* at Okhimath, and basic shelters for the pilgrims en route.

G8: TO TUNGNATH

At 3680 metres, close to the summit of the Chandra Shila peak, Tungnath is the highest temple in the Garhwal Himalaya. From Okhimath there is a local bus to Choptra, 17 km further on, and from there it's a steep 6 km climb through the forests to the temple. The entrance to the Tungnath Temple is guarded by two sculptured lions, and behind them rises a short pagoda-like tower, capped with a wooden roof and golden spire.

G9: TO RUDRANATH

From Chopra take a bus 16 km along a fair-weather road to Mandel. From there the trail branches north and climbs gradually to the temple at Rudranath. It is dedicated to Rudreshwar (Shiva) who is said to have slewn the demon Andhakasur here. There is a *PWD Bungalow* at Mandel, and basic shelters along the trail.

G10: TO KALPESHWAR

This shrine, at 2786 metres, is approached from Helang, on the Rishikesh-Badrinath highway. From Helang the trail runs northwest and climbs 13 km to the temple in the village at Urgam. For the more devout pilgrims, there is a direct cross-country trail from Rudranath to Kalpeshwar. This avoids the road and can be completed in two stages.

G11: TO KHATLING GLACIER

The Khatling Glacier lies at the head of the Bhilanga River, one of the main tributaries that eventually flow into the Ganges. The glacier is in the heart of the Tehri Garhwal,

with Gangotri to the north and Kedarnath to the north-east. From Rishikesh it is a 5 hour bus ride to Tehri (about Rs 50), and a further 3 hours to Ghuttu, where there is a small hotel with rooms for Rs 50 per night. Little in the way of supplies is available, so it is advisable to bring food for the trek with you from Hardwar.

The trek takes a week to complete, with the trail passing through villages on the initial stages of the trek. From there, the trail winds through thick forest to the high meadows, and these extend to the moraine at the base of the glacier. Spectacular mountain views are, from all reports, the highlight of this trek.

Stage 1: Ghuttu to Gangi

From Ghuttu the route follows a jeep track as far as the village of Deolang. The track has not been maintained, and rock avalanches block the way for vehicles. Past Deolang, the trail continues through terraced fields and small settlements to the village of Reeh Channi. From there, it is a steady climb to the village of Buranschauri. 'Buran' means rhododendron, and the countryside is dotted with trees which come into full bloom during late spring. It is easy to miss the village as it is well above the main trail. There is a *Forest Rest House* here if you decide to stop early.

After passing Buranschauri there is a steep climb before the trail continues to Gangi, the highest village in the valley. Accommodation here is restricted to the school shelter, but there is a camping site further up the trail. If you are going strong, the trek from Ghuttu to Gangi can be completed in about 8 or 9 hours.

Stage 2: Gangi to Kharsali

From Gangi, the trail initially descends to the river. Here the track splits; the trail to Khatling heads along the river path. (The path which diverges to the left leads up a steep incline to Sahastra Tal and a series of lakes, and eventually takes you along a rough trail to Uttarkashi.)

From the river, the trail to Khatling crosses several side streams that may be a problem to ford either early on in the season before the Gujar have rebuilt the bridges, or during the monsoon when they can be swept away. Apart from that, the trail ascends gradually through the forest to the camp at Kharsali, a large meadow surrounded by giant conifers and oaks. Time from Gangi to Kharsali is about 5 to 6 hours.

Stage 3: Kharsali to Bhedikharg

From Kharsali the trail crosses the main river and continues along the forest track, with plenty of ups and downs, to traverse the side streams before reaching the alpine meadows of Bhedikharg. There is no shortage of camp-sites here, and it is an ideal base from which to explore the Khatling Glacier. The area is renowned for wildflowers during the summer.

Stage 4: Bhedikharg to Khatling Glacier & Return

Khatling Glacier is 11 km beyond Bhedikharg, and it takes a full day to get to the glacier and back. There are a number of hanging glaciers above the valley floor, and the peaks of the Jogu group (6463 metres), Tholay Sagar (6902 metres), Rudugaira (5364 metres), and Kirti Sambh (6578 metres) make this a spectacular setting.

Getting Away The return to the roadhead can be completed in two stages, making this an ideal one week trek.

Badrinath

Badrinath has traditionally been the resting place of Vishnu. According to legend it was once the abode of both Vishnu and Shiva, but the arrangement didn't work well. Shiva offered to move to Kedarnath and Vishnu, as an act of gratitude, stipulated that all pilgrims should first pay homage to Shiva at Kedarnath before making the journey to Badrinath.

The temple opens in the first week of May and remains open to the end of October, when the priests return to Joshimath for the winter.

The journey from Rishikesh to Badrinath involves a drive of 10 hours to Joshimath, and from here it is another 44 km and 2½ hours. An overnight stay in Joshimath is recommended.

Joshimath Area

Two treks are outlined in this section: to Hempkund and the Valley of the Flowers, and to Rupkund Lake.

Ever since Frank Smythe's discovery of the Valley of the Flowers in the 1930s, it has been a popular destination. Between mid-June and mid-September the valley is an enchanting vision, filled with a bewildering variety of wildflowers. Snow-clad mountains stand in bold relief, creating an impressive backdrop. The dimensions of the valley, nearly 10 km long and 2 km wide, are not large enough to support a stream of trekking parties throughout the season, and for this reason some restriction on numbers was necessary.

Hempkund provides a different attraction. In the Sikh holy book, the *Granth Sahib*, the Sikh guru Govind Singh recounts how, in a previous life, he had meditated on the shores of a lake surrounded by seven snow-capped mountains. Hempkund, according to the Sikhs, fitted that description and was designated a holy lake. Each year many thousands of devotees come to the lake, at an altitude of 4370 metres, and immerse themselves in the icy waters.

The Valley of the Flowers, actually the valley of the Bhyuntar Ganga, has been declared a national park, and no overnight camping is permitted at present. However, it is possible to trek up to Hempkund near the entrance of the valley, although it is best to check with the authorities as the regulations change quite frequently.

There are also restrictions on entry to the Nanda Devi Sanctuary, so the trek to the Rupkund Lake is included as an alternative.

This can be arranged in a simple fashion without a huge army of porters though a local guide, tent and supplies are necessary.

As in the rest of the Garhwal, the post-monsoon period is the most settled time to trek in the region, but the Valley of the Flowers is at its most attractive during the rainy months of July and August. For those particularly interested in wildflowers, a trek to the meadows at Dodital, or to the *bugyals* (meadows) on the approach to Rupkund, may provide an alternative if the restrictions over entry to the Bhyuntar Valley continue.

Joshimath can be reached by bus from Rishikesh. It takes a full 10 hour day and the cost is Rs 58.

G12: TO HEMPKUND & THE VALLEY OF THE FLOWERS

Both Hempkund and the Valley of the Flowers can be reached from the roadhead at Govind Ghat, 10 km from Joshimath on the road to Badrinath. Porters and guides can be arranged at Joshimath, although it is easy to rely, for a few days, on the many teahouses-cum-hotels which line the main pilgrim route.

Stage 1: Govind Ghat to Ghangaria

From Govind Ghat it is a 14 km trek to Ghangaria on the first stage of this trek. The first few km to Bhyuntar are easy, but from there on the climb becomes steeper. Hundreds of Sikh pilgrims, in various stages of physical fitness, use this well-marked trail, and there are tea stalls along the way to relieve the climb.

Ghangaria, also known as Govind Dham, is set between high mountain walls and dense forest at 3084 metres. As a large pilgrim complex there is a *gurdwara* (Sikh temple) with free board and lodging, some small *hotels* and a *Government Bungalow*. The camping ground is about 2 km further up the track.

Stage 2: Ghangaria to Hempkund & Back

Two km above Ghangaria the trail splits: one trail goes to Hempkund, the other to the Valley of the Flowers. The trail to Hempkund is well defined, although the ascent is quite steep and it takes 3 or 4 hours to cover the 6 km to the lake.

Stage 3: Ghangaria to the Valley of the Flowers & Back

The alternative trail to the start of the Valley of the Flowers involves a trek of 5 to 6 km. This trek includes a descent down to the Bhyuntar Ganga, which is crossed by bridge. The trail then climbs gradually for 2 km to the entrance to the alpine valley.

You can walk into and around the valley, but you can't camp there. It is possible to recognise some of the trek options at the head of the valley. These include the Bhyuntar Pass that leads to Joshimath, and the Khulia Pass, from where it was once possible to trek to Badrinath. To trek these routes special permission must be obtained.

DEBAL TO RUPKUND LAKE

At an altitude of 4778 metres, Rupkund Lake is steeped in local legend. It has often been referred to as 'the mystery lake', on account of the many skeletons of humans and horses discovered and preserved in the snows close to its waters. Many interesting theories have been forwarded. One of the most plausible is that the skeletons are those of pilgrims who were caught in inclement weather while on their way to the nearby Homkund Lake.

There are a number of approaches to Rupkund. The first is from Joshimath across the Kauri Pass and then on to Homekund and Rupkund. The second is from Ghat, a village 20 km from Nandprayag in the Nandakini Valley. The third approach is from the south via the village of Debal in the Pindar Valley. With each of these options, a local guide is recommended as the trails frequently criss-cross the local tracks. A tent is also necessary, unless you are prepared to take a chance on sleeping in the various cave shelters that the shepherds and porters use throughout the season.

Note that Rupkund Lake appears at the south-east corner of the Garwhal map. Only the very last part of this trek is on the map.

Stage 1: Debal to Lohajang

There is a daily bus service from Rishikesh to Thardi, and from there you take a local bus on to Debal. The cost is Rs 48. From Debal the road has been constructed up the valley as far as Mandali. Jeeps cover this stage for Rs 12 per seat.

From the roadhead, the trail leads through a number of small villages and continues steadily uphill to Lohajang where there is a *Forest Rest House*.

Stage 2: Badni Bughal

The next stage involves a gradual 14 km climb to the village of Wan. The time taken is about 5 hours. There is a *Forest Rest House* here, but there is ample time to continue up through the forest to the delightful meadow of Badni Bughal.

Stage 3: Badni Bughal to Bhogubasa

From the Badni meadow it is a further stage to the high camp at Bhogubasa where there is a cave shelter. It's frequented by shepherds during the season, but favoured by the local porters as a convenient night halt before continuing to Rupkund the following day.

Stage 4: Bhogubasa to Rupkund Lake & Back

From Bhogubasa it is a 7 hour return trek to the lake. The trek involves quite a steep climb over boulders to the rim of the lake. Views of Trisuli and Nanda Kot are a great attraction.

Option If you're self-sufficient, the trek from Rupkund can be extended by climbing the rocky ridge via the Joara Gali to Homekund.

Darjeeling & Sikkim

Treking in the areas of Darjeeling and Sikkim is not developed to the level that it has been in the West Himalaya of India. The huge dimensions of Kanchenjunga can be appreciated from both Sikkim and Darjeeling, while the approach walks lead through tropical and temperate forests that support flora and fauna not found in the West Himalaya.

A trek out of Darjeeling is quite easy to organise, and an ideal way to spend a few days in the hills.

In contrast, the treks out of Sikkim are difficult for the individual to undertake. Trekking groups must comprise at least four people and the trek must be organised prior to their arrival India, through a local agency recognised by the Sikkim tourist department. The itinerary is restricted to the region from Yuksam to Dzongri and on to the Sikkim-Nepal border. However, regulations are forever changing and the current easing of restrictions on individuals sightseeing may eventually extend to trekking.

History

The region was originally populated by the Lepchas, a tribal people thought to have migrated from Assam in the 13th century. The Lepchas were essentially nature worshippers, moving from one forest clearing to the next as they spread throughout the valleys of Sikkim. With the coming of the Tibetans to Sikkim, during the 16th and 17th centuries, the Lepchas moved to the more remote regions of the country.

In 1641 the Dalai Lama in Lhasa appointed Penchoo Namgyal as the first king of Sikkim. At this time the country included part of eastern Nepal, part of the Chumbi Valley in Tibet, some of the western valleys of Bhutan, Darjeeling, Kalingpong and territory down to the Indian plains.

In the 18th century Sikkim was involved in a series of wars with Bhutan that resulted in the loss of much of the southern foothills,

as well as Kalingpong, on the important trade route between India and Tibet.

More territory was lost after 1780, following the Gurkha expansion in Nepal. The balance of power was again to change following the conflict between the British East India Company and the Gurkhas. The Treaty of Siliguri in 1817 ensured that the territtory lost to the Gurkhas was returned by the British to the raja of Sikkim. In return, the British assumed control over Sikkim's external affairs and its trade negotiations with Nepal, Tibet and Bhutan.

In 1835 the British pressured the Raja to grant them Darjeeling, which they wanted as a cool Himalayan hill station away from the summer heat of Calcutta, and also as a means of securing a hold on trade with Tibet. An agreement was reached and an annual payment made to the raja. The raja was not totally comfortable with the agreement however, and Tibet also voiced concern as it still regarded Sikkim as one of its vassal states.

In 1849 matters came to a head. A high-ranking British official and a renown botanist, who were touring Sikkim with the permission of the raja and the British government, were arrested by the Sikkim government. The British took this as an affront to their position and, after the release of the prisoners, they temporarily withdrew the raja's stipend and annexed the area between the Sikkim border and the Indian plains. This effectively redrew the borders of Sikkim, cutting it off from the plains except through British territory, and at the same time gave Darjeeling direct access to the rest of British India.

Further British expansion lead to the declaration of Sikkim as a protectorate in 1861, and a further delineation of its borders. The Tibetans, however, were becoming increasingly suspicious of British expansion, and in 1886 they invaded Sikkim to reassert their authority. This was resisted by the

British and the powers of the raja were further reduced.

The British were keen to develop the country. Workers from Nepal were attracted to the tea plantations in Darjeeling, and many settled there, and also in Sikkim. When India became independent in 1947, Sikkim became a protectorate under the Indian Union.

In the early 1960s the Nepalese constituted some 75% of Sikkim's population. The Sikkim raja upheld a policy to prohibit further immigration and to restrict the right of Nepalese to citizenship. Demonstrations followed and the raja sought refuge in India. India intervened, the raja was pensioned off and Sikkim was declared the 22nd state of India.

Darjeeling

Getting Ready

The trekking season in Darjeeling is very similiar to that in eastern Nepal. The post-monsoon season in October and November brings clear days and warm temperatures, particularly in the valleys. The temperatures drop considerably in December and January, although this should not preclude the short treks out of Darjeeling. The spring season, from March through to May, has many attractions. The days are longer and the rhododendrons come into bloom, remaining in full colour until the first of the monsoon rains reach the area in mid-June.

When undertaking a trek, it is recommended that you bring your own sleeping bag, although you may be able to hire one from the Youth Hostel in Darjeeling. You could get by without a tent, as there are PWD huts or forest rest houses along most of the trek routes. Food and provisions can be purchased in Darjeeling, while guides and porters are available from the local agencies. Guides rates vary around Rs 100 per day and porters around Rs 60.

As of September 1990, a permit to visit Darjeeling is no longer required.

Things to See & Do

Tiger Hill, the highest point in the area, is about 11 km from Darjeeling. It is a pleasant walk from town taking about 2 to 3 hours. To appreciate the dawn views over Kanchenjunga you must make an early start, or stay overnight at the local *Tourist Lodge* which can be booked from the tourist office in Darjeeling.

From Tiger Hill it is a short trek to the Ghoom Buddhist Monastery, about 8 km from town. It is the most famous monastery in the Darjeeling area, with its statue of the Maitreya Buddha.

Also recommended is a visit to the Himalayan Mountaineering Institute, about 2 km from town. It has a museum with a collection of mountaineering equipment and memorabilia, a relief model of the Himalaya and samples of local flora and flauna.

Places to Stay

Like most Indian hill stations, Darjeeling has a wide variety of accommodation. At the top end is the *Windamere Hotel*, on Observatory Hill, where a room with all meals costs about Rs 500/700 for a single/double. A little cheaper, but with a similiar atmosphere, is the *Darjeeling Club* (formerly the Tea Planters Club), with singles/doubles for around Rs 550/400, including meals. Accommodation comes complete with comfortable lounges and fans in the bedrooms.

At the other end of the scale, the *Youth Hostel*, above Dr Zakir Hussan Rd, is popular with trekkers. It has two rooms, at Rs 30, and dormitory accommodation at Rs 10 per person per night. The hostel is well maintained with a friendly manager. It also rents out trekking gear and keeps an informative log of trekkers comments.

Other hotels recommended include those run by Tibetan families, including the *Shamrock Hotel* and the *Hotel Pagoda*, with rooms for about Rs 60 to Rs 70 a double. Both are close to the main bazaar, and if they are full there are plenty of other budget hotels in the vicinity.

Getting There & Away

The nearest airport is at Bagdogra, near Siliguri, about 90 km from Darjeeling. There are daily flights from Delhi (US$128) and Calcutta (US$50).

There are numerous buses throughout the day from Siliguri to Darjeeling. The drive takes 3 to 4 hours, and costs Rs 15. Taxis are an alternative and cost Rs 100 per seat.

Broad guage trains run to to New Jalaiguri, near Siliguri, from where the famous miniature railway, or 'toy train', runs to Darjeeling. The Assam Mail, from Delhi to New Jalaiguri, takes about 36 hours and costs Rs 601 1st class, and Rs 174 2nd class. The Darjeeling Mail operates overnight from Calcutta to New Jalaiguri, takes 12 to 13 hours and costs Rs 281 1st class, Rs 102 2nd class. Alternatively there is a faster video coach from Calcutta to Siliguri which costs Rs 100 and operates overnight, arriving in time for the morning toy train departure for Darjeeling.

Services on the miniature railway were discontinued in 1986, following political disturbances and damage caused by landslides. The political problems have been resolved and repairs have commenced, so hopefully the toy train will be running by the time you get there. The trip to Darjeeling takes 7 hours and costs Rs 73 for 1st class and Rs 25 for 2nd class. It's a memorable journey and one you shouldn't miss.

From Nepal It is 12 hours by bus from Kathmandu to the border at Karabitta. The border is open 24 hours a day. A taxi going directly from the border to Darjeeling takes a further 3 to 4 hours, and costs about Rs 200 per seat if you share. Alternatively you can take a bus to Siliguri (about 45 minutes) and then pick up a shared taxi (Rs 100 per seat), catch the bus or take the toy train.

DARJEELING TO PHALUT & RETURN

The trek to Phalut via Rimbik and returning

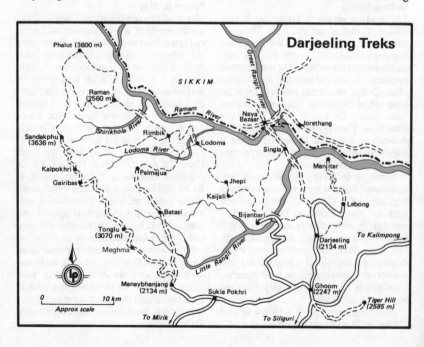

via Sandakphu is the most popular trek out of Darjeeling. The views from Phalut across to Kanjchenjunga are breathtaking, while the approach walk through the luxuriant forest makes this an ideal break away from Darjeeling.

In many respects it is is similar to trekking in Nepal, with lodges and small hotels along the main trail. Advance bookings are necessary if you intend to stay at the *Youth Hostels* at Rimbik, Raman and Sandakphu. There are also *Dak Bungalows* and *Forest Rest Houses*. These also require advance booking, but if you just turn up you are unlikely to be refused. Food along the trail is also available, although it is advisable to bring chocolate and dried fruit for the daytime. The trail is not hard to follow and porters can be hired from Rimbik for about Rs 60 per day.

Unfortunately, the magnificent forests attract their fair share of leeches, particularly in the months of October, November, March and April, so some medication should be carried, plus the mandatory box of waterproof matches.

From Darjeeling there is a regular bus service to Rimbik that takes around 5 hours and costs Rs 15. There is accommodation, and supplies are available in the bazaar if you intend to cook on your trek.

From Rimbik it is a 4 hour walk to Raman. The trek is initially quite level before dropping steeply to the Shirikhola River. From there the trail levels out for 9 km to Raman. There is a *Youth Hostel* in Raman and camping spots in the vicinity.

From Raman the trail continues to the Raman River, then there is a steep ascent, through forest and rhododendruns, to Phalut. The distance from Raman to Phalut is about 11 km, and the average walking time is around 6 to 7 hours. At Phalut there are magificent views of Kanchenjunga, and the peak of Everest can also be seen on a clear day. Phalut is at an altitude of 3600 metres, and it is not unusual to experience some snow conditions there, especially in December and January.

From Phalut it takes one day back to Sandakphu. There is a steep zig-zag descent, followed by a taxing climb to the ridge at Sandakphu. Views are on a par with those from Phalut, and jeeps ply the track, via Tonglu, to Darjeeling. Alternatively, you can walk the final stage back to to Rimbik in a morning, with time to catch a bus back to Darjeeling the same day.

Sikkim

Getting Ready

The trekking season in Sikkim is the same as in Darjeeling. In spring the rhododendrons are at their best, and the variety of blooms is particularly impressive through till the end of May. However, the higher elevation of the treks requires more preparation, and groups in December and January should be prepared for snow conditions above 3000 metres.

A sleeping bag and tent are necessary when trekking in Sikkim, as the huts on the higher camps out of Dzongri are inadequate. Tinned food can be brought from Darjeeling or from Gangtok.

The permit requirements for Sikkim have been relaxed during 1990. If you're sightseeing in Sikkim, it's no longer necessary to apply for an entry permit before you arrive in India. A 15 day permit can be issued by the Sikkim authorities on your arrival in Delhi or Calcutta.

For trekking however:

Applications for permission for trekking in West Sikkim should reach the office of the Deputy Director, Sikkim Tourism, New Sikkim House, Chanakyapuri, New Delhi two months prior to the date of the intended trek.

What this adds up to is that you need to have a minimum of four starters in your group, your arrangements must go through a local agency recognised by the Sikkim tourist department, and the trek is restricted to the Yuksam-Dzongri for a maximum length of seven to 10 days.

Regulations are forever changing and you

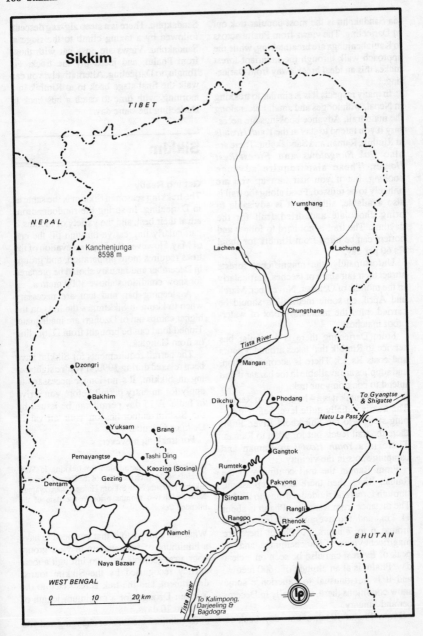

Sikkim

TIBET

NEPAL

▲ Kanchenjunga
8598 m

Yumthang

Lachen ●   ● Lachung

Chungthang

Tista River

Dzongri ●

Bakhim ●

Mangan ●

Yuksam ●   ● Brang

Phodang ●

Dikchu ●

To Gyangtse & Shigatse

Pemayangtse ●   ● Tashi Ding

Natu La Pass

Gezing ●   Keozing (Sosing) ●

Gangtok ●

Dentam ●

Rumtek ●

Pakyong ●

Singtam ●

Namchi ●

Rangli ●

Rangpo ●   Rhenok ●

BHUTAN

Naya Bazaar ●

WEST BENGAL

0   10   20 km

To Kalimpong,
Darjeeling &
Bagdogra

should double check the details when applying.

Things to See & Do

Gangtok consists of a series of modern, rather ugly, concrete buildings set across a ridge above the Ranipod River. From the bazaar it is a short distance to the Institute of Tibetology and the Orchid Sanctuary.

The Institute of Tibetology was founded in 1958 and possesses one of the largest collections of books on Mahayanna Buddhism. The Institute is situated in the Orchid Sanctuary where you can see many of the 454 species of orchid found in Sikkim. From the sanctuary it is a short walk up the hill to the Deer Park and the Royal Chapel, which also houses a large collection of Buddhist scriptures and tankas, but is not always open to visitors.

A visit to Rumtek Monastery can be made on a day trip out of Gangtok, or on the way

Silversmith

to Pemayangtse or Yuksam. The monastery is 24 km from Gangtok across the Ranipod Valley and is open to visitors. The main monastery has been recently constructed and is the seat of the Gyalwa Karmapa, the head monk of the Karpya sect, one of the older sects of Tibetan Buddhism. There are a number of small hotels if you want to stay overnight.

Pemayangtse is the second oldest monastery in Sikkim, and is affiliated with the Nyingma sect – the Tantric sect established by the Indian guru Padmasambhava in the 8th century.

Places to Stay

The upmarket hotels in Gangtok cater mainly to organised sightseeing groups, and include the *Norkhill Hotel*, the *Tashi Delek* and the *Hotel Ashok Mayur*. All are similiarly priced at Rs 400/500 for a single/double, including all meals, or Rs 225/300 for rooms only. The *Hotel Tibet*, on Stadium Rd, with rooms from Rs 120 to Rs 200, has been recommended.

At the budget end, the *Gangtok Tourist Lodge* has rooms for Rs 50 upwards. The hotel is managed by the Government of Sikkim tourist department, and transport to the hotel is available from the tourist office above the bus stand.

Getting There & Away

The bus trip to Gangtok from Siliguri, or from the airport at Bagdogra, takes about 5 hours and costs around Rs 50. The buses are always crowded and overbooked. The minibus service is a good alternative but it also is heavily booked, so plan well in advance.

From Gangtok there is a daily bus service to Pemayangtse, taking about 8 hours and costs around Rs 40. After a visit to the monastery, there is a daily bus service to Yuksam where you can commence your trek. Taxis are a good way of getting around in Sikkim if you want to save time. The cost is high, around Rs 1000 to Rs 1500 from Gangtok to Pemayangtse via Rumtek, but it's very convenient if time is at a premium.

YUKSAM TO DZONGRI & RETURN

The trek out of Yuksam to Dzongri can be completed in four to five days, allowing time for acclimatisation and day-walks out of Dzongri. From Dzongri there is the option to trek further towards Kanchenjunga, to the Gocha La at 4940 metres. The trek out of Yuksam (1780 metres) involves quite a steep ascent to Dzongri (4030 metres), and additional days for acclimatisation are recommended.

Accommodation on the trek is in basic huts that have been constructed at Bakhim and Dzongri. The Dzongri trek is popular with Indian students, particularly during the May holidays, so it is advisable, for peace of mind, to bring your own tent. A sleeping bag and an insulated mat must also be carried, and supplies that can be purchased at Yuksam.

From Yuksam the trail is level for the first few km, following a well-marked route above the Rathong Gorge. After 10 km the trail diverts and climbs through forest to the Lepcha village of Bakhim. There is a good campsite above the village, but water is a problem.

From Bakhim the ascent continues through beautiful rhododendron forests, then crosses the alpine ridges to the yak herders camps at Dzongri. An intermediate camp at Phetang is recommended unless your party is on a very tight schedule.

From Phetang the trail splits. One path follows the course of the Rathong river to the base of Rathong (6683 metres), while the other climbs the ridge to Dzongri, with views across to Rathong and the tip of Kanchenjunga. A side trek along the nearby ridges reveals a clearer view of the huge Kanchenjunga massif to the north.

From Dzongri it is a comparatively level stage to the camp at Onglathang, and on to Samiti, the glacial lake at the base of the Gocha La. The pass provides some superb views of Kanchenjunga and the other main peaks in the vicinity of the massif. It also marks the limit of the current trekking permit in Sikkim.

Index

TEXT

Map references are in **bold** type.

170 Index

TREKS

Guides to the Indian Subcontinent

Bangladesh - a travel survival kit
This practical guide – the only English-language guide to Bangladesh –
encourages travellers to take another look at this often-neglected but
beautiful land.

India - a travel survival kit
Widely regarded as *the* guide to India, this award-winning book has all the
information to help you make the most of the unforgettable experience
that is India.

Karakoram Highway the high road to China - a travel survival kit
Travel in the footsteps of Alexander the Great and Marco Polo on the
Karakoram Highway, following the ancient and fabled Silk Road. This
comprehensive guide also covers villages and treks away from the
highway.

Kashmir, Ladakh & Zanskar - a travel survival kit
Detailed information on three contrasting Himalayan regions in the Indian
state of Jammu and Kashmir – the narrow valley of Zanskar, the isolated
'little Tibet' of Ladakh, and the stunningly beautiful Vale of Kashmir.

Nepal - a travel survival kit
Travel information on every road-accessible area in Nepal, including the
Terai. This practical guidebook also includes introductions to trekking,
white-water rafting and mountain biking.

Pakistan - a travel survival kit
Discover 'the unknown land of the Indus' with this informative guidebook
– from bustling Karachi to ancient cities and tranquil mountain valleys.

Sri Lanka - a travel survival kit
Some parts of Sri Lanka are off-limits to visitors, but this guidebook uses
the restriction as an incentive to explore other areas more closely – making
the most of friendly people, good food and pleasant places to stay – all at
reasonable cost.

Trekking in the Nepal Himalaya
Complete trekking information for Nepal, including day-by-day route
descriptions and detailed maps – a wealth of advice for both independent
and group trekkers.

Also available:
Hindi/Urdu phrasebook, *Nepal* phrasebook, *and Sri Lanka* phrasebook.

Lonely Planet Guidebooks

Lonely Planet guidebooks cover every accessible part of Asia as well as Australia, the Pacific, South America, Africa, the Middle East and parts of North America and Europe. There are four series: *travel survival kits*, covering a single country for a range of budgets; *shoestring guides* with compact information for low-budget travel in a major region; *walking guides*; and *phrasebooks*.

Australia & the Pacific
Australia
Bushwalking in Australia
Islands of Australia's Great Barrier Reef
Fiji
Micronesia
New Caledonia
New Zealand
Tramping in New Zealand
Papua New Guinea
Papua New Guinea phrasebook
Rarotonga & the Cook Islands
Samoa
Solomon Islands
Tahiti & French Polynesia
Tonga

South-East Asia
Bali & Lombok
Burma
Burmese phrasebook
Indonesia
Indonesia phrasebook
Malaysia, Singapore & Brunei
Philippines
Pilipino phrasebook
South-East Asia on a shoestring
Thailand
Thai phrasebook
Vietnam, Laos & Cambodia

North-East Asia
China
Chinese phrasebook
Hong Kong, Macau & Canton
Japan
Japanese phrasebook
Korea
Korean phrasebook
North-East Asia on a shoestring
Taiwan
Tibet
Tibet phrasebook

West Asia
Trekking in Turkey
Turkey
Turkish phrasebook
West Asia on a shoestring

Indian Ocean
Madagascar & Comoros
Maldives & Islands of the East Indian Ocean
Mauritius, Réunion & Seychelles